Voice in Qualitative Inquiry

D1563125

Voice in Qualitative Inquiry is a critical response to conventional, interpretive, and critical conceptions of voice in qualitative inquiry. A select group of contributors focus collectively on the question, 'What does it mean to work the limits of voice?' from theoretical, methodological, and interpretative positions, and the result is an innovative challenge to traditional notions of voice.

The thought-provoking book will shift qualitative inquiry away from uproblematically engaging in practices and interpretations that limit what 'counts' as voice and therefore data. The rejection of comfort and authority when qualitative researchers work the limits of voice will lead to new disruptions and irruptions in making meaning from data and, in turn, will add inventive and critical dialogue to the conversation about voice in qualitative inquiry. Toward this end, the book will specifically address the following objectives:

- To promote an examination of how voice functions to communicate in qualitative research.
- To expose the excesses and instabilities of voice in qualitative research.
- To present theoretical, methodological, and interpretative implications that result in a problematizing of voice.
- To provide working examples of how qualitative methodologists are engaging the multiple layers of voice and meaning.
- To deconstruct the epistemological limits of voice that circumscribe our view of the world and the ways in which we make meaning as researchers.

This compelling collection will challenge those who conduct qualitative inquiry to think differently about how they collect, analyze, and represent meaning using the voices of others, as well as their own.

Alecia Youngblood Jackson is Assistant Professor of Educational Research at Appalachian State University, USA.

Lisa A. Mazzei is Research Fellow at the Education and Social Research Institute, Manchester Metropolitan University, UK.

Voice in Qualitative Inquiry

Challenging conventional, interpretive, and critical conceptions in qualitative research

Edited by

Alecia Y. Jackson and Lisa A. Mazzei

Routledge
Taylor & Francis Group

LONDON AND NEW YORK

First published 2009
by Routledge
2 Park Square, Milton Park, Abingdon, Oxon OX14 4RN

Simultaneously published in the USA and Canada
by Routledge
270 Madison Ave, New York, NY 10016

Routledge is an imprint of the Taylor & Francis Group, an informa business

Typeset in Times by
Integra Software Services Pvt. Ltd, Pondicherry, India
Printed and bound in Great Britain by
TJ International Ltd, Padstow, Cornwall

British Library Cataloguing in Publication Data
A catalogue record for this book is available from the British Library

Library of Congress Cataloging-in-Publication Data
Voice in qualitative inquiry : challenging conventional, interpretive, and
critical conceptions / edited by Alecia Youngblood Jackson & Lisa A. Mazzei.
    p. cm.
    1. Qualitative research. 2. Discourse analysis—Social aspects. 3. Voice
(Philosophy) I. Jackson, Alecia Youngblood, 1968- II. Mazzei, Lisa A., 1961-
    H62.V624 2008
    001.42—dc22   2008008882

ISBN10: 0–415–44220–6 (hbk)
ISBN10: 0–415–44221–4 (pbk)

ISBN13: 978–0–415–44220–6 (HB)
ISBN13: 978–0–415–44221–3 (PB)

Contents

Acknowledgments

We began our conversation about this book in San Francisco, CA, at the 2006 American Educational Research Association's (AERA's) annual conference. Because we both had interests in voice, poststructural theory, and qualitative research, we became very excited about possibly collaborating on a project that would allow us to combine our interests and make a significant contribution to the field of qualitative inquiry. What began, then, as a short conversation about a possible symposium at a future AERA meeting turned into an ambitious endeavor of working together across two continents to compile this collection. We express our sincere thanks to everyone who helped us as we conceptualized and then produced this book.

This book would not have been possible without the immediate enthusiasm of our editor at Routledge, Philip Mudd. We also thank Amy Crowle for assistance in keeping us organized. We are especially indebted to Phillip Prince for stocking us with food during our editing session in Manchester, UK. We express gratitude to Harry Torrance at Manchester Metropolitan University for generously funding our transatlantic phone calls, and to the Appalachian State University Foundation Fellows Program for travel funds in support of this work. And lastly we are in deep appreciation to our mentors and colleagues who showed interest in this project from the very beginning.

Alecia thanks Lisa for her positive energy, quick wit, smart mind, and easy friendship. She is most grateful to the loving and generous care from Kristian and Silas.

Lisa thanks Alecia for her keen mind, sense of humor, love of theory, and the friendship that developed. She is especially grateful to Phillip for his passion for the impossible.

Three chapters, edited to varying degrees, have been previously published. We thank *Kvinder, Koen og Forskning* (Copenhagen), Taylor & Francis, and the University of Minnesota Press for granting permission to reprint the following:

Lather, Patti. (2000). Against empathy, voice and authenticity. *Women, Gender and Research*, V. 4. Copenhagen, 16–25. [Reprinted with permission of *Kvinder, Koen og Forskning*]

Marker, Michael. (2003). Indigenous voice, community, and epistemic violence: the ethnographer's 'interests' and what 'interests' the ethnographer. *International Journal of Qualitative Studies in Education*, 16(3), 361–375. [Taylor & Francis]

Alcoff, Linda. (1991). The problem of speaking for others. *Cultural Critique*, 20, 5–32. [University of Minnesota Press]

Contributors

Linda Martín Alcoff is Professor of Philosophy, Women's Studies, and Political Science at Syracuse University. Her books and anthologies include *Feminist Epistemologies* co-edited with Elizabeth Potter (Routledge, 1993), *Thinking From the Underside of History* co-edited with Eduardo Mendieta (Rowman & Littlefield, 2000), *Epistemology: The Big Questions* (Blackwell, 1998), *Real Knowing: New Versions of the Coherence Theory of Knowledge* (Cornell, 1996), *Identities* co-edited with Eduardo Mendieta (Blackwell, 2002), *Singing in the Fire: Tales of Women in Philosophy* (Rowman and Littlefield, 2003), *Visible Identities: Race, Gender and the Self* (Oxford, 2006), *The Blackwell Guide to Feminist Philosophy* co-edited with Eva Feder Kittay (Blackwell, 2006), and *Identity Politics Reconsidered* co-edited with Michael Hames-Garcia, Satya Mohanty, and Paula Moya (Palgrave, 2006).

Becky M. Atkinson grew up in the central valley of California and earned her BA in English at Pomona College in Claremont, CA. After completing work for her MA in Education at Stanford University, she taught school for eight years in southern California. She completed her PhD in Educational Research at the University of Alabama after moving to Alabama in 1995. She is now an assistant professor in Instructional Leadership at The University of Alabama. She has co-authored articles published in *Educational Theory* and *Qualitative Inquiry*. Her research interests include teacher knowledge research, narrative research, and semiotics.

Lubna Nazir Chaudhry teaches Human Development, Women's Studies, and Asian & American Studies at State University of New York, Binghamton. She is also affiliated with the Sustainable Development Policy Institute, Islamabad, as a Visiting Fellow. She is the co-editor of a volume entitled *Contesting Nation: Gendered Violence in South Asia* scheduled for publication in 2008 by Zubaan Press, New Delhi. Her current work centers around the impact of different forms of violence, direct as well as structural, on women and children in Pakistan and Muslim women in the United States. She also writes about the quagmires and conundrums of conducting research as a feminist of Third World origins. Recent publications include articles in *Muslim World* and *Cultural Dynamics*.

Bronwyn Davies is Research Professor at the University of Western Sydney and leader of the research node Narrative Discourse and Pedagogy, an inter-disciplinary research group that works at the intersections of the social sciences, the performative, visual and literary arts, and philosophy. Bronwyn is well known for her work on gender, for her work with collective biography, and her writing on poststructuralist theory. Her recent work has focused on the develop-ment of a critique of neoliberalism as it impacts on subjectivities at work, with a particular focus on university work. Her work on body–landscape relations, and on enabling pedagogies, is now turning toward the development of a theory of place in pedagogical settings, and on working across the boundaries between the arts and social sciences.

Karen Dooley is Senior Lecturer in the School of Cultural and Language Studies in Education at Queensland University of Technology. Her research interests are focused on pedagogy for learners of English as an additional language. Previous studies have examined pedagogic provision for Samoan and Taiwanese students in Australian schools. Karen is the Secretary of the Queensland Association of Teachers of English to Speakers of Other Languages.

Alecia Youngblood Jackson is Assistant Professor of Educational Research in the Department of Leadership and Educational Studies at Appalachian State Univer-sity. Alecia holds a PhD in Language Education from The University of Georgia, where she also obtained a Women's Studies Certificate and a Qualitative Studies Certificate. She has publications in *The International Journal of Qual-itative Studies in Education*, *Qualitative Inquiry*, and *Qualitative Research*. Her research interests center on poststructural theories of power and know-ledge and applying those theories to narrative and voice in qualitative research, cultural studies of schooling (with an emphasis on the rural), and gender and education.

Patti Lather is Professor of Education in the School of Educational Policy and Leadership at Ohio State University, where she teaches courses in qualitative research, gender in education, and cultural studies. Her book *Getting Smart: Feminist Research and Pedagogy with/in the Postmodern* (Routledge, 1991) won an AESA 1991 Critics' Choice Award. *Troubling the Angels: Women Living with HIV/AIDS* (co-authored with Chris Smithies, Westview Press, 1997) was designated a CHOICE Outstanding Academic Title for 1998. Lather's research interests are in (post)critical methodology, feminist ethnography, and poststruc-turalism. Her latest book is *Getting Lost: Feminist Efforts Toward a Double(d) Science* (SUNY, 2007).

Felicity McArdle is Senior Lecturer at Queensland University of Technology. She teaches undergraduate and postgraduate students, and is the coordinator of the preservice Bachelor of Education courses for the Faculty of Education. Her research interests are particularly in the arts, and ways of seeing and know-ing. She has over 15 years' experience as a classroom teacher, and has taught children from a wide range of social, cultural, and economic backgrounds, and is committed to principles of equity and sustainability in education.

Maggie MacLure is Professor of Education in the Education and Social Research Institute at Manchester Metropolitan University, UK. She is interested in relationships between methodology, policy, and practice, and is particularly interested in putting deconstruction to work in applied social research. Her books include *Educational Research Undone: The Postmodern Embrace* (with Ian Stronach, Open University Press, 1997) and *Discourse in Educational and Social Research* (Open University Press, 2003), which won the Critics' Choice Award from the American Educational Studies Association.

Erica McWilliam is Professor of Education and Assistant Dean Research in the Faculty of Education at the Queensland University of Technology. Her educational publications cover a wide spectrum, as is evidenced in her numerous publications on innovative teaching and learning, research methodology and training, and leadership and management. She is currently series editor of 'Eruptions: New Thinking Across the Disciplines,' an academic series for Peter Lang Publishing, New York. Erica is also an author and social commentator on some of the charming absurdities of corporate practice.

Michael Marker is Associate Professor in the Department of Educational Studies and Director of Ts"kel First Nations Graduate Studies at the University of British Columbia. He has served on the editorial advisory board of the Council on Education and Anthropology and worked at the Lummi reservation as a high school teacher and as the director of Oksale Teacher education program.

Lisa A. Mazzei is Research Fellow in the Education and Social Research Institute at Manchester Metropolitan University, United Kingdom. She joined MMU from Ohio Dominican University, United States, where she was Associate Professor of Education. She is the author of *Inhabited Silence in Qualitative Research: Putting Poststructural Theory to Work* (Peter Lang, 2007), and also has publications in *Educational Researcher* and *Qualitative Inquiry*. Her current research interests include the study of racial identity and awareness among white teachers and the subsequent implications for pedagogy and teacher education.

Roland Mitchell is Assistant Professor of Higher Education Administration at Louisiana State University where he teaches courses that focus on the history of higher education, college teaching, and educational research methods. He has a B.A. in History from Fisk University, a M.Ed. in higher education from Vanderbilt University, and a Ph.D. in Educational Research from The University of Alabama. His current research interests include theorizing the impact of historical and communal knowledge on pedagogy, and an exploration of the understandings that allow educators to provide service to students from different cultural, ethnic, and social backgrounds. His research has appeared in the *Journal of Excellence in College Teaching, The International*

Journal of Learning, and *The Review of Education, Pedagogy, and Cultural Studies*.

Jerry Rosiek is Associate Professor of Education at the University of Oregon, where he teaches qualitative research methods and the cultural foundations of education. His articles have appeared in leading journals such as *Harvard Educational Review*, *Educational Researcher*, *The Journal of Teacher Education*, *Curriculum Theory*, *Qualitative Inquiry*, and *Educational Theory*. His current research focuses on the nature and content of teachers' practical knowledge, specifically the knowledge that enables teachers to teach across cultural differences in a manner that avoids imperialism and recognizes the cultural contingency of all curricular ideals.

Elizabeth Adams St.Pierre is Professor of Language & Literacy Education and Affiliated Professor of both the Qualitative Research Program and the Women's Studies Institute at the University of Georgia, USA. Her research agenda is grounded in poststructural theories of language and subjectivity and focuses on a critique of both scientifically based research and conventional qualitative research methodology.

Jennifer Pei-Ling Tan is a Research Fellow in the Centre for Learning Innovation at the Queensland University of Technology. Her principal research interests focus on literacy education, innovation diffusion, and equity issues in global educational policy and pedagogy. She specialises in quantitative methodology, structural equation modeling, and mixed-methods research designs. She has lecturing experience in both undergraduate business and education programs. A UK-certified TESOL member, Jennifer has designed English as a Second Language (ESL) curricula for language schools, and over the past seven years, has partnered numerous volunteer organizations to teach ESL in Cambodia, Vietnam, and China.

Introduction

The limit of voice

Lisa A. Mazzei and Alecia Youngblood Jackson

Why voice?

This book is a response to conventional, interpretive, and critical conceptions of voice in qualitative inquiry. We, along with the contributing authors, have become well aware of how voice has frequently been privileged because it has been assumed that voice can speak the truth of consciousness and experience. In these paradigms, voice lingers close to the true and the real, and because of this proximity, has become seen almost as a mirror of the soul, the essence of the self. Qualitative researchers have been trained to privilege this voice, to 'free' the authentic voice from whatever restrains it from coming into being, from relating the truth about the self. This drive to make voices heard and understood, bringing meaning and self to consciousness and creating transcendental, universal truths, gestures toward the primacy of voice in conventional qualitative research.

To solve the problem of voice in conventional, interpretive, and critical qualitative research, methodologists have taken up various practices in attempts to 'let voices speak for themselves,' to 'give voice,' or to 'make voices heard' (see Jackson, 2003, for an epistemological perspective and critique). As Guba and Lincoln (2005) explain,

> As researchers became more conscious of the abstracted realities their texts created, they became simultaneously more conscious of having readers 'hear' their informants – permitting readers to hear the exact words (and, occasionally, the paralinguistic cues, the lapses, pauses, stops, starts, reformulations) of the informants. (p. 209)

Along with this crisis of representation described by Guba and Lincoln, qualitative researchers have recognized the dangerous assumptions in trying to represent a single truth (seemingly articulated by a single voice) and have therefore pluralized voice, intending to highlight the polyvocal and multiple nature of voice within contexts that are themselves messy and constrained. This practice of 'more is better' has indeed highlighted the ways in which voices are not singular, yet the obsession for more full voices side-steps what we view as a more salient feature of the problem: these practices remain attached to notions of voice inherited from metaphysics – voice as present, stable, authentic, and self-reflective. Voice is still 'there' to search for, retrieve, and liberate.

We take then as our starting point such unproblematized notions and practices of voice that posit the presentation of unadulterated participant voices or the inclusion of a multiplicity of voices as attempts to solve the problem of voice. We are convinced, for instance, that innovative practices that attempt to provide voice data that is more authentic, spontaneous, or realistic, whether that be a script for an ethnodrama, a raw transcript, or a photograph, may do little to engage the epistemological and methodological limits of voice.[1] Letting readers 'hear' participant voices and presenting their 'exact words' as if they are transparent is a move that fails to consider how as researchers we are always already shaping those 'exact words' through the unequal power relationships present and by our own exploitative research agendas and timelines. Even those accounts of voice that are more critical and that attempt to equalize and democratize the research process, such as those deployed by some feminist researchers, may do little to make transparent how decisions are made to 'give voice:' Who decides what 'exact words' should be used in the accounts? Who was listened to, and how were they listened to? How might voices be distorted and fictionalized in the process of reinscription? And indeed, how are those voices *necessarily* distorted and fictionalized in the process of reinscription? The task would then be to examine whose interests are served by particular reinscriptions and whose are further marginalized.

Such questioning of the promises, problems, inadequacies, and deficiencies of voice is not new terrain for qualitative researchers under the influence of post-structural theories of language and meaning, nor is it exclusively the territory of those who have contributed to this book. Qualitative researchers have for some time begun to question the ethics of representing the voices of others, interpreting narrative accounts, and the privileging that occurs in the decisions that we make in the questions that we ask (or fail to ask), interpretations that we map onto (or miss), and the ways in which participant voices are portrayed and presented. Some of this questioning has resulted in narrative research (e.g., see Barone, 2001; Clandinin, 2007; Clandinin & Connelly, 1999, 2000), life history (e.g., see Cary, 1999; Munro, 1998; Weiler & Middleton, 1999) experimental writing forms (e.g., see Lincoln, 1997; Richardson, 1997; Stewart, 1996, 2005), and performance ethnography (Denzin, 2003; Gannon, 2005; McCall, 2000) to name a few, as researchers have sought to minimize the corruption and simplification of participant voices that occurs when researchers start mucking around in their attempts to make meaning. However, seeking new ways to present voice does not necessarily result in a straining of voice in ways that complicate meanings, that tangle our voices with those of our participants, that produce different understandings, or that save us from ourselves. It does not always attend to the imperative to 'produce different knowledge and produce knowledge differently' (St.Pierre, 2000, p. 27) but rather can result in the reproduction of the same knowledge with a different literary twist.

Voice has been considered from theoretical perspectives such as social constructionism (e.g., see Cochran-Smith & Lytle, 1993; Hertz, 1997; Lawrence-Lightfoot & Davis, 1997), feminism (e.g., see Belenky, Clinchy, Goldberger, &

Tarule, 1986; Fonow & Cook, 1991; Gilligan, 1982; Nielsen, 1990; Reinharz, 1992), and critical theory (e.g., see Bourdieu, 1986; Colley, 2003; Delgado, 1995; Fine, 1991; Kincheloe, 1997). However, no collection exists that 'troubles' the use of voice, from a poststructural stance, in qualitative inquiry. In the most recent edition of *The Handbook of Qualitative Research*, Guba and Lincoln (2005) claim that voice is one of the major issues confronting the poststructural paradigm, and they call for more work that exemplifies postmodern methods and textual represent-ations. What this text seeks to do, then, is to respond to that gap by offering poststructural perspectives on voice. It attempts to take up the absences in the pre-vious questioning of voice and to grapple with the challenges presented by Patti Lather (2007) when considering, 'what we are to do with what we are told in terms of listening for the sense people make of their lives without reverting to "too easy" ideas about voice' (p. 147).

And so this collection of chapters attempts to resist 'too easy' ideas about voice. It does not suggest how this is done, but presents a series of theoretical excesses, methodological instabilities, and interpretive transgressions that result from a res-istance to uncomplicated notions of voice. Our hope is that these resistances may promote an examination of how voice functions to communicate in qualitative research toward more robust examples of how qualitative methodologists are enga-ging (and avoiding) the meanings present and absent as they work the limits of voice. What is new with this collection of chapters is an attempt on the part of the authors not to give in to a paralysis that can occur by the seemingly limitless interpretations and inadequacies of voice, but in a Deleuzian fashion, to exploit what is produced by the trouble of (or with) voice. All of the authors in the book are asking questions of the very notion of what constitutes voice, the voices we choose (or are able) to listen to, how we listen to them, and why we accept some as true and others not. We reject the notion that presenting data as if it speaks for itself is an answer to the problem of voice, and instead seek practices that confront and twist voice, meaning, and truth.

We do not attempt in this book to solve the problem of voice, but to deconstruct the epistemological limits of voice. In the same way that we have criticized others of self-pardoning exercises through a presentation of unadulterated voices, multiple voices, and giving voice, so too we must criticize our own practices in this book of self-pardoning through the choice of language that attempts to unburden voice, but that in some cases, further implicates us in this charade. In the translator's preface to *Of Grammatology*, Gayatri Spivak cautions that 'To make a new word is to run the risk of forgetting the problem or believing it solved' (1976, p. xv). Rather than giving up on voice, or substituting a new word in hopes that we can leave behind the problems of voice, we wish to 'strain' the notion of voice. As we strain the notion of voice and refuse 'too easy' conceptions of voice, we search for new ways of considering voice that engage with the power relations that produce voices (Arnot & Reay, 2007, p. 312). We do not celebrate multiple voices, a critique of 'voice research' leveled by Moore and Muller (1999), but instead entangle ourselves in the layers of voices present and the epistemological assumptions that continue to haunt our methodological practices.

Voice in an era of evidence-based research

Qualitative researchers are currently positioned in an era of evidence-based policy and research-funding practices. Debates in qualitative research circles are taking up the question of evidence and truth and what these terms mean for qualitative inquiry.[2] While targeted sessions at major research conferences have not explicitly dealt with voice, the peripheral attention to the politics of voice as evidence/data signals a need for a focused and multi-perspective treatment.

As we have described previously, the privileging of voice in traditional qualitative research assumes that voice makes present the truth and *reflects* the meaning of an experience that has already happened. This is the voice that, in traditional qualitative research, is heard and then recorded, coded, and categorized as normative and containable data. Given such traditional privileging of voice we ask: How do we go about working the limits of voice? and why should we be engaged in such a practice? How does putting privileged understandings of voice under poststructural scrutiny result in a positioning of voice as *productive* of meaning – as excessive and unstable voices that surprise us, both pleasantly and uncomfortably, with previously unarticulated and unthought meanings? We assert that in our zeal as qualitative researchers to gather data and make meaning, or to make easy sense, we often seek that voice which we can easily name, categorize, and respond to. We argue that a more fertile practice, and one that is advocated in this collection by the authors, is to seek the voice that escapes easy classification and that does not make easy sense. It is not a voice that is normative, but one that is transgressive.

What is the place for these transgressive and productive voices in an age of accountability and in an era of demands for evidence? How can we promote a thinking of voice that is not reductive and that succumbs to evidence claims? There are no simple answers to these questions, but the authors in this collection grapple with what to do with voice, provide exemplars of refusing the simplistic conflation of 'voice as evidence,' and promote new ways of thinking through the dangers and dilemmas of innocent knowledge claims that 'count' as evidence.

Voice and poststructuralism

This is a collection of writings that challenges traditional criteria of voice by shifting qualitative inquiry away from uncritically engaging in practices and interpretations that limit what 'counts' as voice and therefore data. This text challenges those who conduct qualitative inquiry to think differently about how they collect, analyze, and represent meaning using the voices of others, as well as their own. The methodological implications of this view demand that readers of this collection question what they ask of voice, question what they hear and how they hear (their own privilege and authority in listening and telling), and deconstruct why one story is told and not another. As Cixous and Calle-Gruber (1997) write, 'all narratives tell one story in place of another story,' (p. 178) and authors in this text attempt to scrutinize the practices that lead to the telling of one story in place of another or the privileging of one voice over another. Qualitative researchers, while engaging with this text, will learn how other researchers have attempted to examine how voice is mediated, constrained, determined, and even commodified. Chapter authors render voice as a vulnerable site for making meaning from authenticity, and they demonstrate how the loss and betrayal of comfort and authority lead to new disruptions and irruptions in making meaning from data. We believe that these chapters add inventive and critical dialogue to the conversations about voice in qualitative inquiry.

Toward this end, the book specifically addresses the following objectives:

- To promote an examination of how voice functions to communicate in qualitative research;
- To expose the excesses and instabilities of voice in qualitative research;
- To present theoretical, methodological, and interpretative implications that result in a problematizing of voice;
- To provide working examples of how qualitative methodologists are engaging the multiple registers of voice and meaning; and
- To deconstruct the epistemological limits of voice that circumscribe our view of the world and the ways in which we make meaning as researchers.

In trying to organize a book like this and in attempting to provide some guidance for the reader, it is difficult to know whether 'divisions' are useful or obtrusive. Given the theoretical underpinnings of the text, to say that some chapters belong in a section that addresses method and that others belong in a section that addresses interpretation is to create a false division (or binary) that can result in a calcifying process, potentially leading to rigidity and intransigence. At one point we argued against any divisions and for merely placing the chapters one after the other. Succumbing to our desire to be more transparent about our intentions than is possible with our language and in remaining faithful to the idea of excess, we opted to create categories that at least frame the charge presented to our authors, and that also provide a framework to work both within and against.

The book is organized in two sections. Part 1, 'Straining notions of voice,' focuses primarily on a questioning of Method and epistemological assumptions about voice. Part 2, 'Transgressive voices: Productive practices,' primarily enacts certain methodological questions raised in Part 1 and pushes the limit of voice into uncharted territory. All of the chapters provoke questions of method, listening, and interpretation; however, the excesses and productive possibilities of straining and listening are more explicit in Part 1, while the authors in Part 2 are more intentionally performing interpretive transgressions that result from employing various methodological approaches to the problematization of voice. Following Part 2, Elizabeth Adams St.Pierre, in her afterword, titled 'Decentering voice in qualitative inquiry,' evokes questions, tensions, and possibilities of the contributors working the limits of voice.

What follows is an introduction to each of these sections and a brief discussion of how the authors are responding to poststructural practices of listening, interpretation, and representation.

Part 1: Straining notions of voice

The chapters in Part 1 shift qualitative inquiry away from uncritically engaging in practices and interpretations that limit what 'counts' as voice, and therefore data. The authors, through an engagement with data and a questioning of Method, expose the excesses and instabilities of voice in qualitative research that result in a problematizing of voice. All of the authors writing in this section have given up on the promise of voice and instead seek those voices that escape easy classification and that do not make easy sense, exploring the slippages that occur when researchers ask participants to speak with a voice that is understandable to the researcher.

What is to be gained when researchers engage in practices that explore a straining of what constitutes voice? The chapters in Part 1 collectively question a fullness, an incompleteness, a productive insufficiency of voice, and further examine why researchers take up these questions. They collectively acknowledge that a desire for clarity and meaning still haunts their practices in ways that are both productive and troubling, and yet they continue to seek these hauntings. In other words, the authors writing in this section engage readers to ask how voice is laden with assumptions. Drawing on poststructural theories of language and meaning, contributors imagine voice to be something other than a mere reflection of the real and theorize the multiple meanings, functions, and deployments of voice in qualitative research. It is such a theorizing that permits the excesses to inhabit the methodological practices of qualitative researchers. As they strain the voices of their participants, the authors attend to voices that defy classification – and consequently any stable methodology – to enable a better understanding of the implications for research design and for a further irruption of a debate as to what counts as voice and subsequently data.

Patti Lather's chapter, 'Against empathy, voice and authenticity,' directly asks questions of the historical burdens and assumptions placed on voice that are central to all of the chapters in this book. In her chapter, Lather explains how the demand for feminist research to be centered by such concepts as 'empathy,' 'voice' and 'authenticity' has been central for the movement away from scientistic thought. This chapter presents a genealogy of knowing as narration and representation of the other based on comfortable and comforting, empathetic, mutual, dialogical knowing, critiquing such knowledge practices as violence, as imperial sameness once again. It asks, what is it to claim empathy, voice, and authenticity as the grounds of research? To explore the contemporary demands for feminist research to be a space where the researcher practices empathy and offers or facilitates the voice of the researched and the researcher toward more 'authentic' knowing, Lather unpacks poststructuralism in order to challenge the typical investments and categories of ethnography and probes what is at work in the concepts of 'voice' and 'authenticity' in ethnographic work, concepts that are taken up and challenged by authors throughout this collection of chapters.

Michael Marker in the chapter 'Indigenous voice, community, and epistemic violence: the ethnographer's "interests" and what "interests" the ethnographer,' directly addresses, through examples, ways in which ethnographers, especially those ethnographers who research Native communities for their own gain, make decisions about what is authentic, what is to be believed, and how we judge some stories as truthful based on a commodifying process inherent in the tradition of ethnography. He moves some of the historical burdens and assumptions discussed by Patti Lather into the present with examples from research on/with Native peoples. He specifically takes up some of Lather's discussion regarding the violence and imperial sameness that can and does occur in challenging researchers to examine how truth telling is negotiated around the performance of a story and the power imbalances of the space in which the story is listened to. For example, he states that in North America, 'the public has been willing to accept – and even "celebrate" – the stories of Aboriginal people when they are about ancient times, mythic events, folklore and anything else that is removed from commentary on the actual economic and political conditions that tribal people experience,' pointing to the difference in how the native and non-native listen to subaltern voices. He suggests a 'listening' to the cultural assumptions and histories that shape the voices that are heard and how those stories are represented.

Continuing a challenging of the typical categories of ethnography and qualitative inquiry initiated by Lather, Lisa Mazzei in her chapter, 'An impossibly full voice,' contests the very notion of what constitutes voice and puts forth a fullness of voice not 'captured' in spoken utterances, a move that is further developed in the concluding chapter of Part 1 by Maggie MacLure. Mazzei is specifically interested in practices that both elicit and account for the shifting and uncertain voices spoken by research participants with words, with images, and with silences toward more subtle, more nuanced, more startling meanings. In so doing, she imagines a counter-practice that opens up a thinking of voice not previously possible. She seeks an undisciplining of voice that does not make easy sense and that transgresses the domesticated voice that we are accustomed to hearing, knowing, and naming. Such an undisciplining results in the claiming of an excessive silent voice that we cannot 'hear' but that speaks to us nonetheless. The chapter ends with an example of her 'listening to herself listening' as she deconstructs transcripts in an attempt to make space for the impossible fullness of voice.

The chapter 'Voicing objections,' by Erica McWilliam, Karen Dooley, Felicity McArdle, and Jennifer Pei-Ling Tan takes as its starting point the desire to 'let voices speak' that has been such an important imperative in critical educational research. The authors seek to echo the challenges made by Lather and others that researchers can and should 'hear' subjugated voices, then re-present those voices in some authentic and unadulterated way. Based on their work with 'empty suitcase refugees' in Australia, they interrogate the means by which educational researchers go about the business of hearing and documenting 'subjugated' voices, locating their tactics and techniques in the context of more time-honored fantasies about the nature and purposes of educational work. In considering what possibilities remain for a liberating educational project, the paper asserts the usefulness of Anna Freud's dictum to 'do the least harm,' understanding that dictum as a powerful and important imperative for educational research, rather than a retreat from research as proactive intervention in the lives of less privileged others. They end the chapter by providing instances of the ways that our qualitative research methodologies seem to fail us, and what we are learning from the instructive complications of such failures.

The context for Roland Mitchell's chapter, ' "Soft ears" and hard topics: race, disciplinarity, and voice in higher education,' is an examination of how membership in a scholarly community or academic discipline *disciplines* the voices of educators in a higher education setting. Focusing on an analysis of one case-study from a larger sample, he illustrates the ways in which the disciplinary discourses discipline the ways that one particular faculty member thinks about the relationship between her racial identity, approach to pedagogy, and subsequent interactions with students. To develop more sophisticated approaches to hearing and then reporting the voices of their participants is the challenge for researchers seeking to understand better and ultimately benefit from the knowledge that comes from the insights of those who, like the professor in his case study, teach across cultural and racial boundaries. The type of hearing that he is advocating in this chapter entails listening to the voices of participants with 'soft ears' – or ears that are malleable and open to more nuanced understandings and interpretations. In what follows, he offers that poststructuralist theory, and particularly a discursive reading of the relationship among voice, race, and disciplinarity, provides several analytic tools that can assist with such inquiries, demonstrating the ways that an appeal to poststructuralism affords researchers a broader framework for better understanding the obvious as well as the surprising and more complex aspects of their participants' experiences.

The final chapter in Part 1 by Maggie MacLure provides a traversal between the question of Method which is a focus of Part 1 and the interpretive transgressions that are modeled in Part 2. In her chapter, MacLure is interested in what she refers to as 'the disappointments of voice in qualitative research – in the many ways in which voice falters or fails.' In so doing, she examines how the insufficiency of voice – its propensity to be too much and never enough – is unavoidable. Rather than dismissing these insufficiencies as troublesome, she approaches them as productive. She is interested in

> 'voice research' that would attend to such features as laughter, mimicry, mockery, silence, stuttering, tears, slyness, shyness, shouts, jokes, lies, irrelevance, partiality, inconsistency, self-doubt, masks, false starts, false 'fronts' and faulty memories – not as impediments or lapses to be corrected, mastered, read 'through' or written off, but as perplexing resources for the achievement of a dissembling, 'authentic' voice.

The chapter ends with the case of humor as one such troubling property of voice that complicates writing, truth, and method. MacLure is both listening to how we listen and at the same time introducing the possibility of productive practices resulting from an engagement with transgressive voices.

Part 2: Transgressive voices: Productive practices

Building upon the work presented in Part 1, this section explores the interpretive transgressions of employing various methodological approaches to the problematic of voice. The chapters in this section provide working examples of how qualitative methodologists are engaging the meanings present (and absent) as they work the limits of voice. As they try to make (or avoid) meaning, the authors enact practices that refute the notion that voice is a mere reflection of the real and theorize the multiple functions and deployments of voice in qualitative research. Such work permits novel ways of inhabiting the methodological practices of qualitative researchers and moves us toward descriptions and inscriptions of how voice works to produce new knowledge and new knowledge differently. The interpretations and analyses in these chapters push the limits of voice beyond its territories.

All of the chapters in Part 2 engage in a trouble-making that does not reject theory (or method); instead, they use a certain bit of skepticism to upset the easy story that method would have them tell. The authors engage theory not to merely interpret data but to show how approaching data in a Deleuzian, Foucauldian, or Derridean way pushes researchers' consideration of voice toward a different interpretive stance. The authors writing in this section are theorizing voice from a poststructural perspective to emphasize the ways in which meanings and assumptions of voice are historically grounded in positivism, interpretivism, and critical theory. When such philosophy of voice is examined and criticized from a poststructural perspective, the ways in which voice exceeds itself become apparent. Drawing on poststructural theories of language, power, discourse, and subjectivity, contributors re-present data (voices) that challenge the position of the researcher in relation to voice and accentuate the movement of language and voice (a performative act that destabilizes the real). The transgressive voices in Part 2 refuse any illusion of unification or authenticity, any desire for mastery, or any equalization or coherence of voice. Instead, they reveal the productive possibilities for qualitative research when voice is examined not as pure and full but as a failure – not as an intention of the subject but an effect of discursive and material conditions.

Linda Martín Alcoff's chapter, 'The problem of speaking for others,' delegitimizes the authority, validity, and neutrality of the speaker – the academic researcher – for Others. She describes her chapter title as an intentional conflation of 'speaking *for*' and 'speaking *about*,' as she argues that both practices are entangled in the same epistemological and metaphysical claims. Alcoff's critique begins by rendering the location of the speaker as simultaneously privileged and dangerous. The solution, for Alcoff, is not to demarcate and define who can speak for whom – a highly problematic practice because defining social location once and for all assumes fixed, rather than complex, identities. If, as she argues, speaking for others (or even for the self) momentarily creates and reproduces a possible Other in a certain way and from a specific subject-position, then the 'rituals of speaking' are discursive practices that are bound to positionality and power. Alcoff moves away from an emphasis on the *meaning* of the discursive speech event to the importance of the *movement* of social location, possibilities of understanding, and the status/value/significance of truth. Of particular relevance is a list she offers of interrogatory practices that researchers should engage in when they speak for (or about) Others. Her suggested practices shift voice from intention to effect; she writes, 'One must look at where the speech goes and what it does there.'

Alcoff's call for voice as an effect of movement, discourse, positionality, and power are taken up and exemplified by Lubna Nazir Chaudhry, who gives us three vignettes that exemplify the interplay of voice and violence in her chapter, 'Forays into the mist: violences, voices, vignettes.' Chaudhry's vignettes are based on fieldwork in different contexts of violence in Pakistan. They are complex stories of listening, being reflexive, and attempting to represent accounts of violence that are further complicated by her own positioning as a Pakistani feminist academic researcher. Voice, in these vignettes, becomes a site for exploring what enables a certain type of speaking and listening about violences, grounded in the social locations (e.g., gender, class, caste) of both the tellers and hearers. Chaudhry focuses not only on the 'voicing' of violence but also on the interpretive and epistemic colonization that goes on when stories are circulated in discursive and material contexts to the point of destabilizing truth. Chaudhry scrutinizes and reframes the politics of voice – of truths – by examining the effects of voicing violences, effects that are as complex as the stories themselves.

Alecia Youngblood Jackson's chapter continues an examination of the effects of voice. In her chapter, ' "What am I doing when I speak of this present?": voice, power, and desire in truth-telling,' she draws on a Foucauldian question of modernity to consider how the contradictory subject positions, taken up by research participants, shape what they do when they speak of their present, or tell truth(s). She does this by analyzing an interview transcript – and subsequent member check data – with one of her participants in a study of southern women. Rather than going after a meaning of narrative voice, she emphasizes the discursive and performative dimensions of voice that surface as subjects attempt to tell truth(s) about themselves. By examining pieces of data from the interview, she offers a Derridean reading of speech and writing to collapse the binary to be inclusive of voice, a Foucauldian reading of power and truth to expose the discursive fields in which voice is produced, and a Butlerian and Deleuzian reading of desire that enables a new production of the self (and what the self tells about its self). Her concluding point is that power and desire produce nuances of voice that belie all possibility of coherence and presence.

Becky M. Atkinson and Jerry Rosiek also disrupt the continuity and authenticity of voice in their analysis of the discursive contexts in which teachers' voices are made possible. Their chapter, entitled 'Researching and representing teacher voice(s): a reader response approach,' uses as its starting point the tradition of teacher knowledge research with its aim to liberate teachers' voices from the shadow of more formal academic research on education. They argue that the valorization and romanticization of teacher knowledge narratives ignore how their voices are ideologically, semiotically, and socially mediated.

A more robust approach to interpreting teacher voice, and one that they advocate, is grounded in reader response theory, particularly the work of Wolfgang Iser and Stanley Fish. They do this interpretive work by examining how a group of eight teachers talk about teacher narratives, and they focus their analysis on the discursive influences and experiences shared by the group of teachers. Their conclusions point to new ways of rendering teacher voice in teacher research, ways that avoid recreating a regulative ideal of portrayals of teachers' work and that promote voices and narratives as indeterminate and as epistemologically limited (and limiting).

The final chapter by Bronwyn Davies, 'Life in Kings Cross: a play of voices,' is a radio play in which she experiences – and experiments with – a Deleuzian, fictional approach to writing. Davies uses a play of voices to allow lives to emerge in the folds of place. She introduces her play with a preamble titled, 'Writing on an immanent plane of composition: opening oneself to difference,' in which she explains how she was guided by two principles of Deleuze that provide an alternative approach to 'speaking for the other' by emphasizing the movement of 'language, voice, and subjectivity toward the as-yet-unknown.' In the fictional radio play, Davies gives up her authorial 'I' to use herself as a site of becoming within the place; this transgressive use of voice opened her up to difference, to seeing differently, to being different. In transgressing traditional, social-science uses of voice with the imperative to represent the real, Davies produces the unfamiliar and shakes the burdens of old habits of writing and voicing. It is in this final chapter that, in performative fashion, Davies collides many of the tensions and possibilities raised in the previous chapters to produce different voices, and voices differently.

Acknowledgments

Our thanks to Maggie MacLure for her comments on an earlier draft of this chapter and for reminding us that we owe much in our thinking to the 'old régime' of truth and voice, even though we, and the authors writing in this collection, continue to work within and against our received methodologies.

Notes

1 In the article, 'Seeing Voices and Hearing Pictures: Image as Discourse and the Framing of Image-Based Research,' Heather Piper and Jo Frankham (2007) put image-based research under the same scrutiny that other 'voice' texts have undergone. Piper and Frankham specifically take to task researchers who use the practice of giving young people cameras as a popular technique for eliciting student 'voice' as they proceed to deconstruct the representation of student voice through an analysis of young people's images as a medium of expression, focusing in particular on photography.

2 Multiple sessions and symposia on these very issues are being held at conferences such as The International Congress of Qualitative Inquiry, The British Educational Research Association Conference, The American Educational Research Association Conference, The Australian Association for Research in Education Conference, and the Discourse Power Resistance Conference.

References

Arnot, M., & Reay, D. (2007). A sociology of pedagogic voice: Power, inequality and pupil consultation. *Discourse: Studies in the Cultural Politics of Education, 28*(3), 311–325.

Barone, T. (2001). *Touching eternity: The enduring outcomes of teaching.* New York: Teachers College Press.

Belenky, M. F., Clinchy, B. M., Goldberger, N. R., & Tarule, J. M. (1986). *Women's ways of knowing: The development of self, voice, and mind.* New York: Basic Books/Harper Collins.

Bourdieu, P. (1986). *Distinction: A social critique of the judgement of taste.* London: Routledge.

Cary, L. J. (1999). Unexpected stories: Life history and the limits of representation. *Qualitative Inquiry, 5*(3), 411–427.

Cixous, H., & Calle-Gruber, M. (1997). *Rootprints: Memory and life writing* (E. Prenowitz, Trans.). London: Routledge. (Original work published 1994).

Clandinin, J., & Connelly, M. (1999). *Shaping a professional identity: Stories of educational practice.* New York: Teachers College Press.

Clandinin, J., & Connelly, M. F. (2000). *Narrative inquiry.* San Francisco: Jossey-Bass Publishers.

Clandinin, J. (Ed.). (2007). *Handbook of narrative inquiry: Mapping a methodology.* Thousands Oaks, CA: Sage Publications.

Cochran-Smith, M., & Lytle, S. L. (1993). *Inside/outside: Teacher research and knowledge.* New York: Teachers College Press.

Colley, H. (2003). *Mentoring for social inclusion: A critical approach to nurturing mentor relationships.* London: RoutledgeFalmer.

Delgado, R. (Ed.). (1995). Legal storytelling: Storytelling for oppositionists and others: A plea for narrative. *Critical race theory: The cutting edge* (pp. 64–74). Philadelphia: Temple University Press.

Denzin, N. K. (2003). *Performance ethnography: Critical pedagogy and the politics of culture.* Thousand Oaks, CA: Sage Publications.

Fine, M. (1991). *Framing dropouts: Notes on the politics of an urban public high school.* Albany, NY: State University of New York Press.

Fonow, M. M., & Cook, J. A. (Eds.). (1991). *Beyond methodology.* Bloomington, IN: Indiana University Press.

Gannon, S. (2005). 'The tumbler': Writing an/other in fiction and performance ethnography. *Qualitative Inquiry, 8*(11), 622–627.

Gilligan, C. (1982). *In a different voice: Psychological theory and women's development.* Cambridge, MA: Harvard University Press.

Guba, E., & Lincoln, Y. (2005). Paradigmatic controversies, contradictions, and emerging confluences. In N. Denzin & Y. Lincoln (Eds.), *Handbook of qualitative research* (3rd ed., pp. 191–215). Thousand Oaks, CA: Sage.

Hertz, R. (Ed.). (1997). *Reflexivity and voice.* Thousand Oaks, CA: Sage Publications.

Jackson, A. Y. (2003). Rhizovocality. *The International Journal of Qualitative Studies in Education, 16*(5), 693–710.

Kincheloe, J. (1997). Fiction formulas: Critical constructivism and the representation of reality. In W. G. Tierney & Y. S. Lincoln (Eds.), *Representation and the text: Re-framing the narrative voice* (pp. 57–79). Albany, NY: SUNY Press.

Lather, P. (2007). *Getting lost: Feminist efforts toward a double(d) science.* Albany, NY: SUNY Press.

Lawrence-Lightfoot, S., & Davis, J. (1997). *The art and science of portraiture*. San Francisco: Jossey-Bass Publishers.

Lincoln, Y. S. (1997). Self, subject, audience, text: Living at the edge, writing in the margins. In W. G. Tierney & Y. S. Lincoln (Eds.), *Representation and the text: Re-framing the narrative voice* (pp. 37–55). Albany, NY: SUNY Press.

McCall, M. M. (2000). Performance ethnography: A brief history and some advice. In N. K. Denzin & Y. S. Lincoln (Eds.), *Handbook of qualitative research* (2nd ed., pp. 421–433). Thousand Oaks, CA: Sage Publications.

Moore, R., & Muller, J. (1999). The discourse of 'voice' and the problem of knowledge and identity in the sociology of education. *British Journal of Sociology of Education, 20*(2), 189–206.

Munro, P. (1998). *Subject to fiction: Women teachers' life history narratives and the cultural politics of resistance*. Philadelphia: Open University Press.

Nielsen, J. M. (Ed.). (1990). *Feminist research methods*. Boulder, CO: Westview Press.

Piper, H., & Frankham, J. (2007). Seeing voices and hearing pictures: Image as discourse and the framing of image-based research. *Discourse: Studies in the Cultural Politics of Education, 28*(3), 373–387.

Reinharz, S. (1992). *Feminist methods in social research*. New York: Oxford University Press.

Richardson, L. (1997). *Fields of play: Constructing an academic life*. New Brunswick, NJ: Rutgers University Press.

St. Pierre, E. A. (2000). The call for intelligibility in postmodern educational research. *Educational Researcher, 29*(5), 25–28.

Stewart, K. (1996). *A space on the side of the road: Cultural poetics in an 'Other' America*. Princeton, NJ: Princeton University Press.

Stewart, K. (2005). Cultural poesis: The generativity of emergent things. In N. K. Denzin & Y. K. Lincoln (Eds.), *The Sage Handbook of Qualitative Research* (3rd ed.). London: Sage Publications.

Spivak, G. C. (1976). Translator's Preface. In J. Derrida, *Of grammatology*. Baltimore: The Johns Hopkins University Press.

Weiler, K., & Middleton, S. (Eds.). (1999). *Telling women's lives: Narrative inquiries in the history of women's education*. Philadelphia: Open University Press.

Part I

Straining notions of voice

Chapter 1

Against empathy, voice and authenticity

Patti Lather

The demand for feminist research to be centered on such concepts as 'empathy,' 'voice' and 'authenticity' has been central for the movement away from scientistic thought. This demand is much troubled by critiques of the coherent subject that presupposes subjects who speak for themselves; subjects capable of knowing others; and subjects in charge of their desires and identifications. This essay presents a genealogy of knowing as narration and representation of the other based on comfortable and comforting, empathetic, mutual, dialogical knowing, critiquing such knowledge practices as violence, as imperial sameness once again. It asks, what is it to claim voice, authenticity and empathy as the grounds of research? Can there be a research that refuses such grounds, residing in messy 'spaces in between' (Robinson, 1994) where centers and margins are both situated and yet constantly changing intersections of interpretation, interruption and mutuality?

To explore the contemporary demands for feminist research to be a space where the researcher practices empathy and offers or facilitates the voice of the researched and the researcher toward more 'authentic' knowing, I make three moves. First, I unpack poststructuralism in order to challenge the typical investments and categories of ethnography so as to put under theoretic pressure the claims of scientism. I do so via a move away from what Britzman (1997) refers to as the wish for heroism and rescue through some 'more adequate' methodology and toward a learning that can tolerate its own failure of knowledge and the detour of not understanding. Second, grounded in my 'postbook' thinking,[1] I trouble the ethnographer as 'the one who knows' whose task is to produce the persuasive text that elicits reader empathy, in this case, for women living with HIV/AIDS. Finally, I probe what is at work in the concepts of 'voice' and 'authenticity' in ethnographic work.

Against scientism: A (gay) science 'after truth'

Scientism is not so much the actual practices of science as the infusion of the standard elements of scientific attitude into all aspects of the social world (Hayek, 1952; Sorell, 1991). Many logically distinct positions can be called scientism: claims that the laws of physics can subsume everything which, in turn, can be studied best using an idealized, ahistorical and formalized notion of the methods of the physical sciences; objectivism, pseudo-exactitude and de-contextualization;

and the capacity of science for leadership in the development of social values. Poststructuralism troubles the foundational knowledges that undergird such claims (Haraway, 1997; Hollinger, 1994; Lather, 2007).

What do we speak of when we speak of a poststructural science? Rather than heroism or rescue through some new methodology, Britzman (1997) argues that we may be in a time and place where we are better served by research if it is a means to see the need to be wounded by thought as an ethical move. 'Incited by the demand for voice and situatedness' (p. 31), she writes about the curious history of research's mistaken identities. How do we come to think of things this way, she asks, and what would be made possible if we were to think research otherwise, as a space surprised by difference into the performance of practices of not-knowing.

The theoretical and methodological competitiveness of 'successor régimes' (Harding, 1991) that continues to characterize social inquiry often positions qualitative research as some sort of savior. To the contrary, Britzman (1997) points out that qualitative research is filled with sacred objects to be recovered, restored and centered. There is a tendency to avoid the difficult story, to want to restore the good name of research with these 'new' and 'better' methods. But research 'can't seem to get it right' (p. 35), and, she writes, too often our efforts fall back into the too-easy-to-tell story of salvation via one sort of knowledge practice or another. As Britzman goes on to note, what is at stake when research is at stake is whether research can be a mode of thought that refuses to secure itself with the consolations of foundationalism and nostalgia for presence, the lost object of correct knowledge, the security of understanding. This is a move out of the sort of 'devotional scientism' that underwrites the Christian-capitalist-industrialist creed and toward what Nietzsche (1974) termed a 'gay science,' a science based in the very splintering of the mechanisms of control and the resultant incredulity about salvation narratives of scientific progress, reason and the over-administered world. Hence, my argument is that the research of most use is that which addresses how knowledge remains possible, given the end of the value-free notion of science and the resultant troubling of confidence in the scientific project, a science 'after truth' (Tomlinson, 1989). To explore what such a practice might look like, I turn to Chris and my efforts in our book on women living with HIV/AIDS.

Against empathy: A methodology of getting lost

Western feminist ethnographic traditions of romantic aspirations about giving voice to the voiceless are much troubled in the face of the manipulation, violation and betrayal inherent in ethnographic representation (Visweswaran, 1994). At the limits of intelligibility, *Troubling the Angels* works across various layers and shifts of register in order to construct an audience with ears to hear. This was Chris's and my task as we live out the ambivalent failure of the uses of research toward something more productive than an enabling violation of its disciplining effects. Inhabiting the practices of its rearticulation, 'citing, twisting, queering,' to use Judith Butler's words (1993b, p. 237), we occupy the very space opened up by the ruins of the concept of ethnographic representation.

'The too easy to tell tale' (Britzman, 1998) would have delivered the women to the reader in a linear, tidy narrative. Instead, refusing easy identifications, the reader comes to know through a form of textual dispersal of discontinuous bits and multiples of the women's stories. Thus the text works to elicit an experience of the women through the very failures of the book to represent them in order to set up a different economy of exchange that interrupts voyeurism and the erasure of difference.

AIDS activist and theorist Douglas Crimp (Caruth and Keenan, 1995) argues that empathetic understanding gets constructed in relation to sameness. Empathy, then, actually 'solidifies the structure of discrimination' (p. 264) and diffuses any confrontation with death. Similarly, Elizabeth Ellsworth (1997) speaks against empathy as 'the beautiful fit.' Instead, she advocates counter-practices of queering, disidentifying, denaturalizing and defamiliarizing: producing difference instead of the sameness. Reading for some empathic union of two selves in a mirroring relationship is NOT helpful in unfixing categories. Instead, Ellsworth argues, we need to act from the abject space of the between, to make that space material so that we keep it unsettled. Here, our task is to not remain within the same logic of identity and difference from which we presume to escape. Rather, the task is to produce processes and movements beyond the fixedness, or limited mobility, of presently conceptualized categories of difference.

In Deleuzean language, this is not about empathy so much as about becoming (Deleuze and Guattari, 1983). To argue against empathy is to trouble the possibilities of understanding as premised on structures that all people share. The issue is the limitations of cognitive access to other individuals and what one can experience of another, 'the riddle of intersubjectivity' (Sawicki, 1997, p. 126). It is also about audiences and issues of resisting competent readers and intentionality, some rhetoric outside of persuasion, some focus on what we cannot know, a move away from fantasies of mutuality, shared experience and touristic invitations to intimacy.

In a book less argued than enacted, Chris and I have written an 'uncooperative text' that refuses mimentic desire. It constructs a distance between reader and subject of the research, producing a kind of gap between text and reader. Refusing the liberal embrace of empathy that reduces otherness to sameness within a personalized culture, casting doubt on our capacity to know, it refuses the mutuality and dialogue that typify an empathetic approach to understanding.

As Sommer (1994) notes, these points are double-faced, both epistemological and ethical. They are about what we can know but also what we, perhaps, ought not to assume we have the right to know. What Sommer terms a recalcitrant rather than a persuasive rhetoric questions enlightenment views of understanding as necessarily liberating (p. 542). Forcing understandable identities, overlooking differences 'for the sake of a comforting, self-justifying rush of identification,' the will to understand the Other is therefore a kind of violence, 'an appropriation in the guise of an embrace' (p. 543). This is how empathy violates the other and is part of the demand for totality. A recalcitrant rhetoric is about inaccessible alterity, a lesson in modesty and respect, somewhere outside of our desire to possess, know, grasp. Here, 'interpretive reticence' makes sense (p. 548) as we learn to listen to what the Other has to say without the mutuality presumed by empathy. To withhold the anticipated intimacy that invites conquest, teaching the reader how to read at some distance, with respect for the distances: this is the readerly response our text tries to constitute, a defiant book that teaches unanticipated lessons by being 'hard to read.'[2]

Defying our personalized culture, easy identifications and sentimentalizing empathy, this argument foregrounds the inadequacies of thought to its object. Empathy is situated in relation to sameness and 'solidifies the structure of discrimination' (Caruth and Keenan, 1995, p. 264). Denying the 'comfort text' in moving away from fantasies of mutuality, shared experience, dialogue and touristic invitations to intimacy, the book declines the too easy to possess knowledge and reader entitlement to know.

Against voice and authenticity: Representation and the new ethnography

Questions of authenticity and voice are at the heart of claims to the 'real' in ethnography. Indeed, in the 'new' ethnography, which comes after the crisis of representation (Marcus and Fischer, 1986), the authority of voice is often privileged over other analyses. Confessional tales, authorial self-revelation, multivoicedness and personal narrative, all are contemporary practices of representation designed to move ethnography away from scientism and the appropriation of others. At risk is a romance of the speaking subject and a metaphysics of presence that threatens to collapse ethnography under the weight of circumscribed modes of identity, intentionality and selective appropriation (Atkinson and Silverman, 1997; Hargreaves,[3] 1996).

But one example is *The Education of Little Tree* (1976), a so-called autobiography by 'Forrest Carter.'[4] In writing of authenticity and voice in his discussion of Carter's fraud, Henry Louis Gates (1991) castigates 'the ideologues of authenticity' (p. 2) and explores concepts of true lies, pseudoslave narratives, 'the real black writer,' the authority of experience in policing genre boundaries,[5] and the intertextuality of *Uncle Tom's Cabin* where slave narratives were influenced by Stowe and Stowe by slave narratives. The key, Gates argues, is to see 'the troublesome role of authenticity' (p. 2) as linked to 'imputations of realness' that elide how, while identity indeed matters, 'all writers are "cultural impersonators"' (p. 3). Whatever it means for a writer to speak 'as-a' (Miller, quoted in Gates, 1991, p. 4), authenticity is much more complicated than singular, transparent, static identity categories assumed to give the writer a particular view.

Given such complications, how are we to think of the problematics of 'authenticity?' 'Heidegger instituted authenticity,' Adorno (1973, p. 17) argues disparagingly, at least in its second generation which betrayed Kierkegaard and Nietzsche in its systematic ontologizing of authenticity as a philosophical concept (Golomb, 1995). To read Heidegger most generously, invested in displacing the dominance of the subject in thought and language, Heidegger's effort was to think on the question of authenticity and voice, turning the question, 'thinking in an aporia' (Scott, 1996, p. 84) of the question. While getting lost is set up as some other way of 'homing in on our being' (ibid.: p. 16), it is Heidegger who thinks the thought of a tradition beginning to overturn itself within itself, in this case, a move away from transcendence or, perhaps better said, a thinking within the aporia of the loss of transcendence.[6]

Less generously, Adorno (1973) situates the 'cult of authenticity' (p. 5) as an existential jargon that is part of the disintegration of aura. Creating a universal understanding that must be negated if we are to escape the 'liturgy of inwardness' (p. 70) and quest for pure identity that 'devours everything' (p. 139), Adorno's disdain for Heidegger follows that of his mentor, Walter Benjamin. Benjamin's interest was the loss of 'aura' versus Heidegger's search for fullness of essence (Golomb, 1995). For Benjamin, what mattered was how to work the ruins of aura toward a living on. The loss of aura was the loss of transcendence under conditions of history as a permanent emergency. Trying to gather the weak messianic power of those who have been passed over by history, Benjamin (1939/1968) worked the ruins of theology to ask just how secular are our supposedly non-theistic forms of thought. The secularized discourse of post-Kantian modernity is not as different from earlier theological discourses as modernists would like to believe – this was Benjamin's turn to theology – against the devaluation of truth in the name of knowledge (Nagele, 1991). To get lost at the limits of representation is to encounter the radical discontinuity of modernism and the secularization that is its basis. This is about the limits of knowledge where the old significance is shattered, 'but the signifiers resist, empty shells for somber ghosts' (Nagele, 1991, p. 195).

In *Troubling the Angels*, the angels circulate among many questions, sharpening problems, making insufficiencies pressing and marking the limits of any easy resolutions of issues around voice and authenticity. 'Trying,' as Derrida cautions, 'not to take advantage of the emotion,' (1976, p. 185) Chris and I mobilized the angel to use sentimentality against itself and to construct a questioning text that signals tentativeness and partiality. The angel, then, is a placeholder, a shell for the ghost of meaning. Our recourse to an old theological symbol insists on the otherness that remains outside of any reconciliation. Like Benjamin's *Angel of History*, the various voices of our text are inverted and perverted, folded and refolded into some non-fixity. This sets up an escape from the general cliches of the Frankfurt School so that thinking might start over about the traces of otherness that cannot be erased by secularization or edified by the self-deceptions of a humanistic rhetoric (Nagele, 1991, p. 53). Hence the angel is the ghost of unassimilable otherness that haunts the house of Reason, self-reflexive subjectivity and historical continuity. Revising constitutive concepts of history and subjectivity, interiority and experience, this is an economy of displacements that condenses something other than individualized and psychologized motivations. Here the angel is an effect/affect that helps organize a less bounded space where we do what we can while leaving a place for what we cannot envision to emerge.

In spite of Fredric Jameson's (1984) claim regarding the waning of affect in postmodernism, a new subjectivity seems part of the landscape that creates a renewed interest in affect, emotional responses, 'feelings' (Massumi, 1995; Sedgwick,

1995). Public discourse is full of first-person voice: AA, therapy, talk show public performance of private pain, affective epidemics of the Right, 'moral panics' that occupy pernicious structures of belonging and identification. This turn to affect is complicated by Benjamin's moves against sentimentality and subjectivism. His historical and sociological impulses were toward a non-subjectivist thinking where affect becomes dynamism, complexity, aggregative capacity (Rochlitz, 1996).

Spivak (1994) asks how terrifying is this 'contamination' of subjectivity against technologism and capitalism. This turn to affect (Sedgwick, 1995) works the pathos of the ruins (Butler, 1993a), what Kathryn Bond Stockton traces as the return of 'sentiment and sobs' (1994, p. xxii). In the age of AIDS, she suggests, 'emotional extravagance' might seem fitting to academic cultural critics. As a way to join public sentiment, 'teasing out sobs' is about learning how to visit loss via a risk of the personal form that is transgressive in its sentiment. Her caution is that such ardor and not sacrifice shadows for sense as she endorses a kind of opaque personal confession outside formulas, personal writing that is scandalous, excessive and leaky but based in lack and ruin rather than plenitude. Hence Benjamin's baroque imaginary of ruin and dislocation is useful in situating questions of authenticity and voice, an imaginary that is not about a lost plenitude but about a loss of aura. This is layered with Stockton's evocation of female potential for otherness and transgression and the question of living on, under conditions of the loss of belief in fullness and epistemological certitude.

Within such questions, is Chris's and my text symptom or index? Given the frenzy of demands to show emotion, voice is an authorizing disclosure that points to the insufficiencies of our Hegelian inheritance of historical teleology, subject-centered rationality and recuperation of the Other into the Same. In what I have come to call the 'validity of tears' in audience's reception of our book (Lather, 1997), I see a desire for personal revelation that constructs the appearance of authenticity as having much to do with the abjection of theory and the reinscription of presence. To touch something outside the authority of interpretive thought, to speak of, to, with, for and in the place of simultaneously (Derrida, 1993) as a way to construct a different relationality: this is the sort of authorial agency in excess of subjectivity and phenomenological apprehension to which Chris and I aspired. But the demand for voice also has much to do with subjugated knowledges and multiple fractured voices, the unheard/unhearable voices of Spivak's (1988) 'Can the Subaltern Speak?'

Hence what I attempt here is not so much 'against' empathy, voice and authenticity as it is a double(d) economy of the text to counter-balance the leveling effects of assimilation into sameness. As a sort of 'pragmatic intervention in the machinery of mimesis' (Cohen, 1994: p. 103), *Troubling the Angels* uses de-authorizing devices such as shifting counter-voices and subtextual underwriting that rupture the narrative and forces reading in two directions; dialogic openness and variability of meaning that undercut rhetorical strategies that position the authors as 'the ones who know'; partiality, chunkiness and deferral rather than depiction to signal that representation is irreducible to the terms of the real; and a refusal of closure that works against ending on the sort of recuperative note typical of 'the religious left' (Gilbert-Rolfe, 1995, p. 56).

Perhaps, then, our book is BOTH symptom and index of an effort to rethink science and culture as constituted by difference rather than consensus without re-situating Chris and myself as romantic god-artists who create sublime moments of unity and totality. Foregrounding sociology and politics, we situate our textual moves within and against the historical and normative status of the 'new' ethnography as we try to not position ourselves as knowing more about these women than they know about themselves. Situating their voices above ours on the split-pages and their poems in boxes out of control by authorial judgment, our aim is not so much verisimilitude as a troubling of authority in the telling of other people's stories. Not at all about avoiding interpretation, the Angel inter-texts signal its inevitable weight and the ruins of the author as either priest or prophet. Resisting the unified subject and universal values, the book marks a methodology of getting lost and an uneasiness in the quest for a less comfortable social science.[7]

Conclusion: Interpretation and its complicities

Grounded in AIDS-related testimony by women, I have attempted a counter-discourse to defamiliarize common sentiments of empathy, voice and authenticity. In a book that works hard to interrupt 'the simplicity of style and popular appeal' (Mehuron, 1997, p. 167) that readers might expect in research intending to honor those struggling within and against this disease, I situate such efforts as a breaking of the hegemonies of meaning and presence that recuperate and appropriate the tragedies of others into consumption, a too-easy, too-familiar eating of the other. Against homogenous spaces of collective consensus and communication, such work is emotive, figurative, inexact, dispersed and deferred in its presentation of truth-telling toward responsibility within indeterminacy.

Notes

1 Patti Lather and Chris Smithies, *Troubling the Angels: Women Living with HIV/AIDS* (Westview/HarperCollins, 1997). See Lather (2002), for 'postbook' musings.
2 See Kushner (1997) on the need 'to demand something tough of an audience,' art that is 'antagonistic to our usual consumption patterns.' See Lather (1996), for an argument on the politics of accessibility and the non-innocence of demands for clarity.
3 Hargreaves writes, 'It is perhaps time to contextualize the study of teachers' voices, knowledge, and experience more, and to romanticize and moralize about teachers' voices in general rather less' (1996: p. 16). Calling unproblematically on empathy and authenticity, Hargreaves' project is not so much to trouble the concept of voice as it is to trouble the over-reliance on teacher voice at the expense of other stakeholders in public schooling.
4 A best-seller, with over 600,000 copies sold, used in myriad multicultural courses as 'authentic autobiography,' the author of *The Education of Little Tree*, 'Forrest Carter,' presenting himself as a Cherokee storyteller, was found to be Asa Earl Carter, a Ku Klux Klan sympathizer who wrote segregation speeches for governor George Wallace. See Carter (1991). Thanks to Ingrid Johnston (1997) for reminding me of this.
5 Another example is *The City of Light: An Authentic Traveler's Tale*, Jacob d'Ancona, Trans. David Selbourne, about twelfth century China, thereby supplanting Marco Polo

as the first European account of China. 'A clever conceit for a novel,' one critic says. 'Authentic it is,' says another (*Newsweek*, October 6, 1997, p. 70).

6 For Heidegger, authenticity is an existence which one makes one's own, 'a grasping of one's own existence which gives it direction and meaning' (Piper, 1997, p. 30). To understand our situatedness is to project forward in our history, particularly toward our own death. To be inauthentic is to be lost in the definitions of others, lost in our thrownness. To be authentic is to be about the possible rather than the given, 'an ethical desire for a grounding presence' (Scott, 1996, p. 15) that recognizes the importance of dislocation in breaking the hegemonies of meaning and presence. For a take on the issue from the perspective of folklore studies, see Bendix (1997).

7 My thinking in this section is inspired by Malini Johar Schueller's 1992 critique of James Agee's *Let Us Now Praise Famous Men* where she situates Agee as paternalistic and liberal in his idealization of those whose stories he tells but, nevertheless, opening a space for subverting narrow and consensual definitions of the tenant farmers who people his book.

References

Adorno, Theodor (1973). *The Jargon of Authenticity* (Trans. Knut Tarnowski and Frederic Will). Evanston: Northwestern University Press.

Atkinson, Paul and David Silverman (1997). Kundera's *Immortality*: The interview of society and the invention of the self. *Qualitative Inquiry*, 3(3), 304–325.

Bendix, Regina (1997). *In Search of Authenticity: The Formation of Folklore Studies*. Madison: The University of Wisconsin Press.

Benjamin, Walter (1939/1968). Theses on the philosophy of history. In *Illuminations* (Hannah Arendt, Ed.). New York: Schocken, pp. 253–264.

Britzman, Deborah (1997) The tangles of implication. *Qualitative Studies in Education*, 10(1), 31–37.

Britzman, Deborah (1998). *Lost Subjects, Contested Objects: Towards a Psychoanalytic Inquiry of Learning*. Albany, NY: SUNY Press.

Butler, Judith (1993a). Poststructuralism and postmarxism. *Diacritics*, 23(4), 3–11.

Butler, Judith (1993b). *Bodies that Matter*. NY: Routledge.

Carter, Dan (1991). The transformation of a Klansman. *The New York Times*, October 4, p. A31.

Caruth, Cathy and Thomas Keenan (1995). 'The AIDS crisis is not over': A conversation with Gregg Bordowitz, Douglas Crimp, and Laura Pinsky. In *Trauma: Explorations in Memory* (C. Caruth, Ed.). Baltimore: Johns Hopkins, pp. 256–272.

Cohen, Tom (1994). *Anti-mimesis from Plato to Hitchcock*. Cambridge University Press.

Deleuze, Gilles and Felix Guattari (1983). *On the Line* (Trans. J. Johnson). New York: Semiotexte.

Derrida, Jacques (1976). *Of Grammatology* (Trans. G. Spivak). Baltimore: Johns Hopkins University Press.

Derrida, Jacques (1993). Circumfessions. In *Jacques Derrida* (Geoffrey Bennington and Jacques Derrida, Eds.). Chicago: University of Chicago.

Ellsworth, Elizabeth (1997). *The Uses of the Sublime in Teaching Difference*. Paper delivered at the annual meeting of the American Educational Research Association, Chicago, March 24–28.

Gates, Henry Louis (1991). 'Authenticity,' or the lesson of Little Tree. *New York Times Book Review*, November 24, 1–4.

Gilbert-Rolfe, Jeremy (1995). *Beyond Piety: Critical Essays on the Visual Arts, 1986–1993*. Cambridge University Press.

Golomb, Jacob (1995). *In Search of Authenticity: From Kierkegaard to Camus*. London: Routledge.

Haraway, Donna (1997). *Modest witness@Second millenium: Feminism and technoscience*. New York: Routledge.

Harding, Sandra (1991). *Whose Science? Whose Knowledge?* Ithaca, NY: Cornell University Press.

Hargreaves, Andy (1996). Revisiting voice. *Educational Researcher*, 25(1), 12–19.

Hayek, Friedrich August (1952). *The Counter-Revolution of Science: Studies in the Abuse of Reason*. Glencoe, IL: Free Press.

Hollinger, Robert (1994). *Postmodernism and the Social Sciences*. Newbury Park: Sage.

Jameson, Fredric (1984). Postmodernism, or the cultural logic of late capitalism. *The New Left Review*, 146, 52–92.

Johnston, Ingrid (1997, October). Can the non-subaltern speak? Dilemmas of voice and cultural appropriation in literary texts. *Journal of Curriculum Theorizing Conference*, Bloomington, IN, USA.

Kushner, Tony (1997). The art of the difficult. *Civilization*, August/September, 62–67.

Lather, Patti (1996). Troubling clarity: The politics of accessible language. *Harvard Educational Review*, 66(3), 525–545.

Lather, Patti (1997). Drawing the line at angels: Working the ruins of feminist ethnography. *Qualitative Studies in Education*, 10(3), 285–304.

Lather, Patti (2002). Postbook: Working the ruins of feminist ethnography. *Signs*, 27(1), 199–227.

Lather, Patti (2007). *Getting Lost: Feminist Efforts Toward a Double(d) Science*. Albany, NY: State University of New York Press.

Lather, Patti and Chris Smithies (1997). *Troubling the Angels: Women Living with HIV/AIDS*. Boulder, CO: Westview/HarperCollins.

Marcus, George and Michael Fischer (Eds.) (1986). A crisis of representation in the human sciences. *Anthropology as Cultural Critique: An Experimental Moment in the Human Sciences*, Chicago: University of Chicago, pp. 7–16.

Massumi, Brian (1995). The autonomy of affect. *Cultural Critique*, 31, 83–109.

Mehuron, Kate (1997). Sentiment recaptured: The performative in women's AIDS-related testimonies. In *Feminist Interpretations of Jacques Derrida* (Nancy Holland, Ed.). University Park, PA: The Pennsylvania State University Press, pp. 165–192.

Nagele, Rainer (1991). *Theatre, Theory, Speculation: Walter Benjamin and the Scenes of Modernity*. Baltimore: The Johns Hopkins University Press.

Nietzsche, Friedrich (1974). *The Gay Science* (Trans. W. Kaufmann). New York: Vintage.

Piper, David (1997). Lacan, Heidegger, and the future anterior of teaching and learning. *Journal of Curriculum Theorizing*, 13(3), 28–33.

Robinson, J. (1994). White women researching/representing 'others': From antiapartheid to postcolonialism? In *Writing Women and Space* (A. Blunt and G. Rose, Eds.). New York: Guilford, pp. 197–226.

Rochlitz, Rainer (1996). *The Disenchantment of Art: The Philosophy of Walter Benjamin*. New York: Guilford.

Sawicki, Marianne (1997). Empathy before and after Husserl. *Philosophy Today*, Spring, pp. 123–127.

Schueller, Malini Johar (1992). *The Politics of Voice: Liberalism and Social Criticism from Franklin to Kingston*. Albany, NY: SUNY.

Scott, Charles (1996). *On the Advantages and Disadvantages of Ethics and Politics.* Bloomington: Indiana University Press.

Sedgwick, Eve (1995). Affect. *Critical Inquiry*, 21, 496–522.

Sommer, Doris (1994). Resistant texts and incompetent readers. *Poetics Today*, 15(4), 523–551.

Sorell, Tom (1991). *Scientism: Philosophy and the Infatuation with Science.* London: Routledge.

Spivak, Gayatri (1988). Can the Subaltern Speak? In C. Nelson & L. Grossberg (Eds.), *Marxism and the Interpretation of Culture*, pp. 271–313. Urbana: University of Illinois Press.

Spivak, Gayatri (1994). Responsibility. *Boundary 2*, 21(3), 19–64.

Stockton, Kathryn Bond (1994). *God Between their Lips: Desire Between Women in Irigaray, Bronte and Eliot.* Stanford, CA: Stanford University Press.

Tomlinson, Hugh (1989). After truth: Post-modernism and the rhetoric of science. In *Dismantling Truth: Reality in the Post-Modern World* (H. Lawson and L. Appignanesi, Eds.). New York: St. Martin's Press, pp. 43–57.

Visweswaran, Kamala (1994). *Fictions of Feminist Ethnography.* Minneapolis, MN: University of Minnesota Press.

Chapter 2

Indigenous voice, community, and epistemic violence

The ethnographer's 'interests' and what 'interests' the ethnographer

Michael Marker

Introduction

The controversy around Rigoberta Menchú's Testimonio is an old one for Indigenous[1] people. The questioning from those who have the power to claim the space and set the standards and boundaries for what counts as legitimate inquiry has changed little in a hundred years. Rigoberta Menchú, a Guatemalan Indian woman, gave accounts of military atrocities carried out against her people to one anthropologist, only to have the 'truth' of her testimonio attacked by another anthropologist, David Stoll. In his book, Stoll (1999) seems excited to have discovered discrepancies in the numbers of people murdered, the locations where Rigoberta's family members were tortured, and where mass graves were located. He does not, in general, dispute that such things happened in Guatemala; he only exclaims that the 'details' are exceedingly important because they show how Rigoberta Menchú's truth was told – as in Emily Dickinson's recommendation – with a slant. Stoll, of course, has a larger goal. He wants to nudge other anthropologists back into a preceding era of colonial cynicism sealing up the spaces of flux and transformation for listening to the Indigenous voice. The message is, 'Don't be lulled out of a foot-tapping stiffened posture when listening to the Indigenous narrative. These people have an agenda and some of them may be aligned with popular movements on the left; some of them may be trying to stop U.S. corporate-backed military thugs from murdering their people. We must remain stolid and disinterested as scholars. We are only interested in truth; justice is down the hall, in political science . . . or philosophy perhaps.' Stoll demands an empirical, and therefore presumably neutral and objective, interrogation of the Indigenous voice. He views an emergent openness in Indigenous discourse in the politics of identity and representation as a dangerous deference. Hence, his judgment of Rigoberta Menchú becomes a broader assertion about what standards are to be employed and who is to be believed when it comes to understanding the narratives about Indigenous communities. If individuals like Rigoberta Menchú are not authentic voices for oppressed communities, who can then speak for the Indigenous Other? Stolls's favorite? The anthropologist, of course.

Neither Wolf nor Dog: In the academy and the community

Tribal people, have, since contact, tried to tell their stories in ways that have made sense to them, but the colonizers – of all types – who heard these narratives often dismissed them as irrelevant ramblings of the uncivilized mind. The expectation now is that Indigenous people who write books and speak about serious matters will utilize a narrative form that responds to academic conventions. What is not expected, or accepted, is when an Indigenous person attempts to employ discursive forms that are premodern and part of an oral tradition in referencing events and conditions of the recent past and the present. I am referring to the ways that traditional Indigenous people fashion narratives that combine oral tradition and modern conversation patterns, making no distinctions between the two. Linda Smith (1999) has framed the issue clearly, pointing out that traditional Indigenous talk is viewed as 'naive, contradictory and illogical,' but the educated Indigenous intellectual is presumed to be inauthentic and unable to speak from a real Indigenous position (p. 14). This expected and insisted upon dualism, placing Indigenous scholars as too assimilated, not representing the real community and then positioning 'real community' voices as not quite intelligible in the academy, has been the ideal situation for the non-native anthropologist who can act as translator or interlocutor for the community voices. Edward Said (1978) points out that the Westerner could think about the Orient because *he could be there* and was free to construct the meaning of the Other (p. 7). The Indigenous Other has become the object for Western knowledge and the researcher is free to imagine Indigeneity without resistance. By these traveling researchers *who can be there* in Indigenous communities, we are told what is typical and what is not typical in the factionalized communities that *they* describe for us. I must clarify at this point that I do not mean to indict, wholesale, anthropology and *all* anthropologists with broad strokes. I mean to examine some specific and central tendencies of ethnography and the context of how researchers have entered Indigenous communities to study the Other. There are exceptions to the tendencies that I will review here, but they are exceptions. Richard Nelson's (1989) intentions for doing research with Aboriginal people are an example of an anthropologist who has tried to learn something *from* rather than just *about* tribal people: 'I undertook this work, not as a travel guide, but as a guide to non-travel. My hope is to acclaim the rewards of exploring the place in which a person lives rather than searching afar, of becoming fully involved with the near-at-hand, of nurturing a deeper and more committed relationship with home, and of protecting the natural community that sustains all who live there' (p. xii).

The truth that is told and the truth that is sold

In North America, the public has been willing to accept – and even 'celebrate' – the stories of Aboriginal people when they are about ancient times, mythic events, folklore, and anything else that is removed from commentary on the actual economic and political conditions that tribal people experience. Native people do not speak of themselves as simply existing in the past though. As just one example, I have heard plateau elders and leaders employ coyote stories to illuminate the greed and foolishness of the White man and the hydroelectric dams that threaten some salmon species with extinction. However, when the forms and characters of oral tradition merge with stories that implicate or indict the inheritors of wealth and privilege, linking these trajectories to the destruction of Indigenous communities, such narratives are ignored or invalidated. For tribal people, an unnatural dualism is enforced; they can be traditional only if they remain as an exotic artifact of the past, or they can participate in language and society as a modern individual keeping tradition confined within the realm of personal or private knowledge, distanced from informing public life or policy. Certain rules are enforced by the hegemony of this conversation: the past must be segregated from the present; land must be kept apart from identity and ideology.

Debates about the legitimacy of Indigenous narratives parallel the concerns about ethnographic criticism, which are that it 'undermines the ability of social scientists to sort out "true" stories from "false," or that it promotes a sophomoric skepticism at the very historical moment in which feminist and Third World voices begin to challenge the epistemic authority of the white male academy' (Meyer & Klein, 1998, p. 188). In other words, after the recent decades of Indigenous struggle to gain a place in the academy, the potency and stature of *all* claims to truth have deteriorated in a climate of relativistic doubt. But, Indigenous people did not come to the academy to play word and idea games.[2] In general, Native people have come to the university to have their stories forged into concrete-change for their communities. The change that is needed must be built on a community conversation that listens to the collective histories and moral narratives about place that frame the possibilities and vision. It is at once a narrative that is political, describing the economic and cultural conditions of tribal peoples, and at the same time an ethnohistoric telling of precontact conditions and values that were dislocated by colonialism. The intellectual self-determination of Indigenous people is woven from the translucent vision of an era where things were very different and from a serious assessment of how things are now. It is an open desire to acknowledge the mythic[3] proportions of historic community reality while confronting the present conditions of that community.

It is this syncretism of Indigenous narrative that is so contentious and so problematic within the academy. That is, when Indigenous people speak in storytelling ways that blur conventional distinctions between rationality and ethnopoetics, they are dismissed both as not being colorful and 'pure' enough to be interesting to the outsider gaze and, at the same time, not 'truthful' enough to be taken seriously with regard to what counts as evidence and cogency in universities, courts of law, and public opinion. However, for Aboriginal people, this blending of older ways of seeing and knowing with contemporary awareness and technological skills offers a sustaining and transformative education. This transformative Indigenous vision is quite outside the ideologies of both the Left and the Right.

The Stoll book reverberates around ideologies related to individualism, the marketplace, and underlying assumptions about power and history; it relies on a batch of taken-for-granted American populist beliefs. It is thinly cloaked in the shallow language of disinterested scholarship and wholly transparent in its advocacy for neo-liberal forms of social control. While neo-conservative assaults on Indigenous identity and politics have been well-illuminated by the contributors to this volume, scant attention is usually paid to the policies and plagues of materialist social theories. Indigenous goals and values have been trampled on by Marxists as well as by corporate evangelists. The treatment of the Miskito peoples by the Sandinista government in Nicaragua presents an instructive case study on how the Left has misunderstood or ignored Indigenous epistemology and claims to land. Thomas Berger (1991), in writing about the Nicaraguan setting, has commented that 'Marxism, like capitalism, is a European ideology which sees no place for indigenous peoples' forms of land tenure' (p. 109). It must be observed that the situation for Indigenous communities in Latin America is unique, immersed in the histories of brutal domination by multinational corporations amid the muscle of US military operations. Likewise, the testimonio, Menchú's contested medium, is a uniquely Latin American form of text that emerges within the space of this history. In this essay I wish to move somewhat outside the specifics of the Latin American context and into a broader discussion of what many anthropologists do in tribal communities; how they operate out of a particular set of interests. I am not greatly concerned with exposing David Stoll's ethnographic conduct since it is extreme, obvious, and will continue to be regarded as dubious and marginal scholarship by mainstream anthropology. This is not to casually dismiss it, as I think it is a dangerous piece of work and will act to fanaticize a quasi-academic populist readership eager to excoriate and dismantle openings to Indigenous experience, struggle, and community development. Rather, I wish here to talk about the more subtle and elusive aspects of ethnographic hegemony at the hands of anthropologists who are not on a neo-conservative iconoclastic crusade, but rather simply doing the mainstream studies that get turned into books and careers. I wish to talk about the truth that gets told, and the truth that gets sold.

A coastal Salish case study of truth-telling and White denial

My work with the Lummi community in the northwest corner of Washington State gives some glimpses into how truth-telling is negotiated around and between the performance of a story and the power imbalances of the space in which the story is listened to. I should be clear at this point that my personal and professional narratives converge in this setting. My 'work' was not simply that of a university researcher, but also the real work of sweeping floors, driving a school van, and moving heavy objects when needed, all this while teaching high school classes and listening to the stories of elders, parents, and kids. See Marker (2001) for a more detailed account of my 'work.' The Lummis are a Coastal Salish people who have had some success in Federal court cases dealing with fishing rights and the interpretations of nineteenth-century treaties protecting their land and resources. The Point Elliot Treaty of 1855 is the most important treaty for Lummis and the signing of this treaty, which guaranteed government obligations and fishing rights, is commemorated each year in tribal ceremony. However, from the beginning of contact, the US government and the White society set the terms for what would count as 'truth' and how that truth would be spoken; the Indigenous voice was constrained and repressed. In the 1850s, territorial governor Issac Stevens, under directives from Washington, DC, to quickly negotiate land deals clearing the Pacific Northwest region for settlement, refused to allow tribal leaders to voice their perspectives in their own languages. Instead, Stevens insisted that the land and resources be talked about using the Chinook Jargon, a crude trading language of approximately 400 words. Developed for negotiations between trappers and Indians, and useful for transactions involving horses, canoes, and utensils, it had an early utility for Indians and Whites. However, relying strictly on the Jargon, it was impossible to convey deep and subtle meanings about Coastal Salish cosmology, relationships, and the sacred meaning of the land. Using the Chinook Jargon at the Point Elliot treaty negotiations reduced the discourse about land, people, and desire to a hurried, commodified exchange which resulted in compressing Native people onto small reservations to be served by a team of government agents, missionaries, and businessmen who would eventually find ways to carve even more land from these destitute communities. Alexandra Harmon (1998), citing Swan, noted that Indians regarded the Jargon 'as a sort of white man's talk' (p. 61). Vine Deloria (1977), in writing about the treaties, emphasized how the Jargon favored the Whites not only because the Indians could not communicate their deepest understandings of land and history, but because the actual intentions of the treaties were obscured by the rough and simplistic quality of the language (pp. 57–58). The Native voice, in 1855, had to be filtered through the crude language of commodification. Even so, the treaty reserved the Indians' right to continue fishing at their accustomed locations. It was this 1855 document that was interpreted by federal Judge George H. Boldt in 1974 to mean that Puget Sound tribes had always reserved 50 percent of the salmon catch for themselves.

The 1974 Boldt decision produced a severe White backlash[4] in Puget Sound communities, particularly in the schools. The conditions for Lummi students, especially at the public high school, were very tense. Many of the teachers were fishermen who were opposed to Indian fishing rights, construed as 'special rights' by anti-Indian neo-conservatives. Narratives about and from Indians became a political rather than a cultural expression. Of course, the political is always cultural, and the cultural is likewise political. However, the American 'melting pot' *zeitgeist* is awash in this kind of false dualism. The mentality behind this narrow populism is that 'culture' should be confined to a kind of personal 'folk festival' and should not enter into the realm of the political, which is viewed as a separate and 'cultureless' realm. Culturally specific forms that favor the dominant mainstream are treated as normative assumptions, while those who are identified as cultural Others are expected to perform their culture in ways that are exoticized or commodified. Lummis could only safely refer to their culture in stereotypical vignettes, and the salmon, a central component of the culture, could not be talked about at all in the explosive climate of the classroom.

When Lummis told about violence and racism in the schools, the White community characterized their narratives as exaggeration or fantasy. Lummis, in telling about their lives at the school, spoke in a kind of general language of indictment that often omitted specific details and dates of events. The White school and community could easily defend against claims about history and identity by pointing out that Lummi narratives were both fanciful and predictable as vague complaints. Usually the tribal perspective, that the public school was a place where they had been pushed to the margins and eventually pushed out by institutional racism, was ignored by the White community. I conducted interviews with both Lummis and Whites trying to get to the 'truth,' not only of what happened at the school and in the community, but of what it meant as a larger pattern of Indian–White tensions and Lummi marginalization. As someone who has lived and worked in both the Lummi and White communities, I traversed a divided landscape asking questions and listening to stories as well as some uncomfortable silences from Whites on the meaning of the school. Indeed, I was a researcher, an ethnographer. I viewed the work as a kind of writing down of community conversations across the cultural barricades. I was both insider and outsider in both worlds. Apart from the listening to and writing down of the variety of interpretations of the meaning of this history in both Indian and White communities, my goal was to understand something about the nature of what happened at one particular high school. My goal was to become more informed about a complicated reality to foster a more intelligent and inclusive conversation. I did not anticipate how contentious even these efforts at conversation would become. A number of Lummi tribal members had suggested I do this study which, as I attempted to understand underlying forms and forces, quickly moved in concentric circles away from the high school. I believed then, and I believe now, that we must not abandon the notion that something happened in the past apart from an endless debate over subjectivities and interpretations. Most importantly, I believe that we must attend to an analysis of power to explain the dynamics of settings. Like William G. Tierney (2000), I avoided looking for an 'absolutist reading of events, histories and circumstances that are inevitably contested.' I was attempting to engage in 'the creation of the real' (p. 112). I tried to describe what happened as I tried to delineate the divided interpretations of what happened. I found documents and testimony that offered a clear indictment of the state educational institutions, including the local university. The most outrageous incident featured a professor who won an academic-freedom case arguing that Lummis were genetically inferior (Marker, 2000). It is a sensational example of more elusive, and perhaps more sinister, expressions of racism. It is outrageous both because of the professor's explanations of Lummi inferiority, applying a fanciful history of west-coast slavery, and because no campus or regional newspaper ever covered the story. When I began to discuss my work publicly, I found that most non-Natives in the educational system – especially at nearby Western Washington University – were not very interested in Lummi narratives about oppression, power, and identity. It became clear to me that the White community never disputed the 'truth' of the stories that Lummis told; they only saw that they had no stake in these truths, and they found them dull. Calling them isolated incidents and exaggerations was a discursive move to discard them rather than a move to refute their validity.

When I began doing the research on Lummi schooling during the fishing wars,[5] tribal people were enthusiastic and encouraged me because they said, 'we've told our stories for years now, maybe if someone like you from a university writes things down in the right way, the people in charge will pay attention and change things. At least they won't be able to say it isn't true what happened to us and our kids.' At Lummi, people were eager to read the research and the community library made a number of copies that always seemed to be checked out. But, one afternoon I began to question the real potency of ethnographic research when a Lummi woman told me that 'it was good to write all this down so outside people know what happened, but in the end, it won't do much because the White people at the university know all this anyway and it doesn't change them.' Having a university researcher show the validity of the stories with empirical evidence and analysis did not solve the fundamental problem: The stories about racism were simply not interesting to Whites.

Looking in all the wrong places

While a number of Indigenous scholars have proposed that non-Natives should not be doing research in tribal communities any longer,[6] this misses the fundamental problem. Elsewhere I have argued that 'the quality of research is not improved *simply* by having Aboriginal people doing the writing. It is improved by a more detailed analysis that includes the perspectives and location of both Natives and non-Natives' (Marker, 2001, p. 31). This means an analysis of history, hegemony, and self. Unfortunately, because of the context of competitive careerism in the academy, ethnographers are both in a hurry and selective about whom they talk to and get information from. They want to get something published, and they need to get the attention of editors and reviewers. Often, the themes of Indigenous communities that *they* are most interested in are the ones that are exotically titillating and sealed off from larger considerations of history and power with regard to dominant state and corporate pressures. Researchers have recently discovered that Indigenous communities are not homogenous and so have been fascinated with the internal disputes, contradictions, and gossip about families and factionalism that reverberates in all communities, Indigenous or not. This has really become simply another chapter in the history of the colonial gaze at the Indigenous other. Instead of perpetuating the myth of frozen exotic sameness about tribal society, these studies become a day in the life of colorful but confused subaltern individuals trying to maintain a sense of ritual and tradition in a world of cell phones and laptops. The text is written more conscious of political correctness, but not necessarily more respectfully. The storytelling theater has been renovated,

but the ventriloquists remain the same. This new self-conscious but not necessarily self-reflective writing has emerged out of some misguided efforts to avoid
essentializations of the Indigenous other. The problem is that such an approach
tends to neutralize a more dialectical cultural comparison and analysis of power.
It must also be admitted that it is the *ethnographers'* needs that are being ful-
filled, not the needs of Indigenous communities. Odawa scholar Cecil King (1997)
laments,

> We acknowledge, with gratitude, the attempts by the National Endowment
> for the Humanities and the American Anthropological Association to regulate
> researchers by guidelines or codes of ethics. However, for most of us, these
> efforts are part of the problem. For we must ask: Whose ethics? (p. 118)

Indigenous scholars, few and far between compared with the numbers of anthropologists and critical theorists who are studying Indigenous people, occasionally
find time to challenge the 'truth' of these 'community studies.' Two good examples
of discord between anthropologists and community-based Indigenous scholars
are Daisy Sewid Smith's (1997) response to Harry F. Wolcott's description of a
Kwakiutl[7] potlatch and Jo-Ann Archibald's (1999/2000) review of anthropologist
Crisca Bierwert's ethnography of Coastal Salish Communities. Both essays raise
questions about what the anthropologists paid attention to and how activities such
as the private spiritual practices of the communities were discussed carelessly
and disrespectfully in a public fashion. Archibald observes that Bierwert's book
'presents Stolo people as fraught with family violence, as suffering exception-
ally low employment, and as wrestling with never-ending fishing issues' (p. 111).
A parallel complaint is that the larger historic and political landscape is communities, or rather the factionalism, internal power struggles, and dysfunctional
relationships in these communities as though they were hermetically sealed off
from the outside world.

There is virtually no analysis of historical and cultural forces outside the tribal
community – forces that have disrupted and distorted traditional social and economic relations while consolidating wealth and power for Whites in these regions.

The categories for what counts as true, significant, and even interesting are constructed by the researchers as they apply their own hierarchy of concepts to the
inquiry process. For example, researchers who write about Indigenous communities are often focused on issues of identity as a fundamental issue. In the case of
Rigoberta Menchú, challenging her identity as a *genuine* Indigenous voice was an
important part of Stoll's strategy. This is a hegemonic move that denies other epistemic possibilities about identity and place. James Clifford (1988) has explored
the substrata of these kinds of tensions:

> Yet what if identity is conceived not as a boundary to be maintained but as a
> nexus of relations and transactions actively engaging a subject: The story or
> stories of interaction must then be more complex, less linear and teleological.
> What changes when the subject of 'history' is no longer Western? How do

stories of contact, resistance, and assimilation appear from the standpoint of groups in which exchange rather than identity is the fundamental value to be sustained? Events are always mediated by local cultural structures. (p. 344)

Too many researchers go into Indigenous communities armed with a set of questions and concepts that they apply to their selective listening to selected Native informants. Identity is one of the taken-for-granted questions. It does not matter if identity, in the way the researcher thinks of it, is not constructed by the community in ways consistent with the researcher's understanding. What if identity is not very important to a particular group of Indigenous people, but rather relationships and a more elusive, more difficult to describe, mythic connection to place are? Are researchers who encounter this shape-shifting willing to let go of their expectations and allow themselves to be overwhelmed by the unsettling sensation of flux and uncertainty about truth? Will they let Indigenous people tell them what is important to study and learn about? Or, will they continue to insist on defining Indigenous people in ways that suit their academic disciplines, their careers, and their political agendas? To really learn about Indigenous communities is to learn about oneself, and researchers are not trained for this encounter. The emphasis on describing the internal intricacies of Indigenous communities without a sufficient analysis of the region's larger history of power differentials encourages anthropologists to use a magnifying glass, when they ought to be using a mirror.

The knower and the known

An authentic listening to the cultural Other should produce more than a fascination with the exotic: it should provoke an awakening to the cultural 'self.' This would mean that conventional assumptions about the history and structure of the researcher's own cultural presumptions would be unraveled by engaging with and actually learning from the perspective of Indigenous people. Of course, this does not mean to reverse the fallacy by suggesting that all activities and structures in Indigenous communities have parallels in dominant postindustrial societies; it is only to suggest that such a learner's stance destabilizes the anthropologist's dubious claim to being the expert on that Indigenous community. Clifford Geertz (1995) points out that 'the mere claim "to know better" which it would seem any anthropologist would have at least implicitly to make, seems at least faintly illegitimate' (p. 5). Vine Deloria (1997) is even more to the point: 'It is now time to reverse this perspective and use the values, behaviors, and institutions of tribal or primitive peoples to critique and investigate the industrial societies and their obvious shortcomings' (p. 220).

Listening to the Indigenous voice in a reflexive mode is consistent with Marcus and Fischer's (1986) recommendation for an anthropology of self-conscious cultural critique recognizing that what anthropologists pay attention to is a political choice as 'there are multiple sides and multiple expressions of possibilities active in any situation' (p. 116). The truth, then, is constructed partly out of what researchers are willing to pay attention to and how they interpret what they are being told.

A number of anthropologists and critical theorists have responded to calls for a more reflexive listening to the Native voice by positioning themselves in a dubious advocacy role with regard to Indigenous community issues. We are subjected to a new version of the old pudding sometimes named collaborative, or dialogic, methodologies. However, this stance is too often a continuation of the neo-liberal goal of offering support to oppressed minorities without challenging the power and cultural position of dominant groups. Laura Nader (1974) challenged anthropology to 'study up' three decades ago. Unheeded, this is still the most fruitful, imaginative, and transformative way to listen to the Indigenous voice, to

> ask many 'common sense' questions in reverse. Instead of asking why some people are poor, we would ask why other people are so affluent? . . . Anthropologists might indeed ask themselves whether the entirety of field work does not depend upon a certain power relationship in favor of the anthropologist, and whether indeed such dominant subordinate relationships may not be affecting the kinds of theories we are weaving. (p. 289)

Aanishinabe scholar and activist Winona La Duke, in talking about her tribal community's struggles, focused on the invisibility of the histories of power and privilege and how Americans have glamorized wealth:

> We quite often do not ask how they got to be rich. We don't ask if they paid fair wages to people who worked in their plants, or if they got rich stealing someone else's land, or stealing someone else's natural resources.
> (Speech at Western Washington University, December 6, 2001)

Eric Wolf (1999b), in exploring the anthropology of power, offers a broader but nonetheless useful prescription:

> Seeking answers to such questions, however, also requires us to go beyond the ethnographic present – the moment in which the ethnographer collects and records his observations – to locate the object of our study in time. It is not the events of history we are after, but the processes that underlie and shape such events. (p. 8)

The processes are, of course, much larger than what goes on in the day-to-day life of an Indigenous community.

It is unlikely that anthropology will take on a general interest in the *culture of power*. The discipline has too much invested in the *power of 'culture.'* Sherry B. Ortner (1994) concluded an essay on changes in anthropological theory by observing that 'practice has qualities related to the hard times of today; pragmatism, maximization of advantage, "every man," as the saying goes, "for himself" '

(p. 403). Anthropologists have developed a set of conceptual tools for dissecting the Indigenous identity and voice, but just like the proverbial high school biology exercise, the pieces of the frog strewn about the lab table do not contain the meaning of the frog. And, like the dissecting tools of the biology lab, the anthropologist's tools work best toward purposes that are directly connected to anthropology's history and development as a colonial enterprise. 'Empowering' or 'advocating' for Indigenous communities is a suspiciously ethnocentric and patronizing goal. Many Indigenous groups would find the language itself offensive and presumptuous, as they maintain that they were never conquered and hence have never relinquished their 'power.' Nevertheless, power of culture remains a popular methodological orientation because it retains the utility of anthropology's fundamental dissecting tools, which are oriented toward analysis of a cultural subaltern. Anthropologists have been generally reluctant to pack up their toolboxes and go off seeking information on cultures of power. Describing identity formation, cultural transmission, voice, authority, and social organization among corporate executives, government officials, and privileged upper class families taxes and problematizes anthropological tools and methods. For too many researchers, it is more fun and rewarding – not to mention safer – to imagine themselves 'adopted' by a tribe and 'collaborating' to help solve some problem that the tribe has. What if the tribe's 'problem' is that too many useless studies have been conducted without any analysis of structures that have distorted and dislocated their community from the traditional values that hold people together? Micaela di Leonardo (1998) has stated the problem clearly: 'American anthropology, as we shall see – despite the vigorous and careful efforts of some – relies on an implicit and therefore entirely untheorized, American "home." Its metropolitan gaze misses its own reflection' (p. 16). It is useless to support subaltern groups without concomitantly exposing and destabilizing the hegemonic forces that continue to oppress them, just as it is useless to listen to the Native voice without paying attention to the countervailing voices of power and privilege. Gregory Bateson (1972) puts it in basic language: 'Tools are for purposes and anything which blocks purpose is a hindrance' (p. 49).

Truth resides in places

From an Indigenous perspective, the 'truth' not only needs to be placed within larger dimensions of history and power, it must be experienced in actual places on the landscape. Keith Basso (1996) in his book *Wisdom Sits in Places: Landscape and Language Among the Western Apache*, explains how Apache people regard the land, linked with the oral tradition, as containing the moral authority that undergirds truth and social structuring. Julie Cruikshank (1998), working with Native women in the Yukon, has made similar observations about the intertwining of land, story, and knowledge. The experience has directed her thoughts to fundamental questioning of dominant conventions about knowledge and texts: 'What are the consequences of categorical practices that distance people from lived experience? How does authorizing knowledge change its social function?

Is a passion for universalizing peculiar to the West, or is it part of a more global process?' (p. 70). A genuine encounter with the Indigenous voice is an engagement that taps into transformative moral dimensions. The oral traditions were structured often so that they would trouble the listener's soul. And the spirits of the stories, dwelling in the soul of the land, would awaken the deepest sense of self in the learner. This awakening has been all too rare as elders have watched researchers

> grow in their knowledge and understanding of our ways. But, unfortunately, many times we have been betrayed. Our honored guests have shown themselves to be no more than peeping toms, rank opportunists, interested in furthering their own careers by trading in our sacred traditions.
>
> (King, 1997, p. 115)

Sometimes though, as in the works of Basso, Cruikshank, and a few others, the researcher becomes the learner, in a space of meaning that is difficult to explain without actually being in that geographic place again.

An archeology student told me this story: She was working with a team that was consulting with Tlingit elders about the location of an ancient village site in Alaska, and as they sat in the town's school gymnasium, the directors of the project were growing impatient with the lack of progress. They showed the elders maps, descriptions of artifacts, and analyses of the geology, but the old people were silent. Frustrated, the anthropologists took a break to decide on another strategy to extract the information they needed for their research. This student had lived with one of the traditional Native families and had worked hard over the summer cooking for a fishing boat. She was well-liked by the local people and, in this context, on the morning while the crew drank coffee and tried to strategize their communication styles, an old man silently took her hand and pulled her outside. 'Follow me,' he said. 'Are we going far?' she asked. The old man simply said, 'you are asking questions about that village, you must follow me.' They walked over ridges and grassy bluffs, through a thick forest and down to a glacier carved coastline. They walked all day and into the twilight of summer night. She was exhausted when they finally stopped, and he showed her an enormous rockslide that rolled out into a remote bay. 'Here,' he said, 'many years ago a terrible earthquake pushed this mountain down on top of the village. Many families died in the terror of this rockslide which has covered the place. If you are very still, you can feel spirits and the sadness here.' She wept uncontrollably, and when she regained composure, the elder said, 'you feel it now, don't you? The questions you were asking at the gym in town don't belong there. The questions you were asking belong here. Now you understand.'

Examining the identity and interests of researchers

I was in the Petén region of Guatemala a few years ago on a teaching and research trip with some tribal college students. While many of these American Indian students had come from impoverished reservations and families, they still, by Guatemalan standards, seemed affluent since they wore expensive sport shoes and carried cameras and CD players. One humid morning, some of the villagers gathered to hear the tribal college students tell about their educational and career goals. The Itsa Mayan youth who sat in the audience had few questions for their American counterparts, but later that day an elder, who was teaching us the uses of Indigenous plants and the complexity of regional ecology, talked about how corporate-media-fueled appetites were poisoning the souls of Indigenous youth *everywhere*. 'In our village "la juventúd" are developing "la enfermedad del espiritu," [spirit sickness].' Because we had spent several days with him talking about the land, the stories, and the legacy of colonialism, we knew that his declaration about the poisoning of young spirits included an invocation of this history and its meanings as a way to crystallize – and cauterize – the political/cultural moment. There were certainly countervailing 'truths' available. Throughout Guatemala, and even in the village, many people would contradict the old man's perspective; that which is called 'poisons' becomes named 'opportunities.' The omnipresent multinational logos and US military uniforms worn by the Guatemalan soldiers saturated the setting for the momentary truth-telling of this elder. Yet, his truth, like Rigoberta Menchú's testimonio, had a compelling force that pushed a small, but profound, space open in a crowded marketplace of noisy truths. It was, in spite of everything, a self-evident truth. He told this truth to us with the compelling intensity of a human being who has seen terrible things. However, had I been, for some reason, dissatisfied with his speech and its assumptions about history, epistemology, and teleology, I am confident that I could have found individuals to contradict his assumptions. Given enough time and resources, it is probable that I could have even found and interviewed individuals who would have defamed the elder and challenged his legitimacy, authority, and identity. Was his exhortation untrue, then? What does this mean then? I think it means that at a certain point in these exchanges we must look away from the speaker and shift our attention to the values and motives of the ethnographer (the listener). It also means that David Stoll's disclaimer that he is not attempting to refute the 'general' history of oppression and genocide that occurred in Guatemala must be viewed with some suspicion. He has shaped an argument, but it is dangerously stripped of an analysis of power and culture. It is not the disinterested academic; there *is* no disinterested academic. Historical analysis stripped of its attention to power differentials is neither good scholarship, nor responsible social discourse. Dirks, Eley, and Ortner (1994) have explained how

> history itself has variable cultural form – that the shape of events, the pace of time, the notion of change and duration, the very question of what an event is – all of these things are not simply objective realities, but are themselves products of cultural assumptions.... Culture as emergent from relations of power and domination, culture as a medium in which power is both constituted and resisted. (p. 6)

I must stop at this point and confess that in revising this essay I became concerned that I was being too hard on anthropologists. Indeed, anthropology is steeped in a vigorous debate about how to transform itself in an increasingly compressed and marketized academy. Eric Wolf (1999b) pointed to 'a basic tension between this major contribution – our critical perspective – and the institutional contexts in which we must gain our livelihood' (p. 38). Still, while anthropologists try to redefine themselves as *not* being intellectual 'summer people,' they continue to view themselves as the advisors and helpers to the 'cultured' poor and not much interested in the culture of the rich. Reviewing some recent issues of *Anthropology News* I came across numerous examples of this kind of self-styled advocacy for the subaltern, but scant appeals to study up. Typical is this commentary: 'Instead of seeing the people among whom we do our research and action as exotic, we will see them as the oppressed and underserved, both here and abroad' (Chrisman, 2002, p. 4). I do not think I am being too hard on anthropologists.

Stoll's book has a particular quality that makes it primarily an American cultural – or media – product. I suspect that in Canada, Australia, New Zealand, and other countries with large Indigenous populations, his writing would seem irrelevant and much ado about nothing. Clearly, the book is specifically marketed for an audience steeped in the discourse modeled by former Secretary of the Interior, James Watt: 'If you want an example of the failures of socialism . . . go to the reservations . . . every social problem is exaggerated because of socialistic government policies on the Indian reservations' (quoted in Esber, 1992, p. 216). Such cold war bigotry is an enduring residue of American attitudes toward Native people. Americans, wanting some good news about the 'intention,' if not the outcome, of US military and economic policy in Latin America could find Stoll's good Indians on the Right and the bad ones on the Left. An exposé of Indians and Leftists is, for this audience, a welcome intellectual analgesic. Again, we should be more attentive to who Stoll is, rather than who the informants are at this juncture. In short, Stoll wants to sell a book and advance a career; in point of fact, he has done both – *like other anthropologists who have written about Indigenous communities*. This book has gotten so much attention primarily because it is ideologically profitable for the media and ideologically unnerving for mainstream anthropologists who want to sell books that advocate for tribal people in *opposition* to corporate 'tribes.' An explication of power and its histories escapes the approaches of both Stoll and the 'other friends' as economic and cultural assumptions go unchallenged.

We should begin to ask ethnographers to identify themselves in terms of these cultural assumptions and histories. Some modest efforts to uncloak these context factors and ethnographic 'choices' for what to listen to might help us to understand that a lie is not simply an untruth told; it is also a truth untold. Vine Deloria (1997) concludes that

> asking anthropology to undertake a new task, particularly a task with such a
> high potential for disturbing the secure financial base from which scholars have

always comfortably moved to examine the exotic tribal peoples of the world, is a rather hazardous request and one likely to be rejected out of hand. But it is a necessary request because it basically asks scholars to develop a personal identity as concerned human beings and move away from the comfortable image of 'scholar.' (p. 221)

Those researchers/learners who adopt a respectful position as concerned human beings might gain unique insights into themselves as they come to understand the reality of Indigenous people. They might also come to see that what 'interests' many anthropologists is only vaguely related to the reality of Indigenous communities and more directly related to their own career 'interests.'

Notes

1 It is becoming a more common practice to capitalize words like Indigenous, Aboriginal, Native, in writing that denotes significant historical, cultural, and political distinctions for the peoples who claim these categories for themselves as a fundamental aspect of their identity. I have chosen to capitalize Indigenous as a way to apply a signifier in this regard.
2 Clearly, Chippewa author and Native studies professor Gerald Vizenor's work should be noted as an exception in that he is primarily interested in 'discovering the play in a word' (Coltelli, 1990: p. 175).
3 Words such as 'myth' are easily misunderstood. I do not mean to perpetuate colloquial notions that myth is not 'true' or somehow less valid than 'science.' I use this term distinctly to refer to ways that Indigenous peoples experienced place, space, and time linked to transcendent moral and spiritual forms. I am also referencing a broad discussion of historiography and metaphysics that reverberates around the works of Calvin Martin (1978), William Cronon (1983), Vine Deloria (1995), and others.
4 Backlash refers to the heightened tensions and attacks on Indigenous people and their claims to space and identity which have accompanied legal victories in the courts in the United States. Anti-tribal ideology is linked to neo-conservative populism and finds expression in media and educational discourse.
5 The 1960s and 1970s have been called the era of fishing wars in the Pacific Northwest. In Puget sound tensions between Indian and non-Indian fishermen became violent as boats were rammed and guns were fired. Boxberger (1989) has chronicled the Lummi experience of the 'fishing wars.'
6 See Swisher (1998) and King (1997) as two examples of the indictment of non-Native researchers. Lomawaima (2000) reviews the history of abuses by researchers and displays the strict guidelines by which present tribal councils grant permission to study 'with' Aboriginal people.
7 More correctly, Kwakwaka'wakw. The spelling and pronunciation have changed over time to more accurately reflect the way Kwakwala-speaking people on Vancouver Island refer to themselves.

References

Archibald, J. (Winter 1999/2000). Review of *Brushed by Cedar, Living by the River: Coast Salish Figures of power. B. C. Studies, 124,* 110–111.
Basso, K. H. (1996). *Wisdom sits in places: Landscape and language among the Western Apache*. Albuquerque: University of New Mexico Press.

Bateson, G. (1972). *Steps to an ecology of mind*. New York: Chandler Publishing.

Berger, T. R. (1991). *A long and terrible shadow: White values, native rights in the Americas*. Vancouver: Douglas & McIntyre.

Boxberger, D. (1989). *To fish in common: The ethnohistory of lummi Indian salmon fishing*. Lincoln: University of Nebraska Press.

Chrisman, N. J. (2002). Toward a mature anthropology. *Anthropology News, 43*(4), 4–5.

Clifford, J. (1988). *The Predicament of culture: Twentieth-century ethnography, literature, and art*. Cambridge, MA: Harvard University Press.

Coltelli, L. (1990). *Winged words: American Indian writers speak*. Lincoln: University of Nebraska Press.

Cronon, W. (1983). *Changes in the land: Indians, colonists, and the ecology of New England*. New York: Hill & Wang.

Cruikshank, J. (1998). *The social life of stories: Narrative and knowledge in the Yukon Territory*. Lincoln: University of Nebraska Press.

Deloria, V. (1977). *Indians of the Pacific Northwest: From the coming of the white man to the present day*. Garden City, NY: Doubleday.

Deloria, V. (1995). *Red earth white lies: Native Americans and the myth of scientific fact*. New York: Scribner.

Deloria, V. (1997). Conclusion: Anthros, Indians, and planetary reality. In T. Biolsi & L. Zimmerman (Eds.), *Indians and anthropologists: Vine Deloria and the critique of anthropology* (pp. 209–221). Tucson: University of Arizona Press.

di Leonardo, M. (1998). *Exotics at home: Anthropologies, others, American modernity*. Chicago: University of Chicago Press.

Dirks, N., Eley, G., & Ortner, S. (Eds.). (1994). *Introduction to Culture/power/history: A reader in contemporary social theory*. Princeton, NJ: Princeton University Press.

Esber, G. S. (1992). Shortcomings of the Indian self-determination policy. In *State and reservation: New perspectives on federal Indian policy* (pp. 212–223). Tucson: University of Arizona Press.

Geertz, C. (1995). Review essay: Culture war. *New York Review of Books, 42*(November 30), 4–7.

Harmon, A. (1998). *Indians in the making: Ethnic relations and Indian identities around Puget Sound*. Berkeley: University of California Press.

King, C. (1997). Here come the anthros. In T. Biolsi & L. Zimmerman (Eds.), *Indians and anthropologists: Vine Deloria and the critique of anthropology* (pp. 115–119). Tucson: University of Arizona Press.

Lomawaima, T. (2000). Tribal sovereigns: reframing research in American Indian education. *Harvard Educational Review, 70*(1), 1–21.

Marcus, G. E., & Fischer, M. M. J. (1986). *Anthropology as cultural critique: An experimental moment in the human sciences*. Chicago: University of Chicago Press.

Marker, M. (2000). Lummi identity and white racism: When location is a real place. *International Journal of Qualitative Studies in Education, 13*(4), 401–414.

Marker, M. (2001). Economics and local self-determination: Describing the clash zone in First Nations education. *Canadian Journal of Native Education, 24*(1), 30–44.

Martin, C. (1978). *The keepers of the game: Indian–animal relationships and the fur trade*. Berkeley, CA: University of California Press.

Meyer, M., & Klein, K. L. (1998). Native American studies and the end of ethnohistory. In R. Thornton (Ed.), *Studying Native America: Problems and prospects*. Madison, WI: University of Wisconsin Press.

Nader, L. (1974). Up the anthropologist – perspectives gained from studying up. In D. Hymes (Ed.), *Reinventing anthropology* (pp. 284–311). New York: Vintage Books.

Nelson, R. (1989). *The island within*. New York: Vintage Books.

Ortner, S. (1994). Theory in anthropology since the sixties. In N. Dirks, G. Eley, & S. Ortner (Eds.), *Introduction to Culture/power/history: A reader in contemporary social theory* (pp. 372–411). Princeton, NJ: Princeton University Press.

Said, E. (1978). *Orientalism*. New York: Pantheon Books.

Sewid Smith, D. (1997). The continuing reshaping of our ritual world by academic adjuncts. *Anthropology & Education Quarterly*, 28(4), 594–603.

Smith, L. T. (1999). *Decolonizing methodologies: Research and indigenous peoples*. London: Zed Books.

Stoll, D. (1999). *Rigoberta Menchú and the story of all poor Guatemalans*. Boulder, CO: Westview Press.

Swisher, K. (1998). Why Indian people should be the ones to write about Indian education. In D. Mihesuah (Ed.), *Natives and academics: Researching and writing about American Indians* (pp. 190–199). Lincoln: University of Nebraska Press.

Tierney, W. G. (2000). Beyond translation: Truth and Rigoberta Menchú. *International Journal of Qualitative Studies in Education, 13*(2), 103–114.

Wolf, E. R. (1999a). *Envisioning power: Ideologies of dominance and crisis*. Berkeley, CA: University of California Press.

Wolf, E. R. (1999b). Anthropology and the academy: Historical reflections. In L. G. Basch, L. W. Saunders, et al. (Eds.), *Transforming academia: Challenges and opportunities for an engaged anthropology*. Arlington, VA: American Anthropological Association.

Chapter 3

An impossibly full voice

Lisa A. Mazzei

Voice happens. But *when* does voice happen? I am no longer certain that I can *know* when voice happens, because it is *always* happening. What I do know is that the voice I have been seeking as an indicator of expressed thought exceeds my ways of hearing, knowing, and understanding. The voice which I have been seeking to 'capture' and tame as clear, pure, and articulable is now only present to me as slippery, shifting, knowable, unknowable, certain, uncertain, audible, inaudible, and certainly unstable. Can I take comfort in this certainty of uncertainty? Can I know that I know *when* voice happens just because it is always already happening?

How does voice happen? Voice clearly happens in spoken utterances 'voiced' by our participants, but does it not also happen when they/we fail to audibly voice an opinion with words and instead voice displeasure, discomfort, or disagreement with silence? Does it not also happen through other nonverbal forms such as art, or dance, or music? Are there not other unthought ways in which our participants voice their thoughts, resistances, and desires?

Where does voice happen? Voice plainly happens in the formal context of an interview or conversation, but does it not also happen in the dreams of our sleep? Does it happen in the spaces and places that name us and claim us? Does it happen *everywhere*?

I could be paralyzed by this certainty of uncertainty, this potential irruption of data everywhere, unable to make meaning, unable to discern the voiced thoughts of those whom I encounter in doing qualitative research. Or, like Derrida, I might relish the possibility of impossibility (Caputo, 1994; Derrida, 1997), the exhilaration of missed meanings, silent meanings, and excessive meanings – of voices and identities [and researchers] in trouble (Jackson, 2004). What then am I to make of this shifting, uncertain, uncontainable voice? This shifting voice that is much more seductive, much more intriguing – at least to me – than some predictable knowable voice. How to account for this elusive voice with its promise of unspoken meanings? If I am no longer to know when voice happens, how voice happens, or where voice happens, then how am I to know what constitutes voice?

A faithfulness to excess

Some might accuse me of posing as a modernist shrouded in a cloak of poststructuralism, shielding myself from the criticism of an underlying attempt to get to the bottom of something – of voice, of meaning, of truth, of silence. Still others might playfully accuse me of poststructural eroticism[1] – teasing with the possibility of what might be revealed beneath the veil of speech in a world of shifting voices. My desire that produces these questions, however, is not a modernist attempt to seek a fixed and certain voice *spoken* by research participants. It is rather my desire to be faithful to the competing voices that are present toward a more complete, more nuanced, more complicated hearing of an impossibly full voice.[2]

What is this impossibly full and enigmatic voice that I seek to confine in an attempt to learn more about the research participants that I engage – their voices shifting and cavorting as they speak with spoken words, with images, with silences. I am urged to consider how I might account for those voices with which they speak in their attempts to articulate a boundless identity in response to my urging that they give an account of themselves (Butler, 2005). To consider how I might both elicit and work the limit of this excessive voice toward more subtle, more nuanced, more startling meanings. If the pursuit of a counter-practice that seeks the silent siren voices is worthy of our imagining, then how might it be imagined at the limit of voice that opens up a thinking of voice not previously possible?[3]

Ian Stronach (2002) writes, 'This space is not yet blank. Before I write, it is overwritten by the polarity of theory/practice' (p. 291). This overwriting, this writing over, is discussed by Stronach as a way in which our research and writing are disciplined and censored before we ever put pen to paper. In much the same way, I am attempting to theorize the ways in which the voices that are given a hearing have been censored and disciplined before we ask a single research question, write a single field note, or record a single response. The voices that have been given a hearing are disciplined in ways that eliminate a silent voice previously ignored because it does not make easy sense and transgresses the domesticated voice that we are accustomed to hearing, knowing, and naming. This excessive silent voice that we cannot 'hear' but that speaks to us nonetheless, requires a different attentiveness and listening in our research settings. This silent voice is only hearable 'within a problematic of silence that is errant, wayward, and that rebels against those practices of censoring and over-writing' (Mazzei, 2007a). This silent voice is one that beckons and constitutes itself in a resistance to classification and a desire for authenticity.

An imperceptible crack

In discussing the linguistic aspect of voice, Mladen Dolar (2006) writes that 'if we speak in order to say something, then the voice is precisely that which cannot be said. It is there, in the very act of saying, but it eludes any pinning down' (p. 15). However as Dolar continues, because voice precedes the Word, the tendency is to progress from voice to meaning (p. 16).[4] As researchers, we then seek that voice which can elucidate, clarify, confirm, and pronounce meaning. And yet, our poststructural sensibility (if such a thing exists) tells us not to give up on voice, but to give up on the promise of voice. By the promise of voice I mean the promise of a voice that can provide truth, fixity, knowledge, and authenticity. Instead, we should seek the promise of an impossibly full voice that challenges such truths and authentic meanings.

If, however, a desire for authenticity is no longer possible as asserted by Patti Lather in the opening chapter of this section, then why the relentless pursuit of voice in qualitative inquiry, particularly in research that depends on the narrative accounts offered by our participants? Or perhaps, a more appropriate question is, what do we seek when we seek to give 'voice' to our participants; what are we listening to/for in our effort to constitute voice? Perhaps though, before we proceed too far toward what we seek, we must first answer the question of what is there, or in the case of my project, *when* is voice.

We should not be so self-assured in the knowledge that we can know our participants' voices or that we can trust their voiced speech to provide meaning and truths, for in a destabilizing of such truths and self-certainty Deleuze cautions that 'it is rather when everything is going well, or everything goes better on the other line, that the crack happens on this new line – secret, imperceptible, marking a threshold of lowered resistance, or the rise of a threshold of exigency: you can no longer stand what you put up with before, even yesterday' (Deleuze & Parnet, 1987/2002, p. 126). What is the crack that happens on this line of voice that once seemed so unproblematically solid and 'real?' A Khora, perhaps, through which the destabilized and silent voices slip, a threshold of exigency such that we can do nothing but to notice/hear/listen differently.

In an installation entitled Shibboleth as part of the Unilever Turbine Hall project at the Tate Modern, London,[5] the artist Doris Salcedo has provided a visual rendering of such a destabilizing crack, beginning imperceptibly, but forcing a noticing of this unsettling presence. Writing of the opening of the installation, Adrian Searle (2007) describes the effect:

> Shibboleth begins with a hairline crack in the concrete floor by the entrance. As insignificant as a flaw in a teacup, as telling as the build-up scenes of a disaster movie, the crack soon widens and deepens, a jagged crevasse making its jagged way the length of the Turbine Hall, 167 metres away, jabbing like a fork of lightning, and deepening and [sic] as it goes. You can never quite see the bottom of it. (p. 21)

The fundamental difference between the visual crack produced by Salcedo and the crack to which I refer is that the crack into which voice slips (or escapes), the crack created by this Other voice, can be ignored. What we risk by plunging into this abyss is a willingness to think voice beyond its recognizably constituted forms. Salcedo (2007) describes her installation as one that 'intrudes in the space, that it is unwelcome like an immigrant that just intrudes without permission.' The crack into/out of which voice slips intrudes, escapes, and opens without our permission, but we must give ourselves permission to tumble into the uncomfortable uncertainty that it creates.

Thinking voice beyond its already constituted forms

In writing of Deleuze's thought, Claire Colebrook (2006) describes his commitment to 'thinking life *beyond* its humanized and already constituted forms' (pp. 16–17). As researchers, our challenge is to imagine those forms beyond our ways of knowing that constitute the cracks, fissures, and gaps worth considering. To no longer stand what we put up with before is to question the efficacy of what we have done previously in order to think interviewing – in fact all dialogic encounters – differently, in ways that think voice beyond its humanized and constituted forms. To do so is to think a repetition of voice in the context of qualitative inquiry that does not merely reproduce the original form, thereby resisting the radical potential possible in a working of the limit of voice, but that transforms the already recognized form that is solidified and calcified to constitute an audible, knowable voice. To do so is to think a repetition of voice that does not 'toe the line' but that *cracks* the contour and risks tumbling into its breach. It is a repetition of voice that compromises words and produces meaning that slips 'around in the shadow of words, hissing through the gaps in their definitions' (Kimmelman, 2007).[6]

An assumption of what counts as voice that merely reproduces the original form limits those voices to which we customarily attend in listening to our participants, circumscribing the devising of follow-up questions, and inhibiting our making sense of what has transpired. These assumptions also have implications for how we describe our participants' voices and how we inscribe or re-inscribe their voices according to our own voices in a manipulation of data (Jackson, 2003, p. 697). Jackson continues in her discussion of the work of Michelle Fine and warns that in this process of description and inscription, we pay attention not only to '*what* voices we hear' but also '*how* we hear them' in order that we not 'idealize and totalize' (p. 697) their experiences as voiced and thereby ignore the messiness that is present. Furthermore, in this repetition of form, are we prone to leave out the silent voices in our narratives and, in so doing, deem them as unimportant or irrelevant digressions? I assert that in our zeal to 'capture voices' and make meaning, or to make easy sense, we often seek that voice which we can easily name, categorize, and respond to – the one that is tame and friendly. We seek the familiar voice that does not cause trouble and that is easily translatable. We seek a voice that maps onto our ways of knowing, understanding, and interpreting. A more productive practice, however, would be to seek the voice that escapes our easy classification and that does not make easy sense – the voice in the crack.

This voice that does not make easy sense is 'out-of-field' (Deleuze, 1985/1989), not within limits, but at the limits, off the track, in the rough, and beyond our easy comprehension. But we seek what is 'out-of-field' of voice/speech in order to work the limit of voice/speech. The aim is not to improve the hearing, nor to probe for deep-seated meanings, but to redefine what it means to hear and to listen to speech and voice. It is to recapture what Deleuze (1985/1989) describes in a discussion of the break between the talkie and silent picture when he describes silent pictures not as silent, but as noiseless (p. 216). It is not that the films were silent in the sense that voice was not projected, but rather the voices of the actors were communicated through the use of a 'seen' image and an 'intertitle' that was read. The intertitles were thus used to convey in addition to other elements, 'speech acts.' Deleuze continues to write that the silent film did not just call for the talkie but 'already implied it' (p. 216). Prompted by Deleuze, we might then consider how our participants give voice not in ways that are deemed absent as silent, but in ways that are meaningful as noiseless. By so doing, we begin to consider the intertitles and images used by our participants that function to convey voice. To consider the voices both performed and projected through these intertitles and images is to consider what is missed if we only rely on one or the other in the viewing of film (or encounter with research participants) as silent rather than noiseless.

According to Deleuze, the silent film spoke through images and titles. If we rely only on the titles, in effect the words spoken, or the easily discernible speech act, then what are the voices that are missed? Do we literally rely on the words in quotation marks, either on the screen or in the form of our transcript, or do we also include the voices spoken in the cracks, the sighs, and the expressions? For example, in viewing the silent image and the intertitle, do we only rely on the scriptural cue that reads, 'he says he is going to kill him' or do we also read the facial and bodily expression of anger and aggression on his face that speaks, 'I am going to kill you' and the facial and bodily expression of the one being threatened that conveys fear and uncertainty? In the same way, what is voiced by our research participants is changed when we pay attention to both the intertitle (that which is literally scripted) and the silent image or voice that provides additional cues.

Just as the meaning made changed (and seemed 'easier') when pictures began to 'talk,' we can too easily slip back into what is voiced in a literal sense in our research settings – that which is spoken with audible words as the source of meaning – away from a 'reading' of the multiple registers of voice, both spoken in a literal sense, and spoken through silence. We settle for an easy reading and thereby lose the possibility of tripping up on a translation that entangles us in the layers and registers of uncertainty. If we settle for this easy reading or hearing, we fail to consider those other voices that speak beyond the limit of our knowing.

A silent voice

In seeking only the voice of our participants that is easily discernible, easily understood, easily translatable, easily heard, what we seek is a normative voice – one that is shared and designed for whoever must and can understand it (Derrida, 2001). We then *limit* such *voice*, or we fail to 'work the limits of voice' (Jackson, 2003) satisfying ourselves with an interpretation, a translation that gets the job done but that ignores the errant voices, the silent voices, those that demand a 'hard listening' (p. 698). In other words, we risk settling for a relevant translation.

> A relevant translation would therefore be, quite simply, a 'good' translation, a translation that does what one expects of it, in short, a version that performs its mission, honors its debt and does its job or its duty while inscribing in the receiving language the most relevant equivalent for an original, the language that is the most right, appropriate, pertinent, adequate, opportune, pointed, univocal, idiomatic, and so on.
>
> (Derrida, 2001, p. 177)

This quote begs the question, what do we seek when we 'listen' to our participants? Is it the relevant translation that performs its mission by being readily discernible, knowable, and transparent? Or do we seek an irrelevant translation that performs its mission by being messy, opaque, polyphonic, and nuanced – one that exceeds our knowing (easily) and understanding (quickly). Does our limiting of what counts as voice, what we *hear* our participants saying, and *how* we hear them speaking serve only to smooth over that which is not knowable, not discernible, and perhaps unpleasant?

What might it mean to seek a text that desires, that searches for, and that demands an irrelevant translation? What might happen if we were to begin to think of, listen for, or orient our researcher selves differently? To take these questions seriously is to move toward a refutation of a normative and 'understandable' voice in pursuit of a troubled and difficult to pin down voice, a voice that is speech/silence rather than speech or silence (Cixous, 2007). A voice that is unconventional and subtle.

Deleuze (1964/2000) wrote, 'the truth is not revealed, it is betrayed; it is not communicated, it is interpreted; it is not willed, it is involuntary.' (p. 95). As such, an interpretation that does not mimic voiced speech, that does not merely reproduce meaning and truth, that does not will meaning, might be less normative and more 'authentic' should we not base our interpretations on what we think we hear, but what we might hear, what we might experience, when we invite an irrelevant translation. 'Truths remain arbitrary and abstract so long as they are based on the goodwill of thinking. Only the conventional is explicit' (p. 95). A voice that whispers through the cracks and fissures with its siren call is this unconventional voice worthy of our hearing. A silent voice that is both irrelevant and impossibly full.

What is to become of qualitative research that relies so heavily on making meaning from the stories told by our participants if we are to acknowledge, even insist upon, the presence of a silent voice? The question is not whether there is a silent voice present in conversations and interview encounters, but rather, how we as researchers might responsibly and ethically engage this silent voice in the act of conducting discourse-based research. In working the limits of voice (Jackson, 2003), we must remain cautious of the temptation to echo one's own voice in the silent data. We work the limits of voice to hear the voices that have been silenced, not to fill the silences with yet another voice of our own desire.[7]

In an acknowledgment of the presence of a silent voice, it is essential that we forge this space for the silence to breathe and inform as we listen to the tapes of our conversations and read transcripts and journal reflections, as we pursue strategies for 'tracking the grammar [both silent and spoken] of research case records' (Thomson, 2005, p. 137). This way of listening will encourage us to invite the voices present in the silences rather than avoiding them. It will allow us to hear that which is being erased (silent breath) in the production of the voices, both audible and noiseless, of speech. It will encourage us to permit the expansion of spaces for the silence to fill, rather than filling the spaces of silence with meaningless noise, or with echoes of our own insecure voices.

What I wish to question/consider then is how the dynamic of encounters with our research participants, particularly those dialogic encounters such as conversations and interviews, and the subsequent voice that might be elicited rather than missed, might be re-framed, re-shaped, and re-imagined, if as researchers, we are to begin to bring the silences into our hearing. By that I mean, we are to consciously (as much as possible) frame the silent questions that we ask our participants – the questions that we withhold, the audible responses that we garner, the silences that we overlook – as essential aspects of the dialogue that radically affect the outcome of our interviews, whether we like to acknowledge them or not – the voices silently spoken by our participants through the cracks and fissures. These voices compel us to read/listen/hear the data, not just with an emphasis on the scripted words presented in the intertitled transcripts, but to rethink the very idea of those voices and images that our participants use to give voice and to make meaning. Invoking Shakespeare's Hamlet and Derrida's Specters of Marx (1993/1994),

> What if we dare to meet the specter on the rampart at the stroke of midnight, not to contain the specter, nor to prove the specter's existence, but in a search for the ghostly intensity of voices that we often miss so softly spoken in the mist.
>
> (Mazzei, 2007b, p. 91)

What if we are to engage in a dialogue with the specters, voicing questions that we fear, listening to the haunting replies, privileging the unspoken and the not asked questions, not in an attempt to contain these voices but to use them as the basis for our interactions with and questioning of participants in our field sites?

Such a move, rendering these silently articulated voices as part of the soundscape of voice, requires an acute awareness that not only permits a listening that has been impossible, but further demands an attentiveness and openness that has been absent. To engage this limit of voice in qualitative inquiry is to begin the process of *listening to ourselves listening* (Mazzei, 2007b, p. 91) in order that we might be attentive to our own silenced/silent voices and those of our research participants. 'We do not therefore speak of a dualism between two kinds of "things", [or two kinds of voice] but of a multiplicity of dimensions' (Deleuze & Parnet, 1987/2002, p. 133) – not more voices, but more differences, contradictions, and entanglements.

Prompted by Deleuze, the task then is to rethink the dualism that is speech/silence toward a different conception of voice, toward a shifting of thinking, that escapes dualism completely. 'But what defines dualism is not the number of terms, any more than one escapes from dualism by adding other terms' (Deleuze & Parnet, 1987/2002, p. 132) or, in this case, other voices. And so to merely think more voices is not what I am proposing, but in keeping with Deleuze, an assemblage of multiplicities that is at the same time sense and nonsense, speech and nonspeech, spoken silence and silences spoken.

> You only escape dualisms effectively by shifting them like a load, and when you find between the terms, whether they are two or more, a narrow gorge like a border or a frontier which will turn the set into a multiplicity, independently of the number of parts. What we call an assemblage, is precisely, a multiplicity. (p. 132)

This process then is one of beginning to rethink not only what constitutes voice in the crack but of the multiplicity of the dimensions of voice in the gorge, and what it means to listen to our research participants given such an understanding. In writing of multiplicities, or in my co-opting of Deleuze's notion of multiplicities, I resist the temptation that more voices are an easy solution to the problem, but rather accept that the notion of 'a' voice is a misnomer and that to begin to untangle meaning one must recognize the disparities, incongruities, and smooth surfaces that seem to form a coherent and meaningful voice but that enact what I have previously referred to as an impossibly full voice, one that intentionally relies on subtleties of phrasing and oblique responses.

This multiplicity or plenitude I am gesturing toward refuses a dualism of speech/silence and of certainty through articulated voice and instead encourages a rethinking of the research process and the dualism between voiced speech and silent speech, of a multiplicity serving to tangle and untangle meaning at the same time. It refuses a dualism between what is voice and what is not voice. It does so in the recognition that voice is always happening as we consider those questions to ask and those that we consider too sensitive to ask, as we listen to what participants are saying and at the same time pay attention to what might be silently voiced, when we focus on what is said and what is not said, and as we construct follow-up questions and simultaneously begin the process of analyzing what is readily present and what is absently present in an attempt to listen at the limit of voice.

Listening at the limit

To listen at the limit of voice calls first for a grappling with the nature of this limit or 'frontier' that I consider and how it might help me think the construction of research narratives in a way that rejects dualistic thinking about voice and speech. In turn, I must seek productive practices for purposely eliciting those narratives that have previously gone unnamed, unnoticed, and unthought. How might I attempt to put this idea of listening at the limit into motion rather than re-presenting current practices with different words and voices that do nothing more than enact the same methods?

To put into practice a listening at the limit would mean to render visible the current boundaries of research and the specters that silently slip across the border beyond our reach. It is to enact what Patti Lather (2007) describes as a responsibility not to seduce or persuade but to 'implicate by setting up the obligation to see how we see' (p. 96), or in the case of what I am attempting, to listen to how we listen. Hélène Cixous said, 'By asking the question already being inscribed, you are trapped in the text. It changes everything when you change shores' (2007). So to change shores would mean not simply to re-imagine the boundaries, but to re-map the boundaries if you will from a completely different vantage point. To do so is to let the errant voices intrude without permission in the same way that Salcedo evokes the unwelcome immigrants in her art installation. It is to re-image in a way that resists a tracing of the familiar coastline and that prompts a rupture of that which has come to define what is knowable, askable, and possible in terms of data that we have previously missed or not counted. This listening at the limit requires a thinking of methodological practices that do not merely repeat our comfortable methods, but that seek disruptive and undisciplined practices. Such a listening does not ignore the obvious voices, but treats those voices with the same level of mistrust with which we have come to accord the errant silent voices.

To think data and research differently, I am prompted to reconsider the question not just of when and what is voice, or data for that matter, but how data/voice is enacted and presented by participants in the field. Instead of the one-dimensional way in which we often treat data on the page in the form of field notes and transcripts, our data may speak to us differently with a multiplicity of voices in the context in which it was presented, in the form of multi-dimensional performances in our research sites. What then might it mean to consider the performances as producing silent voices in qualitative research?

In a discussion of silences in the plays of William Shakespeare, Phillip McGuire (1985) writes about silences that are given to the characters in the form of a silently articulated voice. Such an acknowledgment of these intentional silences or open silences as referred to by McGuire – silences that are open to interpretation – requires that we acknowledge the limits of textual authority in the plays, the literal words, and that we can only hear these other voices in the context of a performance.

> For such understanding we must turn to performances. What we can learn from performances is something other than, something different from, something outside of the knowledge that the text can provide. It is something without which our knowledge of the play is less than complete.
>
> (pp. xxiv–xxv)

If we are bound *to* the text, be it the text of the transcript or the script that is spoken by our participants, then we are bound *by* the text, or the intertitle as the place where we can track voice in order to make meaning. Listening to the voices and inserting the silent questions as intertitles alongside those obvious ones is a beginning step in including the open silences in the performance given in our research settings. Such practices are a return to a tracking of the grammar (Thomson, 2005), not in an effort to predict the next word, but in order to tease out or elicit the unexpected. It is a poststructuralist understanding, particularly a deconstructive reading that considers not what the text tends to say, but engages a deconstructive openness to expect, even encourage, an interpretation of the text that does not consist in 'providing ready-made responses' (Malabou & Derrida, 2004, p. 239).

Because we know from the early writings of Derrida (1967/1976) that we have privileged voice as presence, we often mistakenly assume that a voice spoken by our participants, or by ourselves, is the voice to be given weight in the accounts given and heard, in deciding what gets 'kept in' as voice and what gets left out. By resisting this privileging might we rupture the dualism of what counts, not by inserting meaning or voice or silence into the dualism of absence/presence, but by 'shifting the load' (Deleuze & Parnet, 1987/2002) toward a multiplicity of meanings, voices, silences, and data? Working from this place of resistance we may then be able to 'hear' how we have privileged presence, or what counts as presence, in deciding the voices that our participants use to 'speak,' or as Patti Lather (2007) writes, to mine the tensions of our methodological encounters toward a formulation of 'a kind of feminist research not yet overcoded in the face of received understandings' (p. viii).

Steiner Kvale (1996) wrote that the postmodern approach to interviewing 'emphasizes the narratives constructed by the interview' (p. 38). I want to think not of how the narratives are constructed, but how we obstruct the narratives and voices as we continue to listen to/listen for those voices that fit into our over-coded and received ways of knowing without paying attention to listening how we listen. The practices that I propose are intended to focus on the narratives con-structed in the context of the interview, and also aim to purposefully elicit those silent narratives inhabiting the shadows that we fail to notice, those voices and narratives that we prevent from entering the field of play. The practice of eliciting these silent narratives means that as researchers, we must listen for, listen to, and ask questions not just in response to an answer voiced, but to ask questions of a withheld response, a nonresponse, or a masked response. Rather than a mapping that traces the outline of our humanized notions of voice, I propose that we attempt a mapping that permits a performance of the voices in their multiple and tangled forms.

Consider the following response by one of the teachers in my study as Anne described herself as being different from other members of her family and friends in my 'first' encounter with her. As you *listen to how you listen*, and perhaps even more tellingly how conventionally I listened at the time, note the multiplicity of voices slipping in and through the words that I failed to 'hear.' In some cases these voices were heard by me but ignored for fear that the imperceptible crack if noticed would release too many uncomfortable voices to contain.

ANNE: I never really saw myself as prejudiced, but then I never really had to deal with any 'other people.' So I was raised this way and now I've come to a *very, very*, very liberal, *very* open-minded understanding as far as my friends. I'm also a single mother, as far as people who I go out on dates with, political views, everything and it's very, *very* conflicting with my parents.

Not really, like my sisters with my generation, but its very hard for me because I'm confused a lot of the time, I'm torn.

You know, I want to do things with the person that I'm going out with right now and its wrong and I'm thinking, you know what's the difference if I get along with somebody or if my friend is Hispanic, or you know, what's the big deal. . . . So I'm just real torn and my whole paper was just about how torn I am and how now that I'm, you know, I'm thinking how you always find out who you are and sometimes I think that my family must look at me and say, 'How in the world? Where did she come from and why is she like this? How could that happen?'

In this first listening, I am bound to the text, and therefore bound by the text or the intertitle as the place where voice resides. My eyes/ears are fixed on these intertitles so as not to miss a word spoken. I track the grammar and obediently follow the cues. I too easily seek the ready-made responses provided by Anne. Perhaps I desire them and nurture them as they are safe and thus allow me/us to stick within the confines of the script of the play without threat of falling into the crack of destabilized voices.

   In a relistening, or a listening at the limit, I turn a focus not on what is evident, but a return to Deleuze's notion of the crack that happens on the new line and how a noticing of the crack produces a listening that can no longer be ignored. It is this imperceptible crack through which the destabilized and silent voices slip. A listening at the limit then does not ignore the hairline fractures, but notices the pain and uncomfortableness present within them. For example, in the same way that an interviewer uses a pause or a gap to allow a respondent time to reflect on her or his answer, the interviewer might also use a question to create a productive opening that will allow the silence to be given voice. Consider this 'second' exchange with Anne and how a refusal to ignore the crack through acknowledgment and questioning of the silence on my part might have led to a much more nuanced response on her part and subsequent understanding on mine. In this 'second' exchange I have, in the brackets, inserted the questions I might have asked in response to Anne's assertions, both silent and spoken.

ANNE: I never really saw myself as prejudiced, but then I never really had to deal with any 'other people.' [**Other people? Who do you mean by Other people?**] So I was raised this way and now I've come to a *very, very*, very liberal, *very* open-minded understanding as far as my friends. [**When you say liberal, you mean . . . ?**] I'm also a single mother, as far as people who I go out on dates with, political views, everything and it's very, *very* conflicting with my parents. **[How is that conflict lived out in your relationship with them?]**

Not really, like my sisters with my generation, but its very hard for me because I'm confused a lot of the time, I'm torn. **[Confused and torn, that sounds like another conflict. Why are you torn?]**

You know, I want to do things with the person that I'm going out with right now and its wrong **[How is it wrong? Why do you say that?]** and I'm thinking, you know what's the difference if I get along with somebody or if my friend is Hispanic, or you know, **[We don't know. What do you want us to know? Tell us what you mean?]** what's the big deal. . . . So I'm just real torn and my whole paper was just about how torn I am and how now that I'm, you know, **[Again, what do you want me to know?]** I'm thinking how you always find out who you are and sometimes I think that my family must look at me and say, 'How in the world? Where did she come from and why is she like this? How could that happen?' **[Boy, you just said a lot. Can you be more specific about how your values are in conflict with theirs?]**

In the 'first' exchange with Anne, she leaves unsaid what she assumes I know, or perhaps what she hopes I do not know, or maybe have forgotten. What if, as indicated in the 'second' exchange above I were to have asked at the time 'What are you not saying?' or 'Who are you not naming?' or in response to a long pause or gap in the conversation, 'Why the pause?' or 'What is the pause saying?' What if I would have been practiced enough and courageous enough to have asked the silent questions that I have since inserted in the brackets or even to have been more pointed in the response, to veer off the path of safety and into the crack of not knowing? The questions may not have elicited a spoken clarification, they may not have resulted in a 'desired' response, or Anne might simply have nimbly avoided the faint opening. Even so, what may result in such an interaction is the creation of a productive tension, an opening for Anne to momentarily reflect on what she is not saying, or to identify (whether for herself or for me) what she is not saying. What may result is a spacing or interplay of conflicting views both audibly and inaudibly expressed. What does result is that the silences and denials are at the very least given a living presence. This approach also serves to prompt other participants in the context of a group interview to consider their own silences and what they may be revealing and withholding in these silences. These internal conflicts, the group knowledge that lives without words, even the complicities of phrases such as 'you know' are now acknowledged and ready to be 'heard.'

For instance, I knew at the time of the group interview that Anne was in a relationship with a black man but I am not sure if the others did. As presented in the excerpt from the first group session, she alluded to her relationship without speaking directly to it. She spoke emotionally of the values and actions that she holds which are in conflict with those of her parents; however, she never came out and directly said that she was in a relationship with an African American man. What is she saying with this silent voice? Did she fear how we might respond to her because of her projected attitudes regarding Others vs. whites? Is she unsure herself whether the relationship is acceptable (not only to others but also to herself)? Does she censor herself based on the context and what she perceives to be acceptable in a given situation or with a particular group of people? As researcher, I must consider not just her motivation regarding her behavior but also why I remained silent. Was I hiding behind the veil of a nonthreatening and 'safe' feminist methodology?

A further quandary that this re-listening and re-questioning of Anne exposes is a consideration of the possible markers of silence that may provide cues for the silences yet to be named and noticed.[8] When Anne says, 'you know,' is the assumption that we in fact do know? Has 'you know' become a commonplace way of saying something without articulating it, or do we ignore this signal as a substitute for a pause or moment of gathering our/her thoughts. For the speaker to decide that you in fact do know, so as not to have to state the obvious, or that I would rather you not know so I assume/pretend/convince myself that you know what is meant, or that I do not really know how to say what I mean so I conceal my 'real' feelings with this seemingly innocuous statement is the implicit/explicit function of silence. By attending to these and other such markers (you know, I mean, like, whatever) we orient ourselves to receive these placeholders not as diversions, excuses, or an instance when the participant is at a loss for words, but to receive them as an announcement of something worthy of our attention. We shake ourselves out of a complacent listening (and questioning) that focuses solely on the words spoken as being that place where meaning resides and actively seek to engage the impossible fullness of a silent voice.

To continue to hide behind the veil of a safe methodology is to revert to the predictability of a first reading. It is to stay on the safe path, avoiding the signposts of the silent cues and the imperceptible cracks in the floor into which we risk tumbling with the shadows of words. It is to be so reliant on the intertitles present in the silent performance given by our participants that we miss what is happening behind our back or in front of our faces. It is to be so intent upon the map that we fail to notice the beauty of the landscape for fear of losing our way. It is a desire to retrace our footsteps and journey to the destination we anticipate rather than setting off on errant paths trusting that in the end we will arrive where we need to be. It is the richness and unpredictability of these errant paths in the doing of qualitative research that will allow the voices of silence to have a hearing.

A mapping at the limit of voice

If we were all more lost we would be better off.
John D. Caputo

When we set off on a journey with a reliable map, and with a destination in mind, we plot our course, follow the shortest route (generally) and arrive at our destination more or less as planned. We seek a truth (a fixed location), we rely on a map to guide us, and confirm the truth (accuracy of the map) when we arrive at our final destination. Such a journey is one that is more or less predictable and certain. Such a journey makes no space for a 'voyage *without truth*' (Malabou & Derrida, 2004, p. 28). Such a journey keeps us safe within the confines of what is known (and knowable) in order that we avoid the unforeseen detours and unmarked roads that might take us in an unknown direction with an unpredictable outcome. If it works, then why be reckless and risk the peril of the cracks in the road?

To trust Caputo's claim that we would be better off lost is to trust a different reason for going in the first place. To give ourselves permission to be lost may be to acknowledge that where we went before wasn't really where we wanted or needed to be. To listen to Caputo is to set off on Derrida's 'voyage *without truth*, one that "would never again reach the thing itself, . . . would above all never touch it. Wouldn't even touch the veil behind which a thing is supposed to be standing" ' (Malabou & Derrida, p. 28). Rather than a traveling or voyaging that assumes going from one place to another, it is a traversal (pp. 45–53) that elicits a to and fro, that moves counter to the path that is cleared and that like a five-year-old with a shiny new pair of rubber boots, splashes in every puddle she encounters just because the puddles are there and because they hold unanticipated surprises. It is a traversal that seeks what is often overlooked in the ordinary in our rush to reach a destination, whether that be the end of a journey or the end of a research project. This ordinary that is found in the mud and the puddles is 'the ordinary that opens up and shows it treasure, which is, precisely, ordinary' (Cixous, 1991).

A methodological traversal without certainty is not about avoiding interpretation, but is about a troubling of the authority of interpretation (Lather, 2009) and the certainty of voice. Veering from the path then is not about an abdication or avoidance of the responsibility of interpretation, but is a troubling of the authority of interpretation so that we are not taken in by the easy story that we can readily hear. We veer from the path in hopes that we encounter the errant voices traveling on the sideroads easily overlooked because of their 'ordinary' appearance but often with the most interesting stories to tell. An encounter with these errant voices requires an openness to the Other. But an openness is not enough. One must become estranged from the usual expectations and the rush to complete the journey or to find the 'best' map.

This methodological traversal or voyage without truth then requires a mapping at the limit of voice that depends on an openness to the 'epistemic shifts that dislocate us' (Butler, 2007). It is a Deluzian mapping that allows us to move around, but does not merely re-create or re-present the soundscape as it is known to us. It is a mapping that dislocates in order that we encounter voices from that 'unuttered zone where, mute but distinct, the most essential things are said, minuscule things, infinite things, inexpressible outside in the sharp air, because of their fragility and beauty' (Cixous, 1991, pp. 136–137). It is a mapping that is against a Global Positioning System (GPS) – that not only shows us (and sometimes tells us) where we are, but *traces* where we have been, where we are going, and exactly how to get there and back again, allowing no room for 'error' or errant wandering. The methodological mapping that I seek attempts to re-map the boundaries from a different vantage point so as to encounter the fragile voices mute but distinct. This mapping seeks to estrange us from ourselves in order that we may encounter that which is unexpected at the limit of voice.

An early brush with estrangement occurred when I wandered off the path in an unexpected encounter with these errant voices that I have been writing about. While in the process of trying to make sense of the data gathered in the project with Anne and the other white teachers, I attended the biennial Dodge Poetry Festival as a way to cultivate a more interesting writing style for the telling of my research, one that aspired to Laurel Richardson's desire to 'make my writing matter' (Richardson & St.Pierre, 2005). During the Festival a session entitled 'Spoken Poems and Silent Readings' caught my attention. The session was a discussion by four poets of the silences in poetry and how these purposeful pauses are not intended as absences or mere breaths in poetry, but are intentionally deployed as essential to the meaning and rhythm of the poems. My openness to an Other voice in my research led to an encounter with the fragile voices that were mute but distinct as I began to consider a reframing of data as a poetic construction (Mazzei, 2003) and to hear the silent voices present in the data. This dislocation resulted in an uncertainty that challenged the easy story I could readily hear and make sense of and depended on a different listening and a methodological traversal in the cracks.

What is to be gained from a traversal and mapping that dislocates rather than a tracing that locates? Why is a return to uncertainty desirable when it comes to research? Where does this get us in the project of voice? Because 'all narratives tell one story in place of another story' (Cixous & Calle-Gruber, 1994/1997, p. 178), and a dislocated mapping might allow for more complicated and tangled tellings of the other stories that get told in the unuttered zone. This uncertainty, this dislocated mapping, this different listening seeks to find the stories that have been cast aside as unimportant, that have become lost in the cracks, that are lying on the cutting room floor, and that don't make the reel designed to appeal to a mass audience. We risk tripping up on these cuttings and getting stuck in the cracks in order to escape being bound to a tracing/text that produces the expected outcome and response.

Such an unexpected outcome requires that as researchers we acknowledge that we don't know. This does not mean that we give up on the promise of knowing, but we give up on the promise of a certainty of knowing. We seek an encounter with the voice of difference on a path not drawn on our map, in an imperceptible crack in the floor, in the words not captured on an intertitle. We admit that we don't know the precise direction to take, and yet we continue on, uncertain of the destination, left with the certainty of uncertainty that impels us forward, 'keeps our passion aroused, and holds us to the other' (Derrida, 1992, p. 24). Cixous describes writing as 'touching the mystery, delicately, with the tips of the words, trying not to crush it, in order to un-lie' (1991, p. 134). Perhaps this is our best hope and our most responsible desire as researchers: to un-lie.

Notes

1 This reference to poststructural eroticism comes from the discussant remarks presented in response to an earlier version of this paper by Pat Thomson at the 2007 British Education Research Association Conference (BERA) held at the Institute of Education, University of London.
2 In the paper 'Broken Voices' presented by Maggie MacLure at the 2007 BERA conference, she writes of an 'impossible fullness' in a discussion of the excesses and insufficiencies of voice.
3 In *The Mystical Element in Heidegger's Thought*, John Caputo (1986) writes of Heidegger as 'a thinker whose thinking is conducted at the limits of philosophy' (p. 1). Throughout the book, Caputo discusses Heidegger's thinking 'post philosophy,' as he describes Heidegger as wanting to shake loose of Western philosophy in order 'to overcome philosophy and take up the task of thought' (p. 266). Heidegger speaks of the end of philosophy as an end to the rationalities and strictures that limit thought. What he pursues is a transgression of these limits and strictures that open him to the beginning of thought, or rather, toward the beginning of thought not previously possible because it was outside or beyond the permissible, seeable, hearable limits. What I pursue then is a movement beyond the limits of methodology as currently understood toward those new limits that result from a thinking beyond the permissible, seeable, hearable limits of our received methodologies.
4 In Dolar's (2006) discussion of the voice and the signifier, he uses the interpretation from Saint Augustine as John the Baptist as the 'voice' and as Christ as the 'word' following textually from St. John's Gospel that proclaims that 'in the beginning was the Word, but in order for the Word to manifest itself, there has to be a mediator, a precursor in the shape of John the Baptist' (pp. 15–16), in other words, a Voice.
5 The Unilever Series is an annual commission that invites an artist to make a work of art especially for the Tate Modern's Turbine Hall. The commission referred to in this chapter ran from 9 October 2007 through 6 April 2008.
6 Speaking of the reporting by William Shirer, a US journalist who artfully reported on the Nazi occupation during WWII, Peter Nadas in an interview with the NY Times (Kimmelman, 2007) commended Shirer on his use of ambiguous sentences and the resulting triumph of meaning conveyed in such a way. Shirer intentionally relied on the use of subtle phrasing, suggestive tones of voice, or US slang not understood by German censors. Similarly, Nadas discusses the way that meaning shifts and slips through the intentional misuse or rather incongruous use of words and 'how deformed the thoughts and actions of someone can become who for years has used their mother tongue for hiding thoughts rather than for expressing them.'
7 See the chapter by Alecia Jackson in Part 2 for a discussion of how desire is performed in the act of truth-telling and the voices that are produced.
8 This idea of the grammatical markers of silence emerged from a conversation with Maggie MacLure. While I mention these markers and provide some possible examples, there is much room to explore more fully these markers and their effects in the process of conducting interviews.

References

Butler, J. (2005). *Giving an account of oneself*. New York: Fordham University Press.
Butler, J. (2007, April). *Sexual politics, torture, and the limits of secular discourse*. Paper presented at the conference Postmodernism, Culture and Religion II: Feminism, Sexuality and the Return of Religion, Syracuse University, Syracuse, NY.
Caputo, J. D. (1986). *The mystical element in Heidegger's thought*. New York: Fordham University Press.

Caputo, J. D. (1997). *The prayers and tears of Jacques Derrida: Religion without religion.* Bloomington, IN: Indiana University Press.

Cixous, H. (2007, June). *. . . a kind of magic?* Paper presented at the conference Hélène Cixous, Jacques Derrida: their Psychoanalyses, University of Leeds, UK.

Cixous, H. (1991). *'Coming to writing' and other essays* (D. Jenson, Ed.). Cambridge, MA: Harvard University Press.

Cixous, H., & Calle-Gruber, M. (1997). *Hélène Cixous rootprints: Memory and life writing.* (E. Prenowitz, Trans.). London: Routledge. (Original work published 1994).

Colebrook, C. (2006). *Deleuze: A guide for the perplexed.* London: Continuum.

Deleuze, G. (1989) *The time-image* (H. Tomlinson & B. Habberjam, Trans.). London: Continuum. (Original work published 1985).

Deleuze, G. (2000). *Proust and signs: The complete text* (R. Howard, Trans.). Minneapolis: University of Minnesota Press. (Original work published 1964).

Deleuze, G., & Parnet, C. (2002). *Dialogues II.* (H. Tomlinson & B. Habberjam, Trans.). London: Continuum. (Original work published 1987).

Derrida, J. (2001). What is a 'relevant' translation? *Critical Inquiry, 27*(2), 174–200.

Derrida, J. (1994). *Specters of Marx: The state of the debt, the work of mourning, & the new international* (P. Kamuf, Trans.). New York: Routledge. (Original work published 1993).

Derrida, J. (1992). Passions: 'An oblique offering' (D. Wood, Trans.). In David Wood (Ed.), *Derrida: A critical reader* (pp. 5–35). Oxford, UK: Blackwell.

Derrida, J. (1976). *Of grammatology* (G. C. Spivak, Trans.). Baltimore: The Johns Hopkins University Press. (Original work published 1967).

Derrida, J. & Caputo, J. D. (1997). *Deconstruction in a nutshell: A conversation with Jacques Derrida* (J. D. Caputo, Ed.). New York: Fordham University Press.

Dolar, M. (2006). *A voice and nothing more.* Cambridge, MA: The MIT Press.

Jackson, A. Y. (2003). Rhizovocality. *Qualitative Studies in Education, 16*(5), 693–710.

Jackson, A. Y. (2004). Performativity identified. *Qualitative Inquiry, 10*(5), 673–690.

Kimmelman, M. (2007). A writer who always sees history in the present tense. *New York Times.* Retrieved November 1, 2007 from http://www.nytimes.com/2007/11/01/books/01nadas.html?pagewanted=all

Kvale, S. (1996). *InterViews: An introduction to qualitative research interviewing.* Thousand Oaks, CA: Sage Publications.

Lather, P. (2009). Against empathy, voice, and authenticity. In A. Jackson & L. Mazzei (Eds.). *Voice in qualitative inquiry: Challenging conventional, interpretive, and critical conceptions.* London: Routledge.

Lather, P. (2007). *Getting lost: Feminist efforts toward a double(d) science.* Albany, NY: SUNY Press.

MacLure, M. (2007). *Broken Voices.* Paper presented at the 2007 British Education Research Association Conference (BERA), Institute of Education, University of London.

McGuire, P. C. (1985). *Speechless dialect: Shakespeare's open silences.* Berkeley, CA: University of California Press.

Malabou, C., & Derrida, J. (2004). *Counterpath: Traveling with Jacques Derrida* (D. Wills, Trans.). Stanford, CA: Stanford University Press.

Mazzei, L. A. (2007a). Toward a problematic of silence in action research. *Educational Action Research, 15*(4), 631–642.

Mazzei, L. A. (2007b). *Inhabited silence in qualitative research: Putting poststructural theory to work.* New York: Peter Lang.

Mazzei, L. A. (2003). Inhabited silences: In pursuit of a muffled subtext. *Qualitative Inquiry, 9*(3), 355–368.

Richardson, L., & St.Pierre, E. A. (2005). Writing: A method of inquiry. In N. K. Denzin & Y. S. Lincoln (Eds.) *The sage handbook of qualitative research* (3rd ed.). London: Sage Publications.

Salcedo, D. (2007). The Unilever series: Doris Salcedo Shibboleth. Retrieved October 1, 2007, from http://www.tate.org.uk/modern/exhibitions/dorissalcedo/default.shtm

Searle, A. (2007, October 9). A study of horror and indifference in the temple of liberal arts. *The Guardian*, 20.

Stronach, I. (2002). This space is not yet blank: Anthropologies for a future action research. *Educational Action Research, 10*(9), 291–307.

Thomson, P. (2005). Developing the textual turn: Tracking the grammar of research case records. *Educational Action Research, 13*(1), 137–159.

Chapter 4

Voicing objections

Erica McWilliam, Karen Dooley, Felicity McArdle and Jennifer Pei-Ling Tan

Flashing lights

Over a decade ago, Patti Lather (1991) made the point that 'advocacy research' was in many respects an oxymoron. This assertion came after Elizabeth Ellsworth's (1989) warning about the unintended effects of critical pedagogy's mission to 'empower' students in the classroom. Over a decade before that, Michele Le Doeuff (1977) expressed her concerns about the dangers of feminist projects that seek to end oppression in all its forms. Two decades later, Deborah Britzman (1997) questioned the 'wish for heroism' that so often comes with the desire to 'let voices speak'. A year later, this theme was echoed in Lather's paper 'Against Empathy, Voice and Authenticity' (1998; reprinted in this book), a paper that troubles the notion of 'a coherent subject' who 'speaks for themselves' (p. 1), and again in Erica McWilliam's warnings against being 'stuck in the missionary position' (McWilliam, 2000). By the end of the century, poststructuralist scholars were flashing orange lights at anyone and everyone looking to empower others through qualitative educational research.

Notwithstanding all this scholarly ambivalence around 'emancipation through giving voice' from poststructuralist scholars, 'letting voices speak' continues to be a powerful imperative in educational research a decade later. A new generation of qualitative researchers has been mobilised by the moral–ethical calling of 'hearing subjugated voices' through appropriate data collection strategies and then 'letting them speak' in a relatively unproblematic way through the text work of the research. It is assumed that uncovering what is 'silenced' *can* and *should* lead to emancipation or empowerment for those whose voice is captured in the display of research data. This proposition is related, in turn, to the twin fantasy that education *can* and *should* be able to overcome any and every social problem if it is done properly (see McWilliam and Lee, 2006). With hypercompetitive economic globalisation implicating governments worldwide, we are seeing formal education and educational research charged with more responsibility and accountability for national economic and social outcomes. This includes 'making a difference' to the stubborn statistics that continue to show so little change for the most socially and economically disadvantaged.

Doing the least harm

It is easy to criticise naïve assumptions about the power of research to change the lives of people for the better, just as it is easy to criticise scholars of research methodology for investing more in an 'undoing' project than a 'doing' one. We are not interested in staying within the boundaries of either of these meta-projects. Our interest is to work at their nexus – at the intersection of the push to overcome disadvantage and the pull away from naïve assumptions about 'voice' in qualitative research. In a sense, we want to move on from both the romance about emancipation through voice and the sort of paralysis that can result when we find our methods come wrapped in barbed wire. We want, in Anna Freud's terms, to ask how we can 'do the least harm' in our attempts to work *with* and *for* the educationally, socially and economically disadvantaged.

In the current political and moral climate in education, 'doing the least harm' is not easily understood as a high calling. At a recent conference where 'do the least harm' was claimed as a high ideal by one of the authors, the predominantly educator audience expressed their disappointment with this as a lukewarm goal of educational research and practice. Educators should always do 'the most good'. Anything else was at best a disappointing concession to 'the real world' and at worst a selling out of high ideals in favour of fashionable disinterest. For us, it has been important to make this thinkable as an ideal in order to keep our 'best intentions' under scrutiny.

While academic educators continue (as they should) to debate ontological, epistemological and methodological matters that pertain to educational purposes, we are constantly being reminded by what we see and hear elsewhere that disadvantage continues to plague the lives of millions of people in this world, and that our rarefied debates bring them little direct comfort. It is not that 'advocacy research' has achieved nothing for disadvantaged people, or that academic debates are rarefied and pointless. 'Trouble-making' is not about stepping away from debates about Method, but trying to deliver on the promise implicit in Karl Popper's first attack on non-critical rationality, and in Paul Feyerabend's championing of an 'ever more imaginative and wild' irrationality (Bernstein, 1988: p. 4). In refusing methodological 'purity' and insisting on research methodology as a 'game of truth and error' (Foucault, 1985: p. 6), rather than a search for Truth itself, we understand our work to be part of a trouble-making tradition of thinking Method, not a rejection of theory. We have tried to put methodological skepticism about work in 'acid test' problem situations, and to keep making trouble for what we can think (and therefore say and do) as educational researchers. In Elizabeth St.Pierre's terms, we have been seeking to 'produce different knowledge and to produce knowledge differently' (St.Pierre, 2000: p. 27) about educational disadvantage and those who experience it and inquire into it.

The acid test

An opportunity to 'acid test' our own thinking about methodology presented itself in a project involving possibly the most disadvantaged group of young people that has come to Australia in its recent history. They are empty suitcase refugees[1] from the Horn of Africa, many of whom, though perhaps 14 or 15 years old, cannot speak English, hold a pen or sit on a chair. They come from a number of African refugee camps where they have been for who knows how long. The principal of the school, whose job it is to prepare these young people for mainstream high school entry, asked us to help her make a difference to their educational and life futures through a program of school-based research.

In the conduct of that research (which we are yet to complete), we have come to question a number of propositions about 'letting subjugated voices speak' that had, to some extent at least, gone without saying. We have questioned the usefulness of 'voice-centric' research methods and the 'word-centric' cultural assumptions that underpin these methods. We have begun to ask questions about how our well-meaning research techniques are being read by the research subjects, about the politics of interpretation and translation, about the meanings that their silences and utterances connoted and about the importance of critical numeracy and cultural agility in the collection and analysis of research data.

In what follows, we elaborate how our thinking was challenged in the operationalising of the project. We do so by providing a description of the nature and purposes of the project, including empirical data about the refugees under study. We provide instances of the ways that our qualitative research methodologies seemed to fail us, and what we are learning from the instructive complications of that failure. Finally we discuss what we understand to be the implications for conducting this sort of 'well-meaning' cross-cultural research.

Disadvantaged subjects

Australia receives approximately 12,000 humanitarian settlers to its shores annually. The composition of this intake has changed dramatically over the past six years with a sharp increase in the number of 'Horn of Africa' refugee migrants, from approximately 23 per cent in 1999–2000 to a significant 56 per cent in 2006–2007 (Department of Immigration and Multicultural and Indigenous Affairs, 2007). This 'new wave' of African refugee migrants brings with it a diverse range of pre-migration experiences, including war trauma, religious persecution, poverty and starvation, with a large number comprising young people with varying degrees and quality of education and English language proficiency.

Middle-school aged youths from this group typically arrive in Australia with disrupted educational backgrounds, and social and emotional experiences that serve to challenge the expertise and resources of Australian schools, including schools with histories of successful work with students of English as an additional language. As resettlement begins, these young people are typically enrolled in reception (or 'bridging') intensive language schools with the aim of developing both their English language skills and social capabilities before they are transferred to mainstream education in their local secondary schools. It is at this point that they are likely to find that existing educational and social support structures are inadequate to facilitate productive engagement in, and successful transition to, mainstream schooling.

Statistics collated by the local 'transitional' school (Milpera State High School, 2006) identified a 'new wave' of African refugee students (a majority of whom come from Sudan and Burundi) with unprecedented problems. It is worth noting here that 'African' is something that these young people 'become' in Australia. While the fact of their blackness, as Franz Fanon puts it, gives them a particular and problematic visibility in the context of Australian 'whiteness', their 'African-ness' is a process of becoming that starts 'out of Africa' – it is not a given. These young people find themselves constituted as 'African' for the first time in their lives after they enter Australia. The extent to which ownership of an 'African' identity is a necessary precursor to an 'integrating' identity of the sort that renders them 'school-able' is one of many issues that confronted us and the teachers whose job it is to 'integrate' them into mainstream schooling in as short a time as possible. In other words, their identity work involves them in owning and eschewing 'African-ness' simultaneously.

'African' students had been identified through the school records as spending a substantially longer period of time than other refugee groups in the foundational and beginner levels at the school, where the inculcation of basic socialisation skills and the provision of intensive English Second Language tuition occur. The data certainly indicated that length of time required to prepare these students for integration into local secondary schools had increased in comparison with the time taken by earlier groups of 'African' refugees. Our challenge as researchers was to investigate the sort of pedagogy that might speed up the process and make for a more productive engagement for these young people during the process of transition into 'the mainstream' schooling sector.

Good intentions

The three-year longitudinal study was collaboratively developed and funded by various partner organisations,[2] with the aim of building robust mutual understanding of the social capital resources and learning experiences of African refugee migrant youths on arrival and in transition to mainstream schooling. To analyse our 'findings', we would draw on frameworks that bring social theoretical concepts (e.g., Bourdieu, 1986; Goldstein, 2003) to a field historically conceptualised in psycholinguistic terms (e.g., Collier, 1995). It was agreed that we use qualitative multiple case studies, with the first phase of the study entailing observations and interviews with students, parents and staff at the Queensland flagship reception school for adolescent migrants, Milpera State High School (MSHS). The multiple case study approach was adopted to allow for cross-case searches of patterns so that multiple data sources could provide contrasting or replicated results (Yin, 2003) if clear patterns emerged. The longitudinal design would allow us to explore the selected students' learning and transition experiences in MSHS (phase one) and later in the local secondary school to which they would progress (phase two).

At the point of writing, we have completed phase one of the study. A range of data collection methods have been employed, including classroom observations, field notes and document analysis, but the predominant form of data collection has been through semi-structured interviews with the eight students, their parents, bilingual teacher aides and teachers. In line with 'student-centred' principles, we had intended to privilege the student experience over all else, anticipating that their 'voices' would offer us most in terms of 'authentic' understanding of their social reality, and that the 'voices' of teachers, para-professionals and parents would be, though interesting for what they provided as background, of less importance to the study. This depended, of course, on the students' desire to speak, not just our desire to listen.

In the conduct of the interviews with a small number of 'African' students and their parents over the past year, we have gained insights into social and learning experiences of these students, which we hoped to represent accurately and clearly as the study progressed. We were not prepared, however, for the extent of some of the challenges we encountered in the interview process, and these have led us to examine more closely the robustness and appropriateness of requiring that subjugated voices speak on cue and through the 'word-centric' technologies of ethno-methodology inquiry.

Instructive complications

The interview questions were to address opportunities for social, language and academic and cognitive learning in home, school and community contexts, focusing in particular on conditions that have been associated with engagement and social capital (e.g., Finn, 1989; Goldstein, 2003; Kalantzis & Cope, 2005). Student interviews lasted approximately 30 to 45 minutes, while parent interviews ranged from 40 to 60 minutes in duration. With the exception of one Sudanese parent who could speak fluent Arabic and English, interviews with parents and students involved a Kirundi, Arabic or Tirgrinya interpreter.[3] Most of the interviews entailed liaison interpreting, that is, the interpreters were physically present during the interviews and provided consecutive interpreting (as distinct from simultaneous interpreting typical of international conferences). In one case, however, unanticipated difficulties required telephone interpreting in a consecutive mode. Some sight translation of ethics documents was required at the beginning of each face-to-face interview, although this occurred in the context of an oral explanation of the documents provided by the interviewers.

We sought to ensure the quality of the interpreting by employing interpreters with relevant interpreting training and histories, expertise in professional educators' language, and experience of schools in Africa and Australia and of African life in Australia. To clarify the purposes of the interviews, we conducted pre-interview briefings with the interpreters. Although it has been suggested that this procedure potentially compromises the neutrality of the interpreter in the interviewee's eyes (Gentile et al., 1996; Roberts-Smith et al., 1990), we thought it necessary, given the fact that some of our questions (e.g., 'Do you read junk mail?') might otherwise seem banal in a formal educational context.

Once again, we found that this was not the only banality in the entire process, viewed from the 'outside'. For some of the parents and para-professionals (and no doubt for many of the students) invited to speak about matters 'within' and out-side school, there was not a little confusion about the need for, or desirability of, 'outsider' engagement in educational matters at all. In one interview, an African para-professional pointed to significant differences in professional–community relations: 'the only problem here . . . it is a cultural thing, in Africa, . . . my parents they would never be consulted'. Similarly, in response to a school administrator's request for an interview 'to help inform provision for African students', a parent countered with an alternative view of the pedagogic work of the school vis-à-vis that of the family or the community: '*You* must decide'.

In Tom Popkewitz's (2003) terms, parent and community 'pedagogicalisation' through research of this kind was being read as an insufficiency on the part of the school to conduct its own proper business, not an appropriately progressive invitation to participate in a community of educational practice. We have found similar reactions to such 'invitations' from other groups of migrant parents, for whom non-engagement with schooling is understood to be a marker of respect for the work being done by school staff. This remained so despite the disappointment of staff that the parents did not share their view about the importance of parents' being 'more involved'. This has been a timely reminder to us of the *tyranny*, as well as the desirability, of insisting on inclusive participation from all families and communities. Perhaps more importantly for this chapter, it raised issues about requiring parents to speak with a voice that is about and for the school. For a number of these parents, to be silent was to show ultimate respect of the authority of school and support for its aims and its work. 'Speaking out' was not sanctioned regardless of whether that speaking was giving explicit approval or 'voicing objections'.

Some parent interviews were conducted in the homes of the students, whereas others were held in the school, with seating arrangements designed to enable the interviewer to look at both interviewee and interpreter. For our interviews with the students, a room in the administration block of the school was cleared and made available. The room that was at the end of a corridor was chosen in the hope that background noise would not interfere with our audio recording of the interviews. The space also contained the usual assorted paraphernalia of utility rooms in schools. Sometimes, other members of the school community had to pass through this space, to get to their working spaces. It need hardly be said that, while conducting the interviews we were constantly aware of actual and potential interruptions and distractions. These problems are endemic to the physical settings of schools and militate against the intense concentration required for optimal inter-preting performance (Gentile et al., 1996). Once again, we were reminded that this was the pedagogical reality of the teachers – there could be no retreat into some ideal working or learning environment.

The 'interrogation' effect

In addition to issues around the physical space, we became acutely aware of the interaction of physical and social dimensions of the space within which we were working. A large table was set up, with chairs for researcher, interpreter and student. Each of the students was withdrawn individually from their normal classroom setting, and brought to the interview room. We placed our small digital tape recorder on the table, and the researchers had notebooks for entering field notes. The presence of the digital tape recorder would also not go unnoticed, since it was important that we placed this as close to the interviewee as possible. In accordance with our ethical-clearance protocol, we explicitly drew the tape recorder to the students' attention as we sought their permission to audio-tape the interview.

Physically, then, the young interviewees entered a space that was not familiar to them; they were alone in a room with two or three adults, the attention of all focussed on them. In comparison with their classrooms, the interview room was smaller and quite dim. It might well have appeared more like an 'interrogation' space than a space for social communication. This impression would not have been mitigated by the care we took to speak to the interviewee directly and to look at them during both their responses and interpreting of their responses – in fact, given culturally divergent communicative norms, it might well have exacerbated the 'interrogation' effect. We understood that our interview required something phys-ical or corporeal from the interviewees, not just something uttered. As McWilliam (2004) has argued elsewhere, such 'examinations' are body-to-body experiences, in which researchers require the subject of the examination to render themselves open to examination. Put another way, the researcher must negotiate a contract with the researched that there will be sufficient 'openness' to allow scrutiny by the researcher. No amount of throat-clearing could allow us to sidestep this issue. We did hope that, by giving brief messages, meaningfully chunked, and using language that was neither too colloquial nor technical, we could mitigate some of the interview's more discomforting bodily effects. However, given the need to create follow-up questions on the spot during the semi-structured interviews, this remained a constant challenge for us. Our efforts to ensure mutual safety and minimal corporeal discomfort were thus constantly thwarted as we struggled to mind our cultural manners and remain true to our 'standard' protocols.

Where two interviewers were available, we worked in pairs, with one of the pair taking a clearly defined leading role in each case. The aims included: (i) establishing similarity of data production procedure across the interviews; and (ii) enhancing data analysis by enabling team members to bring experience of the interviews to as much of the data set as possible. All the interviews were audio-recorded and transcribed to facilitate accurate data capture and analysis. Transcription was limited to the English segments of the audio-tapes. Consistent with established research practice (e.g., Goldstein, 2003) analyses of the data were informed by linguistic and cultural input sought from the interpreters after the interviews.

Care was taken to keep this overtly interpretative role separate from the inter-preting role so that the latter might not be compromised (Gentile et al., 1996; Roberts-Smith et al., 1990) – although it was, of course, always already so. The neat protocols that we hoped to maintain as a form of methodological table manners had already collapsed even as we struggled to follow the ethical and methodolo-gical protocols of 'good' research. We were compromised by our failure, in Lisa

Mazzei's (2004) terms, 'to attend to how the social situation of the speaker might be communicating more in the pauses and silences than in the speech' (p. 29). Listening to pauses, silences and hesitancies was rendered much less important than who was speaking for whom, when and how.

Given the complex histories of some of the team members as students, teachers and interview researchers in multilingual education contexts in Australia and Asia, some involving interpreting, we were certainly aware that the interview method would pose inter-cultural challenges, but we were unskilled in meeting the challenge of 'travel[ing the] . . . different *soundscape*' (Mazzei, 2004: p. 27, emphasis in original) posed by this research. We shared ambivalence, at the least, about notions of liberating the marginal voices of the 'Other'. Nonetheless, it was hoped that our approach would allow participants to perform 'speech acts' that might bear upon the actual educational processes of this and other schools seeking more productively to engage such young people.

After the interview, one member of the team conducted a post-interview debriefing with the interpreter, asking for his interpretation (a role separate from interpreting) of the interaction. One of the interpreters pointed to the difficulties faced by students with limited experience of schooling with its demands for articulate verbal displays: 'you have to summarize answers and give a direct answer and that is hard'. When asked about the familiarity of research-style verbal interactions in particular, the interpreter affirmed that these were not common in the 'reserved' culture of the student. He elaborated by saying that such interactions were likely to be associated with 'investigations': 'If you ask questions, people wonder why, questions are only asked if it is a bad situation and there is an investigation going on'. In addition, the interpreter said that it was culturally inappropriate for students to comment in any negative way on the performance of teachers. The interpreter had intervened to ensure the best result from the interview: 'I told her it is good to be doing research and told her to be open . . . without that preparation she would have been more reserved'. There is much here that muddies any pure project designed to 'let authentic voices speak'.

In accord with university ethical requirements, there was a formal introductory protocol that we performed when each student entered for the interview. Through the interpreter we explained the research and the presence of the recorder. We asked the student's permission to record, and had them sign a consent form, a procedure that required a minimal element of spot translation from the interpreter-translator. All this is sensible in terms of everyday, ethical clearance procedures for research, but it is less clear what the young people made of being faced with a tape recorder and being asked to sign a paper. All the students agreed to be interviewed and audio-taped and signed the consent form. One student did shake her head when first asked to give her consent. However, after a little more conversation with the translator, she agreed and signed. She may have been refusing permission to be recorded, or she may have been indicating she had no objection – we were unsure, and were unable to clarify further during the post-interview debriefing.

The desire for 'clarity' emerged as an important issue for us all. The fantasy that 'authentic' interviews conducted 'on location' with those for whom we were seeking to advocate a better, more meaningful schooling experience would deliver 'clarity' was foundering. It was foundering because of what we were unable to see and hear. The empty spaces that we hoped would contain words, just like the empty suitcases, contained things that we could not access. We were not prac- tised at 'creating spaces for the silences to fill rather than filling the spaces of silence with meaningless noise or with echoes of our own insecurities' (Mazzei, 2003: p. 362).

Whose voice?

The position of the interpreter presented us with further complexity. The nuances of interpreting mean that it is not simply a matter of directly replacing words of one language with another, as we knew and understood. In any language, translation rather requires conceptual transferences, and a degree of interpretation on the part of the translator, at all steps in the conversation. This is at times exhausting – it is a bodily experience that demands of both examiner and examinee a continual negotiation of power as much as it requires a negotiation of the space between languages. We wondered – but will never know – how much was filtered through the translation. We likewise wondered about the implication of fatigue in decisions to move on to the next topic, rather than to dwell on the current topic. There is evidence in the transcripts that fatigue was interactively salient: in several interviews we assured the students that 'we've nearly finished'. A year later we cannot know how this might have contributed to the brevity of some students' answers.

At the same time, alternative explanations are possible. During the interviews, some students were reluctant to look at, or call on, the translator, and appeared to be determined to conduct the conversation with us in English, without the support of the translator. In some instances, this may be an explanation for the brevity of their responses. The irony of our aim of researching the students' social and cultural capital and identity issues, and connections with language and communication needs, was not lost on us as we proceeded with our 'data capture' strategy. That is, we saw that we were, in Haraway's (1991) terms, 'holding incompatible things together because both or all are necessary and true' (p. 149). We were making demands that rendered these students 'Other' at the same time that we were working quite productively with their teachers to imagine a more culturally appropriate schooling. We were not anticipating that our advocacy could be done in some deodorised space, but continued to revisit the idea of 'doing the least harm' and what this had come to mean – or had ceased meaning – at each stage of the project.

The process of interviewing the students individually was problematic, in part, because the young people found themselves alone in a room with two (or three) adults, including strangers (outsiders). The 'stranger effect' is cause for concern. In one post-interview briefing, the interpreter responded to the interviewer's ques- tion, 'Is she always so quiet?' with the observation: 'She doesn't know you'. Moreover, a number of respondents appeared to be second-guessing, wanting to please the researcher by providing the 'correct' response. After the third consec- utive interview in which the students indicated that they would like to become a doctor, the interpreter spontaneously offered an interpretative comment: 'I think [the interviewees] . . . are all friends . . . maybe they talk together to see what to say and what they want to do'. While this might well be anticipated given the power relations of the interview situation, it is nevertheless drawing a long bow to announce that we were somehow 'capturing' something authentic about these young people and their experiences. There was no doubt, however, that we were very much implicated in their production of aspirational 'speech acts'.

Making trouble

It comes as no surprise, then, that we found ourselves struggling to make new sense of what we had set out to do. In Richard Rorty's (1989) terms, we began 'a labour of re-description'. Re-description, as Rorty explains it, is 'ironic' scholarship, because it is a project that refuses a final vocabulary of explanation (Rorty, 1989: p. 73). It does not tidy up, nor does it provide a vision splendid; it does not condemn, nor does it redeem. So the point is not to 'underwrite or dissolve doubt' but to maintain and insist upon it as useful and important. Language becomes a matter of positioning, never inviolate and always able to be exceeded. In this way, we would accept the proposition that we were not working 'within a neutral and universal metavocabulary' nor should we be expecting to 'fight [our] . . . way past appearances to the real' (p. 73). In refusing 'a neutral and universal vocabulary' and also refusing to see ourselves as struggling toward the authentic, we were moving away from any formula for the 'right' pedagogy to engage these young people, and toward the sort of 'self-referential' knowledge (Baert, 1998), that separated us from traditional consensus about 'proper' methodology, rendering our protocols contingent and strange. Put another way, we asked questions about those taken-for-granted knowledges through which we produce ourselves as researchers, understanding how the desire to do the least harm and the most good were both *and neither* necessary and true for the act of researching.

We have thus found ourselves thinking – dangerously – that perhaps control and command instruction might be more useful to these young people than a democratic pedagogy that may be neither understandable to the students or their parents as a cultural form nor particularly practical under the circumstances. Speedy transition to mainstream schooling is very important to these young people and their families. It was clear that the parents understand the learning of English as *the* passport to a worthwhile social future for their children, and thus English teaching as the most important function of the school. While they were pleased by the 'love' shown by teachers in the school, explicit instruction in English was on top of their list of pedagogical priorities. Similarly, the students almost invariably nominated English as their favourite subject, explaining that better English would make it easier for them to communicate, especially in shops and other social situations.

So what does doing the least harm or the most good mean in these circumstances? Does it mean abandoning 'progressivism' or taking the 'bits' from it that we still want to endorse? Or does it mean distancing ourselves from the imperative to improvement altogether, a well-rehearsed tactic of educational researchers when we get ourselves into another tangle? And what might such distancing look like to those teachers who asked us to collaborate with them to design a better educational experience for these students and worked with us to that end? We could certainly spend a lot of time telling them about the instructive complications of our research efforts, but we also anticipate that they might hope for more than our capacity to theorise our 'findings' and with good reason.

New terrains, new times

So what, then, of liberation through 'giving voice' in educational research more generally? We already know that cross-cultural, cross-generational and location issues bedevil qualitative research – indeed, an entire generation of researchers are continuously 'on guard' when it comes to 'context'. What we are less able to wrestle with in the academy, it seems, are the problems that come with word-centrism itself. In a sense, then, we have now come to voice some objections about the centrality of the Word, spoken or written. Our determination that we must finally have the word, or give the final word, makes for a research economy which is not only problematic in terms of power relations, but can easily collapse into a fantasy of what was 'meant'. Yet we continue to shake the 'word' tree, unwilling or unable to value those cultural products – images, sounds, text messaging, network configurations, novel designs and aesthetic forms – that increasingly speak the 21st-century subject beyond the (English) written or spoken word.

In digital times, it might be useful to re-think the word-centrism of our research methods in favour of other forms of data capture, including the sorts of visual and sound collages that young people enjoy creating in virtual environments, where they may be much more practised and sophisticated than baby-boomer researchers. Certainly we intend in the second phase of our research study to engage more fully the nexus of the social and the technological than we have done to date. The study will move out of the 'interrogation' room and into spaces, including digital spaces, which are more familiar and comfortable to these young people than they are to an older generation of researchers. We will seek to learn otherwise about who they are becoming and how they are most likely to learn what they need to know.

According to Lawrence Lessig, author of *The Future of Ideas* (2001), the capacity to edit reality – to organise it and re-organise it by mixing form and content, to juxtapose through display, to compare texts to understand difference – is one that is still to be authorised and/or acknowledged through mainstream research, despite the fact that it is the predominant capacity that young people need in this new century. While digital technologies have enormous potential in terms of a newly subversive politics and a new flowering of cultural life, our insistence on the (Anglo) voice as word-centric text is more likely to *exclude* rather than include all young people, not just those who are rendered vulnerable by their economic and social circumstances.

In looking beyond word-centrism, we are invited to inspect broader definitions of what it means to communicate and to strategise in spaces that exist between or outside languages using ideas not adequately represented by one viewpoint or in one language. This includes but is not limited to artistic ways of know-ing, involving the integration of significant modes of communication, where the textual is also related to the visual, the audio, the spatial, the multimodal, the beha-vioural, and so on. Just as 21st-century workplaces are changing the nature and purposes of knowledge work, so too we may anticipate new sets of skills for the culturally agile and communicatively competent researcher. As 'creative workers' (McWilliam, 2007), we might hope to include among our research skills a wider range of artistic capabilities, as well as greater competency in digital navigation and interface construction, pattern recognition, creation of novel analogies and mental models, the ability to cross-disciplinary domains, knowledge of schema for problem-solving, understanding intellectual property complexities, and greater fluency of thought for a range of purposes – occupational, civic and aesthetic. With these new skills, we may not be able to 'know the real world' of those whose voices we are seeking to 'hear'. However, we might be better equipped than we currently are to recognise the *when* and *where* and *how* of data, in the interest of greater explanatory power than our 20th-century tools have allowed.

Notes

1 These are refugees who come with few or no personal possessions – they may arrive with or without other family members.
2 Partner organisations include the Australian Research Council, Queensland Studies Authority, Multicultural Affairs Queensland, The Queensland Program of Assistance to Survivors of Torture and Trauma, and Milpera State High School (a flagship reception school for African migrant youth in the middle years of schooling).
3 Procedures for working with the interpreters followed established protocols (Department of Education and Training, 2005; Gentile et al., 1996; National Accreditation Authority, 1990; Roberts-Smith et al., 1990).

References

Baert, P. (1998). Foucault's history of the present as self-referential knowledge acquisition. *Philosophy and Social Criticism*, 24 (6), 111–126.
Bernstein, R. J. (1988). *Beyond Objectivism and Relativism: Science, Hermeneutics and Praxis*, Philadelphia: University of Pennsylvania Press.
Bourdieu, P. (1986). Forms of capital. In J. E. Richards (ed.) *Handbook of Theory of Research for the Sociology of Education*, New York: Greenwood Press.
Britzman, D. (1997). The tangles of implication. *Qualitative Studies in Education*, 10 (1), 31–37.
Collier, V. (1995). *Promoting Academic Success for ESL Students: Understanding Second Language Acquisition for School*, Jersey City: New Jersey Teachers of English to Speakers of Other Languages, Bilingual Educators.
Department of Immigration and Multicultural and Indigenous Affairs. (2007). *Fact Sheet 60: Australia's Refugee and Humanitarian Program.* Accessed 4 April 2007 from website: www.immi.gov.au.
Ellsworth, E. (1989). Why doesn't this feel empowering? Working through the repressive myths of critical pedagogy. *Harvard Educational Review*, 59 (3), 297–324.

Finn, J. (1989). Withdrawing from school. *Review of Educational Research*, 59 (2), 117–142.

Foucault, M. (1985). *The Use of Pleasure: The History of Sexuality, Vol. 2* (Trans. Robert Hurley), London: Penguin.

Gentile, A., Ozolins, U. and Vasilakakos (1996). *Liaison Interpreting: A Handbook.* Melbourne: Melbourne University Press.

Goldstein, T. (2003). Contemporary bilingual life at a Canadian high school: Choices, risks, tensions and dilemmas. *Sociology of Education*, 76 (3), 247–264.

Haraway, D. (1991). *Simians, Cyborgs and Women: The Reinvention of Nature*, London: Free Association Books.

Kalantzis, M. and Cope, B. (2005). *The Designs for Learning Guide.* Altona, Victoria, Australia: Common Ground Publishing.

Lather, P. (1991). *Feminist Research in Education: Within/Against.* Geelong, Victoria, Australia: Deakin University Press.

Lather, P. (1998). *Against Empathy, Voice and Authenticity*, Paper presented at the Annual American Association Conference, San Diego, CA, April 13–17.

Le Doeuff, M. (1977). Women and philosophy. *Radical Philosophy*, 17 (Summer), 3–11.

Lessig, L. (2001). *The Future of Ideas: The Fate of the Commons in a Connected World*, New York: Random House.

Mazzei, L. A. (2004). Silent listenings: Deconstructive practices in discourse-based research. *Educational Researcher*, March, 26–34.

Mazzei, L. A. (2003). Inhabited silences: In pursuit of a muffled sub-text. *Qualitative Inquiry*, 9 (3), 355–368.

McWilliam, E. (2007). *From 'Made in China' to 'Created in China': Changing our education systems for the 21st century*. Paper presented at the 10th China Beijing International High-tech Expo, Beijing Sheraton, 25 May.

McWilliam, E. (2004). Examining the body. In C. Grbich (ed.) *Health in Australia: Sociological Concepts and Issue*s, Frenchs Forest: Pearson Longman Australia, pp. 219–235.

McWilliam, E. (2000). Stuck in the missionary position: Pedagogy and desire in new times. In C. O'Farrell, E. McWilliam, C. Symes and D. Meadmore (eds) *Taught Bodies*, New York: Peter Lang, pp. 27–38.

McWilliam, E. and Lee, A. (2006). The Problem of the problem with Educational Research. *Australian Educational Researcher*, 33 (2), 43–60.

Milpera State High School. (2006). *Student Statistics*, Brisbane: Education Queensland.

Popkewitz, T. (2003). Governing the child and the pedagogicalization of the parent: A historical excursus into the present. In M. Bloch, K. Holmund, I. Moqvist and T. Popkewitz (eds) *Governing Children, Families and Education: Restructuring the Welfare State*, New York: Palgrave Macmillan, pp. 35–61.

Roberts-Smith, L., Frey, R. and Bessell-Browne, S. (1990). *Working with Interpreters in Law, Health and Social Work*, Canberra: National Accreditation Authority for Translators and Interpreters.

Rorty, R. (1989). *Contingency, Irony, and Solidarity*, New York: Cambridge University Press.

St.Pierre, E. A. (2000). The call for intelligibility in postmodern educational research. *Educational Researcher*, 29 (5), 25–28.

Yin, R. K. (2003). *Applications of Case Study Research* (Vol. 34). Newbury Park: Sage Publications.

Chapter 5

'Soft ears' and hard topics

Race, disciplinarity, and voice in higher education

Roland Mitchell

Introduction

DR MASON: I don't think it's my job to talk about issues of . . .

R. MITCHELL: Race?

DR MASON: Yeah, or class or gender. That's just not my job. It's not appropriate for me. I'm teaching a subject matter that's totally different so I wouldn't say that there is a statistically significant difference between blacks and whites on a GRE score. Let's now discuss that philosophically or whatever. I just wouldn't do that.

R. MITCHELL: In that situation would you feel comfortable having that conversation?

DR MASON: Oh no.

R. MITCHELL: Do you think anybody in the class would?

DR MASON: Oh, I don't know. I don't think so. I mean, I just focus on the statistics themselves. Mostly I contrive examples and things like that to illustrate how the stats work but the actual scenario or the research study, that's not really important. We don't have time [to] do that. They can get that over across the hall.

At the time Dr Shelia Mason participated in the interview above, she had been teaching statistics courses for two years at a predominantly European American university in the United States. This interview excerpt represents Dr Mason's insights associated with race and racism as they intersect with her being a member of academic communities or disciplines, and her comments show how these issues influenced the ways that she thought about her teaching in higher education. In this chapter, I focus on a case study of Dr Mason[1] to analyze how although race is such a ubiquitous subject in educational research, the impact of membership in an academic discipline may be overlooked or not as easily observable for researchers and in some cases even for the participants themselves. In fact, the findings from this research suggest that membership in scholarly communities or academic disciplines actually *disciplines* professors to the point that it polices the ways that they think about and voice the relationship between their racial identity, approach to pedagogy, and subsequent interactions with their students.

In addition to drawing out some salient points about the relationships among race, disciplinarity, and voice – especially as it pertains to those of us who are qualitative researchers studying those relationships – I use this chapter to develop a more nuanced approach to hearing and then reporting the voices of those who, like Dr Mason, teach across cultural and racial boundaries (Delpit, 1995, 1998, 2002; Giroux, 1996, 2004, 2006; Ladson-Billings, 1996, 1999, 2001; Rosiek, 2003). The type of hearing that I am advocating in this chapter entails listening to the voices of participants with 'soft ears' – or ears that are malleable and opened to subtle understandings and interpretations. I intend this type of listening to challenge taken-for-granted notions, norms, and conventions at the intersection of both researchers' and participants' understandings. By conceptualizing a listening to voice with soft ears, researchers might move toward 'straining voice' (as described by Mazzei and Jackson in the introductory chapter) and are challenged to become students of the discourses that their participants draw from to make meaning. As a consequence, researchers will need to 'strain voice' in order to view participants' ideas as the product of experientially contingent communal/collective understandings, as opposed to unmediated direct access to another's world. To be specific, if my reading of Dr Mason's comments did not take account of the complex interplay between race and disciplinarity through soft ears, I may have missed the richest and most significant ideas within her remarks.

In what follows, I offer that poststructural theory, and particularly a discursive reading of the relationships among voice, race, and disciplinarity, provides several analytic tools that can assist with such inquiries. Consequently, it provides a framework for analyzing these many intersecting influences on higher education pedagogy, and specifically for the purposes of this study, the ways in which Dr Mason voiced negotiation of these racially informed discourses and how it influenced her teaching. Therefore, an appeal to poststructuralism affords a framework for understanding the relations among teacher identity, student identity, the interpretation of racial signifiers both physical and performed, and the discourses of academic disciplines.

Against this backdrop, the data from this study suggest that the intersection of race and disciplinarity provided emergent insights concerning the participants' reflections about their practice that sometimes differed from my initial understandings and the initial representations of the data as well. Therefore, a key question became for me: What resources can be most useful for inquiry into, and subsequently reporting about, the richest and, in some cases, most surprising nuances voiced by the participants in my study? In this chapter I argue that poststructuralism meets this need as a result of its destabilizing nature, close attention to power relations, and propensity for challenging binaries, meta-narratives, and dominant cultural norms.

In the following section, I offer a description of discourse as it is situated in poststructural theory and make connections to how a discursive reading of race and discipline informs my inquiry.

Discourse

Poststructuralism affords a theoretical framework that recognizes the relationship between a professor's insider–outsider status in certain communities and that professor's subjective experiences in the classroom. Poststructuralism is particularly relevant to this project because it highlights the sutured, fluid, and socially constructed nature of racial identity (Alcoff, 2001; Collins, 1990; Dyson, 2002; Gilroy, 2000; Rushdie, 1991; Spivak, 1988; West, 1999). According to poststructural theory, racial identity is fixed through specific discursive practices. Recognition of these discursive practices provides a theoretical framework for considering the political economy of race in college settings as it relates to institutionalized ways of understanding relationships, activities, and meanings that emerge through language and influence what people in specific institutions take to be true.

For the purposes of this analysis I have chosen to focus on the work of Michel Foucault. In his work, Foucault offers the concept of discourse to establish a conceptual bridge between social dynamics and individual subjectivities. Discourse, as Foucault (1978) uses the term, refers to the system of symbols, signs, and meanings through which a particular topic or issue is understood by a given social group. Thought of in this way, discourses include specialized vocabularies, modes of representation, and conceptions of valid inquiry. For Foucault, an object of inquiry is constituted by the discourse that names it. So in the case of Dr Mason, the interaction and complex workings of multiple discourses, such as race and an academic discipline (mathematics), function to constrain, support, and shape her professional and pedagogical environment and subsequently her subjectivity.[2]

For researchers appealing to a Foucauldian understanding of discourse there is recognition of the constantly shifting and continually reproductive nature of discourse. Obviously, Dr Mason's example illustrated the ways that her racialized identity placed her on the margins of what a statistics professor 'should be' in the environment in which she was teaching. However, my attempting to listen with 'soft ears' (sensitive to overlapping and competing discourses) should resist attaching any static or simplistic meanings to the discursive practices that positioned Dr Mason in this manner. According to Foucault, there are numerous discourses constantly interacting and producing multiple subject positions as well as multiple forms of knowledge. Foucault (1978) wrote,

> We must conceive of discourse as a series of discontinuous segments whose tactical function is neither uniform nor stable ... we must not imagine a world of discourse divided between accepted discourses and excluded discourses ... but as a multiplicity of discursive elements that can come into play in various strategies. (p. 100)

Foucault's notion of multiple discourses moves me to consider what discursive practices make race and disciplinarity salient factors in the professors' teaching.

Accordingly, in examining Foucault's views concerning the nature of discourse, I was led to inquire, 'Who is speaking in a given discourse? Which words are accorded the possibility of making truth?' (Brown, 2000, p. 28). My asking these types of questions of Dr Mason's data offered a discursive reading that revealed not only who she was but *how she was able to speak* within her discourses.

Additionally and simultaneously, discourses constitute the subjectivity of the inquirer, which exists as a relation to the world of objects constituted by the discourse (Foucault, 1977). Both the objects of knowledge and the knower are constituted by discursive practices, and consequently the knowledge and discourse of a discipline (e.g., mathematics) are constructed by members of that disciplinary community. Weedon (1997) describes this robust notion of discourse by writing,

> Discourses, in Foucault's work, are ways of constructing knowledge, together with social practices . . . Discourses are more than ways of thinking and producing meaning. They constitute the 'nature' of the body, unconscious and conscious mind and emotional life of the subjects of which they seek to govern. (p. 108)

Through this definition, Weedon draws attention to the double-move between discourses and the shaping of knowledge and subjectivity. And for researchers seeking to provide new ways of reproducing the experiences voiced by participants, a Foucauldian analysis of voice contends that familiarity with the discourses that intersect to shape the knowledge base and subjectivity of their participants is essential. An example of the discursive relationship between the shaping of knowledge and subjectivities in the data was illustrated at the beginning of this chapter with Dr Mason's discussion of how her membership in an academic community influenced the topics that she considers acceptable to address in class. Armed with some familiarity with the ways that these discourses function individually as well as collectively, a researcher can then conduct a discursive analysis of experiences voiced by participants, an analysis that produces knowledge differently. Furthermore, researchers can also glean insight on how to formulate more insightful questions based on the discursive experiences voiced by participants.

Foucault argued that discourses are driven by power but not in the traditional sense of a centralized or repressive source of power but in a much more omnipresent and fluid manner; and indeed, it is through discourse that power and knowledge are joined together (Foucault, 1978, p. 100). Consequently, for Foucault, knowledge and power merge to produce discourse. As Foucault (1978) wrote, 'Discourse transmits and produces power; it reinforces it, but also undermines and exposes it, renders it fragile and makes it possible to thwart it' (p. 101). Specifically, discourses can serve to transmit and produce power through the disciplining of voices within particular academic communities, be those majority white academic communities, and/or disciplines such as mathematics. I turn now to consider the discursive nature of academic disciplines.

Discourses of discipline

Traditionally discourses associated with mathematics are concerned with a type of data analysis in which the practices include the planning, summarizing, and interpreting of observations of a system possibly followed by predicting or forecasting of future events based on a mathematical model of the system being observed (Lindley, 1985). Preparation to teach mathematics rarely, if ever, requires discussions of racial difference. In fact, as Dr Mason suggested, the discipline of mathematics conspired against establishing the type of environment that explicitly addresses racial difference. Dr Mason stated:

> We don't have an environment that I am totally conscious of that is sensitive to race . . . . I just don't think it's my job to talk about issues of [interviewer finishes the sentence Race?] Yeah or class or gender . . . That's just not my job; it's not appropriate for me. I'm teaching a subject matter that's totally different.

The sentiment that Dr Mason expressed, suggesting that it is not her job to discuss race in class, is an example of her socialization (or being disciplined) into which issues a mathematics professor is required to address. It appears that issues of racial difference are not within these parameters. The problem that arises from an attempt to ignore the influence of racial difference in the classroom is that prior to any discussions of content or subject-matter, discourses associated with gender and race have already shaped the interaction between professors and students. In Dr Mason's case, her perceptions of the student to teacher interactions within her class were influenced by conceptions of the racial and gender difference between she and the majority of her students. Focusing on her race and gender identity, Dr Mason perceived that her students considered her out of place in a college-level statistics classroom. And her desire to stick as closely to what she considered to be the race/gender blind norm within her discipline was led by an inclination to resist, and subsequently detract, attention away from negative stereotypes associated with her race and gender. Instead, Dr Mason emphasized her mastery of her subject matter knowledge. In so doing, her knowledge of statistics placed her in a position of superiority in the classroom conversation, detracting attention away from her racial and gender identity, which would have placed her in a position of inferiority in the conversation.

The ideas associated with discipline that Dr Mason discussed in our interviews conveyed the ways that membership in an academic discipline influenced her approach to pedagogy and the ways she was perceived by her students. In examining her comments closely, I interpreted what appeared to be two interrelated yet separate and distinct definitions of discipline, one of which I take up here. The meaning of discipline most relevant in the case study with Dr Mason was most closely associated with the academy. In this sense an academic is a member of a scholarly community typically represented by a field of study that is both taught and researched. This disciplinary community often encompasses academic journals, college and university departments, and learned societies representing distinct cultures. These distinct cultures exert varying influences on scholarly behavior and significantly inform the structure of higher education (Del Favero, 2002).

However, in some disciplines like ethnic studies, sociology, or anthropology, discussions of racial difference are central to their epistemic foundations. In these cases discourses associated with racial difference influenced the very nature of the language that they used to describe fundamental concepts within their disciplines. For example, Dr Mayo – a cultural anthropologist and another participant in the larger study – stated, 'I was talking about code switching during a lecture on linguistic anthropology and dialects . . . . An African American student and I were talking about African American English as something that has been studied by linguistic anthropologists as a dialect of English.' Dr Mayo's discipline taught her to take racial difference as an important topic for inquiry and analysis as a scholar. It also influenced the way she paid attention to racial difference in her classroom interactions. Through this approach to culturally responsive and disciplinarily informed practice, Dr Mayo established a space within the classroom conversation, which highlighted the relationship between power and language among the voices of the historically dominant and historically subordinate groups in society. The centrality of the analysis of racial and cultural difference within her discipline caused her inclinations to build upon similar racially informed discourses in her practice, and then to subsequently voice the resulting understandings in our interviews about her teaching, to seem almost second nature.

Consequently, membership in a disciplinary community provides an individual the impetus for a particular pattern of thought and action. Further, from a critical perspective these examples illustrate the ways that disciplines can function to classify and control human subjects in both symbolic and material ways. Therefore, membership in an academic community brings together power and knowledge to integrate into a single disciplinary technology (Stangroom and Garvey, 2006). The focus on discipline provides indispensable discursive understandings about which ideas can or cannot be voiced based on the professors' perception of, and orientation to, their academic community. Further, casting academic disciplines as discursive structures shows how classification and control also govern actual statements of truth, what can and cannot be said, and what definitions are acceptable and recognizable (for the purposes of this chapter, statements made by research participants). Later in the chapter, I will further complicate how academic disciplines, such as mathematics, serve to regulate and constrain discussions of pedagogical experiences. For now, however, I continue with applying poststructural notions of discourse to another concept in my analysis: race.

Discourses of race

My analysis of Dr Mason's discursive experiences is significantly enhanced by being familiar with not only disciplinary discourses, but also discourses inherent to historically marginalized communities crossing boundaries. For instance, a common anecdote among the African American community suggests that to be successful in majority white settings, blacks have to perform 110 percent better than their white counterparts. In addition, another adage with similar grounding within historically colonized communities is that an appeal to racism, sexism, or other socio-culture prejudice as a hindrance to advancement or 'playing the race/gender card' is unjustifiable and criticized under the rhetoric of being politically correct. These and similar communal *truisms* did come up in my discussions with Dr Mason and other African American professors who participated in the study. According to this way of thinking, the Civil Rights movement was successful. Supporters of these sentiments would argue that the United States supported the end of race-based segregation; at the time of this writing, an African American man and European American woman were the two front-runners for the 2008 Democratic nomination for President, so some would contend that we as a nation have clearly transcended racism and sexism. Where racial difference is concerned, if we have transcended race then it seems perfectly reasonable to adhere to disciplinary discourses that suggest any allusions to race in a math class are off topic and that regardless of the racial or gender make up of the class, the singular focus on learning statistics affords all similar opportunity and experience.

The understandings associated with race that most heavily influenced discussions with Dr Mason and other participants who were members of minority groups were how their membership in this community of minority faculty led to a grappling with the tension between assimilation and cultural subordination. These tensions are present across all spectrums of American life for people of color. Particularly, for professors of color teaching in majority European American settings, they manifest themselves in numerous ways from isolation or segregation in specific program areas to suspicion from colleagues, difficulty in securing and maintaining employment, high attrition rates, and differing standards for evaluation (Jacobs et al., 2002). In the specific case that this chapter opens with, race and disciplinarity overlap when Dr Mason described her thoughts concerning when and how to voice her feelings of being raced and gendered in the context in which she was teaching. Dr Mason believed that certain aspects of the criticism that she received from her students were more closely associated with her race and gender than with her actual classroom interactions. These feelings were informed by the fact that she was teaching in a majority European American institution with, like most similar institutions in the region, a well-documented history of racially exclusionary practices to both students and professors of color.

This history was not lost on Dr Mason, and the actual student make-up of her class – consisting of mostly white men – further heightened her awareness that as a woman of color, she differed from the norm of most of the other statistics professors in the department. The racial make-up of the American professoriate supports Dr Mason's assertion that race and gender influenced her relationship with her students considering that most of her students had never had an African American woman as a college-level teacher. Data supporting Dr Mason's assertion as published by the U.S. Department of Education (2005) reported that although African Americans made up about 12 percent of the college student population, African American professors represent 5.3 percent of the professoriate. Thus, the

black presence in the faculty ranks is less than half of the black student enrollment figures. Although in our interviews, Dr Mason voiced her recognition and
sensitivity about teaching in this environment, she insisted on not allowing the
resulting sentiments concerning her perceptions about race and racism to influence her teaching. Consequently, Dr Mason voiced in our interviews the ways that
she conceptualized these instances when issues associated with race and gender
impacted her teaching as being heavily informed or *disciplined* by her membership
in a scholarly community or academic discipline that considered discussions of
racial and cultural difference outside the realm of responsible professional practice.

The disciplinary content is the central medium through which the teachers
and students interact. As educational theorist Lee Shulman (1987) has suggested,
'A teacher's content knowledge rests on two foundations: the accumulated literature and studies in the content areas, and the historical and philosophical scholarship
on the nature of knowledge in those fields of study' (p. 9). This is particularly
important in Dr Mason's case because 'the manner in which [this understanding]
is communicated conveys to students what is essential about a subject and what is
peripheral. . . . The teacher also communicates, whether consciously or not, ideas
about the ways in which "truth" is determined in a field and a set of attitudes and
values that markedly influence student understanding' (p. 9). This tacit epistemological influence by and through disciplines is the effect of competing discourses and
was an important part of the type of knowledge and reflection on experiences that
Dr Mason discussed in our interviews. The conflict between discourses associated
with racial and cultural identities that she had lived her entire life and discourses
associated with her acculturation into scholarly communities are apparent in the
interviews with Dr Mason.

In this regard, Dr Mason's membership in an academic discipline functioned
to police the ways that she expressed her ideas about race and teaching. Academic disciplines, which are intimately connected with universities and higher
education in its broadest sense, are a critical territory for these struggles in that
higher education plays an essential role in setting societal norms. The challenge
for educational researchers is to be familiar enough with disciplinary and racial
discourses to be able to conduct inquiry into the information that they receive
from their participants. The following section demonstrates some of the ways that
a researcher who is familiar with racial and disciplinary discourses can analyze
and glean substantive insight from the voices of participants.

A discursive re-presentation of the data

A conception of the voices of participants articulated through a discursive lens
affords me the possibility of thinking of a professor's interpretation of classroom
events through one discourse or another – not in terms of truth or untruth or
an expression of a participant's personal character or politics, but as an effect
of broader institutional practices that make sustaining alternative interpretations
of classroom experiences challenging and even costly for some professors and

difficult to understand for researchers. As opposed to looking for the most obvious ways to either simplify or problematize the linkages that participants voice between racial difference, disciplinarity, and pedagogy, a poststructural analysis acknowledges these nuances as both the product and evidence of different facets of competing discourses. Recognition of these discourses by the researcher provides an expanded landscape for rich inquiry if researchers' ears are attuned to perceive discursive influences inhabiting their data.

The remainder of this chapter will demonstrate the new possibilities enabled through a discursive analysis of the voices of participants. To provide a close reading, I will focus specifically on the intersection of discourses associated with the disciplines or academic communities of which my primary participant Dr Mason is a member (statistics) and her racial identity (African American). By singularly focusing on discourses associated with disciplinarity and race, I do not intend to ignore the existence of other discursive influences such as spiritual or religious beliefs, gender, or sexual orientation. Instead, I simply seek to conduct inquiry into a slice of a very complex system of meaning-making by Dr Mason. My overarching interest focuses on the question of what discourses Dr Mason takes up and uses when talking about her teaching and academic life. As a guide for this discursive reading of the data and responding to the fore-mentioned question, I focus on three listenings: Disciplined Voices within an Academic Life; Disciplined Voices and Representation; Disciplined Voices and Enabling Discourses.

Disciplined voices within an academic life

College classrooms are typically thought of as spaces where students and professors meet with the intention of engaging in the project of learning. Numerous educational theorists have challenged objectivist notions of classrooms as *pure* spaces where students and teachers interact absent broader societal factors (Delpit, 1995; Delpit and Dowdy, 2003; Freire, 1973; Gay, 2000; Mitchell and Lee 2006; Sconiers and Rosiek, 2000). This chapter supports a porous vision of classrooms arguing that not only do societal factors permeate classrooms but also that educational settings are replete with the collective insights and understandings of teachers' and students' home communities. Specific to Dr Mason, these include her communal and collective understanding of her racial identity, the subject matter that she taught, her gender, class, religious and/or spiritual beliefs, sexual orientation, and family background. Further, these discourses are present in the ways that she voiced her ideas about experiences of teaching. This chapter takes up two significant factors – race and discipline – as both are the product and object of intersecting, and at times competing, systems of meaning-making.

Dr Mason's remarks at the beginning of this chapter provide a good space for illustrating the utility of a discursive analysis for understanding the ways that race and disciplinarity influenced her perceptions. Elsewhere in her interview, Dr Mason succinctly described the way that her racial identity (African American), the subject area that she taught (statistics), and gender (female) influenced her students' perceptions of her and her teaching:

R. MITCHELL: Do you think your students respond differently to you than to your colleagues of the same rank and standing of a different color or gender?

DR MASON: Yes I absolutely do and I think that because I am a woman and black that I've had some people tell me that I don't know what I'm talking about. It's been reflected in my course evaluations. I'll never be rated as highly as a white male because most white males teach this course ... but at some point I feel like I will be really good at it however I feel like I will never be recognized for it but that's ok.

These comments suggest that her academic life, work with students and colleagues, and ultimately her subjective experience of teaching is shaped by the perception that as a black woman she is out of place in the context that she was teaching. However, Dr Mason later stated,

I don't think it's my job to talk about issues of race, class, or gender ... It's not appropriate for me. I'm teaching a subject matter [statistics] that's totally different. I wouldn't say, for instance, that there is a statistically significant difference between blacks and whites on a GRE score, let's now discuss what that means philosophically.

This aversion to discuss race explicitly in her teaching seems contradictory to her earlier remarks about race being 'present' in her teaching in regard to student perceptions of her. In fact, these contrasting views may be read in the first example as evidence of her awareness of the racist discourses that structure the context in which she teaches. Dr Mason's latter comments may be read as her 'towing the party line,' supporting the widely held conception of professionally responsible teaching in her field that does not include any significant discussions of race, culture, or gender. Consequently, this example illustrates the way that professors' membership in an academic community might shape the way that they experience their profession and in this case voice their contradictory and even constrained subjective location in a racialized context.

The field of statistics rarely, if ever, requires discussions of racial difference. In light of being a member of the discipline, the sentiment that Dr Mason expressed (suggesting that it is not her job to discuss race in class) is an example of her socialization and acceptance of which issues a mathematics professor is required to address. Further, proof of her adherence to disciplinary discourses was Dr Mason's belief that discussions of racial difference occur in other classrooms, but they have no place in mathematics courses. In Dr Mason's opinion they take the focus off of the primary aim of a statistics class – learning statistics. By adhering to this paradigm a candid classroom discussion about the very structures that keep her and other African American female statisticians on the margins of the field cannot occur. Adhering to this approach to practice seriously curtails the possibility of developing counter-hegemonic discourses from within the discipline that may ultimately eradicate the sexist and racist discourses that she laments. Consequently, her academic life is limited by her pedagogical performance and academic accomplishments being viewed through the lens of the same racist/sexist discursive elements that have historically placed individuals in her subject position on the margins of the discipline. Further, in the classroom her pedagogy and work with students is limited in similar ways in that before she can even begin the process of teaching she must demonstrate to her students that she is qualified to teach the course.

One of the other African American women on the faculty at Dr Mason's university, Dr Maxwell (who was also part of the larger study), provided a useful illustration of this point. Dr Maxwell voiced, in a separate interview, the ways that she often crafted parts of her introductory lectures to explicitly relay to her white students that she has the highest of academic credentials or, as she put it, that she is 'a black woman with a Ph.D. from your institution so give me respect.' Dr Maxwell's reference to her credentials and to the fact that she earned them in predominantly white institutions is a signal to her students that she is credible and has been successful at every level from student to professor.

Through these actions Dr Maxwell spoke directly to racist and sexist discourses similar to Dr Mason's remarks at the opening of the chapter. However, Dr Maxwell has chosen a different strategy of resistance. Regardless of the fact that these discourses may have been implicit and voiced only in the context of our interviews as in the case of Dr Mason, or explicit and voiced in both the classroom and interviews as in the case of Dr Maxwell, they still hinder the progress of black women who teach in these settings. Specifically, they create an environment that causes women of color to prove themselves competent in ways that their white male colleagues do not, before they can even engage in the work of teaching. The most profound insight that I gleaned from our discussions concerned the ways that professors of color like Dr Mason and Dr Maxwell voiced their strategies for how to engage these limiting elements within their teaching contexts. I was left with the understanding that their decision not to discuss candidly issues of racial and cultural difference in the classroom was as much, if not more, of a distraction from teaching the class content as simply addressing these issues head on.

Disciplined voices and re-presentation

The outspoken nature of Dr Mason's remarks from the previous section in which she stated that it was not her job to discuss race in her classroom did not carry over into the portion of our interview concerning her student's racial identity, participation, and performance. Specifically, when discussing her African American students' performance, Dr Mason was somewhat elusive and hard to pin down:

DR MASON: I sometimes see differences in terms of learning and class participation where race is concerned. In many cases my international students tend not to participate as much as US born students . . .
R. MITCHELL: What about your African American students?
DR MASON: I really don't want to share about my black students. Cut that tape recorder off and then we can talk.

Dr Mason acknowledged that she had made observations concerning the students of color in her class. However, when I asked specifically about her African American students, her silence or request that her comments remain off the record illustrated her voice as disciplined and as a result produced an uncharacteristically *loud* silence.

This silence speaks volumes about her comfort level in re-presenting both her work as a professor and her evaluation of her students. Although I will refrain from including our off the record discussion of this matter, it is worth noting that Dr Mason responded to the discussion about her black students' performance in a manner similar to the way she responded to discussions about race and gender in her teaching – no discussion at all. She is aware that there are issues specifically associated with being an African American student, faculty member, or administrator in majority institutions; however, perhaps the provocative, contested, and possibly personally compromising nature of the issues that may arise from these conversations made her hesitant to openly respond in our interview.

For me, that makes essential a discursive reading of the data that Dr Mason is providing in this interview: her silence and particularly an understanding of the factors that produced this silence. It is not the case that Dr Mason is making an appeal to a *color-blind* approach to her practice because she acknowledged the ways within and outside of the classroom being a woman of color impacted her experiences. Therefore she possesses certain understandings about racial and cultural difference, but she has made a measured decision to not explicitly tap into or engage this knowledge base in her teaching. In fact, regardless of her personal frustration with her marginalization, she understands that explicitly challenging these discourses in her teaching further highlights her race and gender and ultimately how she is out of place in her discipline and the university setting.

Instead, Dr Mason represented herself as working hard to continue her impressive publication and service records, thereby adhering even closer to the standards of her academic and university communities. What stood out most for me by understanding the discourses that Dr Mason was using to guide the way that she negotiated these discursive communities was that she was aware of the benefits as well as the hypocrisy of the systems that she was negotiating. Ultimately, however, her decision of what to challenge and what to bear was governed by a merger of disciplinary and communal understandings. Therefore, Dr Mason's voice and her representation of herself was governed by a knowledge base that produced a distinct subjectivity that could be courageous and principled as well as accommodating and self-serving.

Disciplined voices and enabling discourses

The voiced insights that governed Dr Mason's negotiation of discourses associated with race and discipline were more than simply instinct-driven reactions. Our interviews suggest that being at the nexus of these oftentimes competing discourses produced valuable knowledge for improvement to faculty socialization and teaching. However, her negotiations of these competing discourses also functioned to both strengthen and disrupt the enabling discourses within her field. Mathematics is a discipline that has not made race, racial difference, or the subjectivity of African American learners a primary unit of analysis. In fact, as Dr Mason commented, mathematics teachers consider a focus on racial difference a hindrance for teaching mathematics.

A rather interesting example in Dr Mason's department reflects the tension associated with addressing racial and cultural difference within the broader discipline of mathematics concerning the recognition of there being an absence of African Americans in the field. Dr Mason's department was in the process of conducting an academic search to fill a vacant professorship. Dr Mason's department chair felt the need to remind the search committee that despite the personal research and success of a candidate for the position in working in ethnically and culturally diverse educational settings, the committee members should remember that they were in the process of selecting a statistician, not an African American Studies professor. The chair's remarks were in response to their university's targeted hiring program that was intended to address the shortage of minority faculty in their program area. Therefore it appears that the hesitance that Dr Mason voiced to engaging in issues associated with racial difference is not relegated only to classroom settings. Although this is clearly anecdotal for the purposes of this chapter, the chair's comments further demonstrate influential discourses within the discipline, supporting an objective space in which addressing the limited number of blacks in the field is not a concern for the disciplinary community. The chair's sentiments are directly in line with similar discourses voiced by Dr Mason: that racial difference is outside the realm of her responsibilities as a teacher.

A surprising aspect of my research was the prominence of views voiced by mathematics professors of different races, social backgrounds, and genders, views that were similar in their consideration of racial difference as outside the parameters of their discipline. Regardless of their subject position, professors in the larger study voiced clear understandings about why a professor may be hesitant to address racial difference in his/her teaching. My insight is limited if I engage in a simplistic analysis of the voices of professors of color, who may very well be marginalized by adhering to elements within this discourse, by separating race and pedagogy within the discipline. However, a discursively informed analysis helps me to recognize the modernist foundation that under-girds mathematics as a discipline and the search for a value-free, subject-matter-focused classroom.

In her interview, Dr Mason clearly articulated the idea that regardless of race, ethnicity, or gender, the conceptual grounding of the discipline respects no race or creed. This emphasizes the point that $1 + 1 = 2$ whether a student is black or white. This appeal to objectivism can be read as an attempt to bracket out all prejudice, bias, and human frailties and in a sense can provide discursive resources for countering racist practices within the field. From this perspective, as long as the professor is committed to teaching and the students are committed to learning, then racism or a racialized discourse has no place in this type of classroom. Dr Mason and several of her European American colleagues that I interviewed in previous studies were deeply committed to these ideals and they believed that if a mathematics teacher's practice was carried out objectively, then his or her disciplinary training supported these color-blind approaches to pedagogy and all students would have an equal opportunity to succeed.

The virtue of this approach to engaging racial difference in class is that it attempts to go against the grain of institutionalized white supremacy that has historically established conditions that first officially segregated classrooms and then later established conditions that disadvantaged students of color who slipped through the cracks into majority European American classrooms. In this case, the discourses of Dr Mason's disciplinary membership led her to make one of the strategic decisions that Foucault referred to concerning the intersection of discourses in the hopes of disabling the influence of white supremacist discourses within her discipline. By viewing Dr Mason's support of this objective vision of her discipline in this manner I understood Dr Mason to be, as Audre Lorde is often quoted, using the 'Master's Tools' to deconstruct the boundaries that she faced in the context in which she taught. In short, if an objective interpretation of the field meant that subject-matter knowledge was the primary criterion that the professors were evaluated on and not racial or gender identity, religious affiliation, or class status, then Dr Mason sought to position herself within this discourse by demonstrating her mastery of statistics in her classroom while ignoring other aspects of her subjectivity.

On the surface, the greatest limitation to Dr Mason's singular focus on sub-ject matter knowledge in her teaching is the issue of its effectiveness. Historically African American students have not fared well in math-based courses. It may be argued that there is no natural relationship between considering discussions of racial difference, besides the point in mathematics courses and students of color historically not performing as well as their European American peers. However, it seems antithetical to provide culturally responsive service because professors see that a segment of the class is not as actively engaged or experiencing the same level of success, and to turn a blind eye to the possibility that issues associated with racial difference may influence their experience. A color-blind and objective approach is a better method than the explicit bias that many U. S. colleges and universities had against students of color in earlier years; however, I believe the current mani-festation of white supremacy and bigotry calls for much more. Professors must make themselves students of different discourses about race, pedagogy, and their disciplines and work to actively engage the vestiges of institutionalized racism in the classrooms.

If documented and studied, these understandings may provide a starting point for eradicating the vestiges of inequity within academic communities. There is a simple need to support professors' reflection on cultural and racial difference in their classroom and *how they can speak up or speak out about this difference.*

Yet this study points to some specific areas where a poststructural inquiry might profitably focus academic disciplines reflexively by examining the social, profes-sional, and academic discourses that influence the way professors respond to the relationship between race and disciplinarity. In other words, it could be a way to help professors become more constructively self-conscious of the assumptions underlying their classroom practices. And it could assist professors in familiarizing themselves with discourses that are conducive to forming positive relationships with students of color as well as consciously resisting practices that exclude, silence, and alienate students of color in that these students are future professors and researchers within their discipline.

This focus on cultural and racial difference need not come at the expense of the attention to the disciplinary subject matter that has been at the heart of this inquiry. As this study shows, a teacher's thinking about cultural and racial difference is often intimately tied up with his/her disciplinary training. In my opinion, the scope of our responsibility to address issues of equity and justice in our teaching are at least as great as our responsibility to the disciplinary tradition we teach. I have little patience for those who would pit these two important imperatives against one another. I believe the examples from this study and a different listening to Dr Mason's discursively produced voices illustrate not only how they can co-exist, but also how they can enhance one another. Any separation of the two, it seems, is artificially imposed from outside the experience of teachers. This is not to suggest that disciplines like mathematics, chemistry, or physics should change their scholarly focus to reflect socio-political interests that disciplines like ethnic studies or women and gender studies discuss. However, it is intended to highlight the possible benefit of having discussions across disciplines concerning culturally responsive teaching and ultimately strengthening the pedagogical effectiveness of the field. Where Dr Mason was specifically concerned, the parts of these discussions that I gleaned the most insight from were the ways that she voiced a support for discourses that produced her subjectivity. The challenge was not to attempt to smooth them out or develop a master-narrative that made each of these areas fit, but, in contrast, to leave them rough and in subsequent discussions return to them for further engagement and learning.

'Hearing with soft ears': Discursive considerations for researchers

The data on which this inquiry was based are intended to highlight the possibilities afforded by examining professors' reflections on their practice through the discourses that under-gird them. My reference to listening with soft ears is a call for researchers to conceive of the ways that professors conceptualize and ultimately voice their experiences of teaching in ways that recognize the interplay of numerous discursive influences. The introduction to *The Brothers Karamazov* (1992) illustrates this point by framing what I have described as disciplinary and communal discourses as texts with a sense of 'multivoicedness.' When describing, in the novel's introduction, the significance of understanding multivoicedness for a reader, Jones (1990) stated:

> But the 'multivoicedness' of Dostoevsky's novel is not restricted to dialogue between and within the characters and the narrator. It has other important functions. One of them involves the constant echoes of other texts. Of course if one actually knows these texts intimately the echoes are richer and more

thought-provoking. Otherwise they appear as little more than unfamiliar quotations. . . . Still, if one is aware of the precursor voices summoned up through the shared memory of author and reader one still senses that multidimensionality which is one of the glories of *The Brothers Karamazov*. Such awareness may stimulate all sorts of reflections which the author was unaware of, especially if the 'allusions' one detects are to texts which post-date the novel. (xxi–xxii)

Where the afore-referenced remarks show a relationship between the characters in a novel, the reader, and the author, the significance of a common point of reference between all three is synonymous with the type of familiarity with the discourse community of participants that I am calling for by researchers in this chapter. The precursor voices mentioned above are the historic/communal discourses that I have framed as essential for exploration by researchers. As the quote suggests, both participants and researchers bring insights, precursor voices, and reflections to the research process that inform the ways that participants describe their experiences as well as the ways that researchers analyze and subsequently write about those experiences.

Another important point *The Brothers Karamavoz* illustrates for researchers attempting to listen with soft ears is the capacity for the relationship between the author and the reader, or for the purposes of this chapter, researchers and participants, to produce new and unexpected knowledge. The key is that both researchers and participants bring with them prior knowledge and experience as a result of membership in varying discursive communities. The places where these discursive communities intersect and overlap provide rich opportunities for different meaning, and as Jones argues, the resulting interplay can stimulate all kinds of reflections that may not be initially evident. To listen with soft ears a researcher must actually look for the traces of the precursor story or echoes associated with the discourses that may or may not necessarily be shared with participants. Hence the challenge for researchers is to listen with ears that are willing to adjust to roars as well as whispers and echoes voiced by participants.

Couched within this approach to inquiry is the possibility for varying interpretations of the perceptions voiced by participants. Specifically, where issues associated with race, racism, and schooling are concerned, the possibility of developing counter-hegemonic discourses within and across academic disciplines is inspiring. However, for this to occur, researchers must be primed to take advantage of these possibilities. This priming process means researchers must be prepared to make themselves students of the discourses (precursors/echoes) that their participants take up and use in their meaning-making. In the case that this chapter has addressed this means a researcher must be familiar with discourses concerning African Americans, gender, academia, their teaching context, and their specific academic discipline. Singular knowledge of each of these discourses is important but more is needed. Researchers must work to gain an understanding of how these and other discursive influences intersect and overlap to produce and discipline meaning for their participants as well as the ways this meaning is talked about, represented, and incited within related discourses. Lacking this type of insight a researcher has no way of understanding or relaying the nuances of the information that their participants provide. Clearly, this is a strenuous expectation for researchers, and not all researchers will acquire soft ears in the same manner.

Furthermore, based on the research topic, the participants, and the researchers' relationship to the discourses that inform the ideas voiced by participants, some researchers may be primed to work with certain individuals more easily than others. In some cases, this may require the same type of study required as a member of a scholarly community while in others it may require immersion in a community. Still, in others, it may require situating the self within and across communities to become more sensitive to the complexities involved. Ultimately, I do not intend to suggest a one-size-fits-all to acquire the needed insight. Instead I believe that a combination of some or all of these actions is necessary while still recognizing that certain understandings may remain outside the realm of understanding and subsequent representing. However, this understanding of the limitations that exists in and of itself provides advancement as well as an illustration of a researcher who is listening to the voices of participants with soft ears.

If documented and studied, these understandings may provide a starting point for eradicating the vestiges of racially based inequity within academic communities. Beyond the simple need to support the ways that professors voice their reflections on cultural and racial difference in their classroom, this study points to some specific areas where a poststructural inquiry might focus on how they respond to the relationship between race and disciplinarity. In other words, it could foster professors' becoming more reflexive and subsequently voicing the assumptions underlying their classroom practices. And it could assist professors in sustaining the discursive practices that enable their positive relationships with students of color as well as in resisting those practices that exclude, silence, and alienate students of color.

This observation has many complex implications for researchers. First, a researcher must realize that the ideas voiced by their participants are the products of individual and collective histories, experiences, and actions, and that even if the researcher were actually present when they occurred, the researcher may still never truly understand the meaning of the experience for the participants. Second, researchers must also be sensitive to the fact that they also bring to the discussion understandings that are products of their own personal, individual, and collective histories, experiences, and actions. Therefore, a researcher is not only challenged to be a student of the discourses that inform the voices of their participants but also to be sensitive to the ways that their own membership in differing discursive communities inform their analysis of their participants' experiences. And finally, to be knowledgeable – at best – of each of the fore-mentioned intricacies does not foreclose the possibility that a researcher has finally captured the full understandings conveyed by a participant. A discursive approach allows researchers to interpret their participants' ideas differently, but ultimately a researcher can never fully capture the insights provided by his or her participants. Instead, our best hope is to listen to a participants' voice with ears that have been primed and are soft and absorbent but still molded to accept the realization that much will be lost or not completely recognizable. However, familiarity with the discourses that made the voice possible will make resonant the most significant points.

Notes

1 This case study data come from a larger study concerning the insights that allow professors to provide culturally responsive service to students of color. The data for the larger study consisted of interviews and observations with 25 faculty members who were racially diverse, balanced among male and female professors, and representative of a variety of academic disciplines – from musicology to statistics.
2 Subjectivity is the phenomenological experience by an individual of his/her relationship to the world, sense of self, and his/her negotiation of those socially constructed identities and spaces (Weedon, 1997).

References

Alcoff, L. (2001). Toward a phenomenology of racial embodiment. In R. Bernasconi (Ed.), *Race*, Malden: Blackwell Publishers Inc.

Brown, A. (2000). *On Foucault*. Belmont, CA: Wadsworth.

Collins, P. (1990). *Black Feminist Thought: Knowledge, Consciousness, and the Politics of Empowerment*. New York: Routledge.

Del Favero, M. (2002). Linking administrative behavior and student learning: The learning centered academic unit. *Peabody Journal of Education*, 77(3), 60–84.

Delpit, L. (1995). *Other People's Children: Cultural Conflict in the Classroom*. New York: The New Press.

Delpit, L. (1998). *The Real Ebonics Debate: Power, Language, and the Education of African-American Children* (co-edited with Theresa Perry). Boston, MA: Beacon Press.

Delpit, L. (2002). *The Skin that We Speak: Thoughts on Language and Culture in the Classroom* (co-edited with Joanne Kilgour Dowdy). New York: New Press.

Delpit, L. and Dowdy, J. (2003). *The Skin That We Speak: Thoughts on Language and Culture in the Classroom*. New York: The New Press.

Dyson, M. (2002). *Open Mike: Reflections on Racial Identities, Popular Culture and Freedom Struggles*. New York: Basic Civitas Books.

Foucault, M. (1977). *Discipline and Punish: The Birth of the Prison*. 1st American Edition. (Tran. Alan Sheridan). New York: Pantheon Books.

Foucault, M. (1978). *The History of Sexuality an Introduction*. (Trans. Robert Hurley). New York: Vintage Books.

Freire, P. (1973). *Education for Critical Consciousness*. New York: Seabury.

Gay, G. (2000). *Culturally Responsive Teaching: Theory, Research, & Practice*. New York: Teachers College Press.

Gilroy, P. (2000). *Against Race: Imagining Political Culture Passed the Color Line*. Cambridge, MA: Harvard University Press.

Giroux, H. (1996). *Counternarratives: Cultural Studies and Critical Pedagogies in Postmodern Spaces*. New York: Routledge.

Giroux, H. (2004). Cultural studies and the politics of public pedagogy: Making the political more pedagogical. *Parallax*, 10(2), 73–89.

Giroux, H. (2006). *Fugitive Cultures: Race, Violence, and Youth*. New York: Routledge.

Jacobs, L., Cintron, J., and Canton (Eds). (2002). *The Politics of Survival in Academia Narratives of Inequality, Resilience and Success.* New York: Rowman & Littlefield Publishers, Inc.

Jones, M. V. (1990). Introduction. In *The Brothers Karamazov* (Trans. F. Doestoevsky, R. Pevear, and L. Volokhonsky). New York: Knopf.

Ladson-Billings, G. (1996). Silence as weapons: Challenges of a black professor teaching White students. *Theory into Practice*, 35, 79–85.

Ladson-Billings, G. (1999). Just what is critical race theory and what is it doing in a nice field like education? *International Journal of Qualitative Studies in Education*, 11(1), 7–24.

Ladson-Billings, G. (2001). *Crossing over to Canaan: The Journey of New Teachers in Diverse Classrooms.* San Francisco: Jossey Bass.

Lindley, D. (1985). *Making Decisions.* 2nd Edition. London: John Wiley & Sons.

Mitchell, R. and Lee, T. (2006). Ain't I a woman: an inquiry into the experiential dimensions of teacher's practical knowledge through the experiences of African American female academics. *The International Journal of Learning*, 13(7), 97–104.

Rushdie, S. (1991). *Imaginary Homelands: Essays and Criticism 1981–1991.* New York: Granta Books.

Rosiek, J. (2003). Emotional scaffolding: An exploration of teacher knowledge at the intersection of student emotion and subject matter content. *The Journal of Teacher Education*, 54(5), 399–412.

Sconiers, Z. and Rosiek, J. (2000). Historical perspectives as an important element of teacher knowledge: A sonata-form case study of equity issues in a chemistry classroom. *Harvard Educational Review*, 70(3), 370–404.

Shulman, L. (1987). Knowledge and teaching: Foundations of the new reform. *Harvard Educational Review*, 57, 1–22.

Spivak, G. (1988). Can the subaltern speak. In C. Nelson and L. Grossberg (Eds), *Marxism and the Interpretation of Culture*, Urbana, IL: University of Illinois Press.

Stangroom, J. and Garvey, J. (2006). *The Great Philosophers from Socrates to Foucault.* New York: Barnes & Noble.

U.S. Department of Education, National Center for Education Statistics. (August, 2005). Full-time and part-time instructional faculty and staff in degree-granting institutions, by race/ethnicity, sex, and program area. *The Condition of Education 2005*, Fall 1998 and Fall 2003.

Weedon, C. (1997). *Feminists Practice and Poststructuralist Theory.* 2nd Edition. Cambridge, MA: Blackwell Publishers.

West, C. (1999). *The Cornel West Reader.* New York: Basic Civitas Books.

Chapter 6

Broken voices, dirty words

On the productive insufficiency of voice

Maggie MacLure

> The sign of an authentic voice is thus not self-identity but self-difference.
> –Barbara Johnson (1987) *A World of Difference,* 164

Preamble

I am interested in the disappointments of voice in qualitative research – in the many ways in which voice falters or fails. Despite (and because of) a long history of struggles to represent more adequately the authentic voice of research subjects, voice fails somehow to suffice. As I elaborate below, 'voice research' seems always to fall short, or to go too far.[1] Counter-voices from various quarters periodically speak up to repudiate voice and voice research – for failing to be authentic enough; for resisting theory, truth and generalisation; for being naïve or cynical about power and discourse; for dealing in self-indulgence or self-denial; for confounding self-revelation with self-justification. In return, voice is periodically reclaimed as a legitimate and necessary concern of qualitative research.[2] The field of voice research seems to oscillate, then, between surrender and mastery, loyalty and treachery. It is torn between the desire to yield to the 'crystalline address' of the intact, unmediated voice (Derrida, 1976: 115), and the urge to break that voice down: to analyse it until it submits its truths, abstractions or generalisations to the calculations of social science.

But the insufficiency of voice – its abject propensity to be too much and never enough – is unavoidable. Voice will always turn out to be too frail to carry the solemn weight of political and theoretical expectation that has been laid upon it. For voice is also tied to idle, frivolous things that tarnish authenticity, weaken trust or block analysis, at least as these are usually conceived – frivolous things such as performance, appearances, inconsequentiality, vacillation and vested interest. I want to suggest that, rather than trying to repair or deny these necessary insufficiencies, we need methodologies that are capable of dwelling on, and in, those very properties of voice that make it such troublesome material for research. I have in mind a kind of 'voice research' that would attend to such features as laughter, mimicry, mockery, silence, stuttering, tears, slyness, shyness, shouts, jokes, lies, irrelevance, partiality, inconsistency, self-doubt, masks, false starts, false 'fronts' and faulty memories – not as impediments or lapses to be corrected, mastered, read 'through' or written off, but as perplexing resources for the achievement of a dissembling, 'authentic' voice. These insufficiencies, I will suggest, are product-ive: they allow people to mean more than one thing at a time; to fashion mobile and nuanced readings of situations; to connect with others despite not knowing exactly 'who' they themselves are. These mundane qualities of voice also allow people to engage with others without offering to render themselves 'transparent', an important facility in the quasi-colonial contexts of research interviewing and observation.

Qualitative research still tends to prefer a 'poetics of sincerity' (MacLure, 2003: 139) that produces innocent voices that speak a familiar script of revelation, redemption or triumph, in tones that lack idiom and surprise (Carey, 1999; Lather, 1996; Popkewitz, 1998). I want to propose instead a poetics of insufficiency. Such a poetics would recognise the irreparably split nature of the self and the broken voices in which it speaks. It would assert, following Barbara Johnson's opening quotation above, that self-difference is the mark of the authentic voice. This is, of course, a difficult voice for qualitative research. It can neither speak (for) itself, as would, ideally, the authentic voice of the self-identical subject, nor offer itself up unreservedly to the penetrating action of analysis.

Last, and still by way of preamble, I am interested in how the voices that are 'heard' in research texts carry so few of the qualities associated with the spoken voice. At least in that domain called 'the field', qualitative research is pre-eminently a sound- and silence-filled, patchy, vernacular business of more or less satis-factory face-to-face encounters. The problems of transmuting those encounters into written text are well-documented (Clifford, 1990; Geertz, 1988; MacLure, 2003), and indeed are the source of much of the guilt and blame that attaches to the (mis)representation of voice, as I discuss below. These problems of translat-ing speech into writing are never surmountable. I am not proposing to privilege speech over writing, nor suggesting that one could 'capture' the spoken voice more accurately, or authentically, with more fine-grained transcription notations, video records, 'multi-modal' analysis or other methods (though there might still be good reasons for adopting these).[3] Voice always evades capture. Something is *always* lost in translation. I am interested here in *what* is lost in the particular translations of speech into writing in research texts such as interview transcripts, observation notes, reports and articles.[4] The loss that produces voice in research writing does not just involve, as it must inevitably do, a muteness as concerns the 'phonic substance' of speech – its sounds and cadences. It also typically involves the disappearing of those double-dealing, mischief-making qualities that I enumer-ated above – jokes, lies, feints, detours, contradictions, exaggerations and misfires, together with those emissions that lie on the boundaries of language itself, such as laughter, gasps, tears, sneers and silences. In other words, what is lost tends to be those very features of voice that confound both authenticity and analysis.

In the remainder of this chapter, I elaborate on the troublesome ways in which voice has (dis)appeared in qualitative research, in order to open up further space for considering how research might address those aspects of voice that are usually lost in translation. The discussion makes reference to a recent research project involving young men talking about health and explores the possibilities and the dangers for participants when research tries to engage with the antic disposition of voice, and its tendency to confuse and repel. The chapter is written under the influence of Derrida's (1976) *Of Grammatology* – a text that deconstructed the inevitable disappointments of speech and writing, and their implications in the scene of anthropological guilt, well before many of those implications began to unfold in debates about voice in qualitative research.

'The supplementary menace of writing'[5]

Voice has been a fertile site of anthropological guilt and blame. Moreover this guilt and blame is inexorably tied to the problematics of *writing*. The emergence of voice into qualitative research is intimately connected to the realisation that research texts might carry undetected, unwelcome traces of colonialism, racism and gendered privilege in their very structure and poetics. Recognising this troubled heritage – for instance in the representation of subjects as exotic, innocent, primitive or subordinate 'others', or as mere illustrations of their own analytic abstractions – ethnographers and feminist researchers have tried to find forms of analysis and writing that would allow the authentic voice of subjects to be heard more clearly. Or at least they have wanted to call attention to the defining authority wielded by the authorial voice – a voice that had traditionally tried to render itself invisible so that 'science' might speak (Atkinson, 1990; Clifford and Marcus, 1986). The traces of that anthropological guilt circulate in the continuing concern with voice in qualitative research.

This concern has worked itself out, amongst other ways, as textual prescriptions for manifesting the voices of research subjects and/or of researcher-authors. These could be summarised (with oversimplification and with overlap) as three altern-ate injunctions, or writing instructions for researchers: *step back*, *step forward*, or *step away* from the text. Stepping back would involve withholding as far as possible one's own textual and/or analytical interventions, in favour of extensive verbatim quotations and stories from the subjects. An early, and canonical, example is Marjorie Shostak's (1983) *Nisa*, about a woman member of the !Kung people in the Kalahari, substantially built out of Nisa's 'own' words. Stepping away from the text would involve various forms of attempted or forced evacuation, by academic researchers, of the scene of representation in order that participants might speak (in) their own voices and evade the 'epistemic violence' wrought by anthropologists and their writing (Marker, 2003: 361). Recent work in autoethnography and *testi-monio* exhibits such an aspiration. Stepping forward would involve introjecting one's authorial voice into the text so that its representational ruses might be more visible to readers, and therefore more open to critical scrutiny. Patti Lather's and Chris Smithies's book on women living with HIV/AIDS, *Troubling the Angels*, would be one such example: 'rather than only "giving voice" to the stories of others, this is also a book about researchers both getting out of the way and *getting in the way*' (1997: xiv; italics added).

The attempt to rescue the voice of subjects from the perceived threat of writing can be seen as an instance of the desire for 'presence' – for direct access to fundamentals such as truth, thought, meaning or the unbreached integrity of the intact self. Derrida notes how the spoken word has often been considered the 'very condition' of presence in general: as that which seemingly manifests thought without delay or detour, and directly 'presents' self to self and self to other without dropping out into the exteriority of the world (1976: 8). Derrida also notes the specifically anthropological appeal of the 'living voice' as the mark and guarantor of the ideal community whose members are always 'within earshot' (1976: 136). He notes that, for Levi-Strauss, as for Rousseau, speech stands for 'social authenticity': for '[s]elf-presence, transparent proximity in the face-to-face of countenances and the immediate range of the voice' (Derrida, 1976: 138). Writing is always apprehended as a threat to the authenticity of speech – as something secondary and external that muffles the voices and contaminates the innocence of the community.

But Derrida shows that neither speech nor writing can heal the split between self and other, or seal the circle of self-identity. Speech is no less fissured than writing by the fabrications of signs and the necessary spacing or *différance* that divides the self from 'itself', ethnographers from subjects. Speech and writing both emerge from an originary, 'arche-violence', a catastrophic *loss* of presence: 'loss of the proper, of absolute proximity, of self-presence, in truth the loss of what has never taken place, of a self-presence which has never been given but only dreamed of, and always already split, repeated, incapable of appearing to itself except in its own disappearance' (1976: 112). Derrida calls this violence that inaugurates both speech and writing, 'arche-writing': or, simply, writing. Writing, in this Derridean sense, *opens* the question of presence, but opens it as disappearance: 'what opens meaning and language is writing as the disappearance of natural presence' (159). Writing cannot heal the wound that opens ethnography therefore, though this does not mean that ethnographers are thereby absolved from trying to find more responsible ways of writing. But voice and written language will remain *necessarily* insufficient. Neither can deliver the fullness and immediacy that fuels the dream of presence. This helps to explain why voice continues to trouble qualitative method.

'A perpetually reanimated mistrust'[6]

Even in texts that profess the staunchest privileging of subjects' voices, there often turns out to be some insufficiency in the voices that emerge. Researchers find that interviewees seem reticent or resistant – unable or unwilling to speak fully. Or they appear, on the contrary, over-rehearsed or over-compliant, serving up a story they prepared earlier, or trying to be the person they think the researcher wants them to be. They may seem to be putting up false 'fronts' (Woods, 1985: 14), speaking in voices that are not entirely their own as a result of nerves, poor memory, bad interview technique or power differentials. Butt et al., arguing for the authority of teachers' voices, find nevertheless that the stories teachers tell 'are subject to incompleteness, personal bias and selective recall' (1992: 91). Participants' voices are therefore easily found to be *lacking* or *excessive* (which amounts to the same thing): too specific, too general, too biased, too polished, too partial, too practised.

This lack is the opening through which Method enters, in the form of remedies to pre-empt or overcome the silences or failings that interfere with the achievement of 'full' voice: put the subject at her ease; make the interview feel like a conversation; 'triangulate' accounts to check for truth or validity. Woods refers to methodic 'precautions' and 'safeguards' (1985: 17, 18). Carspecken (1996: 165) worries about inconsistency: 'If [a subject] says early on in the interview, "I hated my brother" and then says much later on, "I admire my brother more than any other man I've ever met", you may have problems in taking both statements at face value'. He recommends 'consistency checks' for 'honesty and accuracy' (165). Such remedies are based on the premise that full voice is possible in principle, but in practice never quite transpires. Folded into research texts that sponsor participant 'voice' is a persistent undertone of unease, therefore, about the sufficiency of those voices. Derrida detected a similar misgiving in Rousseau, identifying 'a perpetually reanimated mistrust with regard to the so-called full speech. In the spoken address, presence is at once promised and refused. The speech that Rousseau raised above writing is speech as it should be or rather as it *should have been*' (1976: 141, original emphasis).

The necessary failure of attempts to represent participants' voice, based as they are on the fantasy of presence, means that voice data in research texts is always, inevitably, in *deficit* with respect to some (unstated and unstatable) notion of speech 'as it should have been', in Derrida's formulation. Subjects might always have said something more, or something else, or something deeper, or something more true – if they had felt more at ease; if they had been more honest; if the researcher had asked better questions; or had refrained from asking so many questions; or had 'shared' more of herself; or introjected less of herself; if the interview had been held in a less public place; or a more public place; if it had taken place in a group, or had *not* taken place in a group; if subject and researcher had been of the same sex, or age, or ethnicity, and so on. It is the task of Method to supplement the insufficiencies of voice; to restore it to what it should have been.

There is always *supplementary* work to be done therefore on participants' voice – either midwifery work, assisting at the birth of the true or whole story and the authentic voice or chemical work, distilling/analysing the meanings, themes or significances carried by that voice (cf. MacLure, 2003: ch 7). These two moves correspond to the contradictory moments that Derrida (1998) identifies in analysis, visible in its etymology – one which seeks to return to origins, births and causes (*ana-*), and the other working relentlessly to break down, untie, solve, dissolve, resolve (*-lysis*). Analysis is thus endlessly divided by two incommensurable motifs, the 'eschatological' and the 'archaeological', 'as if analysis were the bearer of extreme death and the last word . . . [yet also] turned toward birth' (20). Pulled or paralysed between birth and death, intact origin and final (dis)solution, analysis is regulated by the structure, or the stricture (Derrida's preferred word here) of the double bind. Pull on one thread and you tighten the other. Caught in the birth–death stricture of the double bind, researchers are pulled in contradictory directions in their engagements with voice. It is that same double bind, between science and surrender, proximity and distance, that Geertz identifies when he writes that ethnographies 'tend to look at least as much like romances as they do like lab reports' (1988: 8).

'This remorse that produces anthropology'[7]

Another problem – perhaps the most significant one – is that the desire for voice is dogged by a kind of repetition compulsion. Each attempt at renouncing the colonialist gesture that suppresses or erases subjects' voices seems to end up re-offending. Thus Pratt (1986), re-reading Shostak's *Nisa*, finds it to be inadvertently caught up in the 'discursive legacy' of colonialism that it repudiates. In trying to extract principles or messages from Nisa and her world that might speak across time and distance, and in particular to 'the American women's movement', Shostak, in Pratt's reading, repeats the colonialist gesture of erasing the cultural specificity of the lives of women in the Kalahari (including the violent history of successive waves of Western colonial aggression) in order to extract life lessons from a putatively more innocent (i.e. 'traditional') society. Pratt notes the recurrence in Shostak's book of a familiar trope of the innocent Other, as the bearer of benevolent personal attributes: '[c]heerfulness, humor, egalitarianism, nonviolence, disinterest in material goods, longevity, and stamina [. . .] all underscored with admiration and affection' (Pratt, 1986: 47–48). Pratt describes these, bluntly, as 'the characteristics that the powerful commonly find in those they have subjugated' (46) and suggests that they are part of an enduring tendency to naturalise, infantilise and decontextualise the subjects of ethnography and of colonialism.

Fuller describes a similar de-historicising gesture in 'eco-discourses' that celebrate the 'Native sciences' of aboriginal peoples as an alternative to Western hard science. Discussing a best-selling popular science book, she points to the ways in which '[n]atives are consistently represented as childlike, pure and most importantly intrinsically connected to the land' (2000: 84). Like Pratt, Fuller emphasises the direct link between this celebratory 'naturalising' of formerly colonial subjects, and the repression of their pre-colonial history. She calls this 'the textual politics of good intentions' (cf. MacLure, 2003: Ch 5). Derrida detects the same colonialist, indeed 'Rousseauistic', gesture in Levi-Strauss' critique of ethnocentrism. This has, Derrida suspects, 'most often the sole function of constituting the other as a model of original and natural goodness, of accusing and humiliating oneself, of exhibiting its being-unacceptable in an anti-ethnocentric mirror'. Levi-Strauss learned thus to know his own unacceptability, and to partake of 'this remorse that produces anthropology' from Rousseau (1976: 176).

Is it fair to identify similar tendencies in the substantial volume of educational research that has sponsored 'teacher voice'? I do not have the space here to do an adequate or fair analysis across different texts, so I will make an example, unfairly, of just one. It is possible to detect something like a 'textual politics of good intentions', I suggest, in this extract from Jean Clandinin's and Michael Connelly's authoritative text, *Narrative Inquiry*:

> There are five people gathered at the table in the Centre on a cold, crisp, sunshine-filled day in winter. It is Saturday and the light filters in the window. The sky is an unbelievable blue but they hardly notice. This is one of their research Saturdays. Chuck and Annie have driven up from Calgary to meet with Janice, Karen, and Jean to talk about and share their research. The tape recorder hums softly in the middle of the table. They are intent on their conversation even though they have been sitting for several hours. [. . .] Jean shares a fragment of the transcript from that conversation (as picked up from the tape recorder), in which Karen [. . .] speaks:

> I think sometimes when you do feel strongly about things though, that marginalises you. I can remember the first year with the principal. I just got red faced arguing with him over these report cards because he wanted every kid to be evaluated the same way [. . .] and I mean I can remember, I was in hysterics almost that he could even be thinking this way. How can you always mark a child as failing? And when I get upset about things, I tend to get really passionate about them.

> (1999: 57)

This fragment carries both Jean Clandinin's authorial voice[8] and the reported voice of Karen, transcribed from the tape recording of the meeting. Jean's voice frames the text, though she also places herself 'inside' it, referring to herself in the third person as one of the participants 'gathered at the table'. The text conjures a warm, convivial space of sharing and conversation around a softly humming tape recorder. This space is also sketched in noticeably *visual* terms – the crisp sunlight, the blue sky, the disposition of the people around the table. This is a familiar ethnographic scene-setting device – describing the scene as if seen from the 'outside', and therefore framing off the subjects, 'providing the knowing observer with a standpoint from which to see without being seen, *to read without interruption*' (Clifford, 1986: 12, original emphasis). Karen's voice (as represented by Clandinin and Connelly) is, I suggest, a recognisable 'teacher voice' of dedication and struggle to realise one's educational values.

The fragment has therefore some of the characteristics of the 'textual politics of good intentions' and the asymmetrical seizure of voice associated with the colonial relation: the tenor of 'admiration and affection' in the authorial voice; the framing of the participants as readable 'without interruption'; the morally engaged teacher voice. I do not mean to suggest that 'Karen' (as reported) is 'lying' or that this is not 'really' her voice. Nor am I suggesting that Clandinin and Connelly are intentionally enacting a colonial relation toward their research participants. But despite the aspiration to go beyond 'univocal' and 'unidimensional' representations of voice (p. 147), the voices conjured lack the specificity and distinctive timbre that the movement for 'voice' has sought. Instead, as so often, what appears is 'the generic shape [and] the universal face' of humanism (Haraway, 1992: 86).

The humanist voice seems to emanate from a subject who knows who she is, says what she means and means what she says. It is a well-intentioned, well-modulated voice that speaks for/from an intact self, or a self who is seeking to restore its intactness, who hopes for redemption or at least reconciliation. Whose voice is that? And whose interests does it serve? Popkewitz argues that such voices are constructed by a 'redemptive culture' of research that 'naturalizes the teacher and child as objects to be rescued' (1998: 423). The 'wisdom of the teacher' that is produced by such rationalising discourses 'assumes a single, universal, and ahistorical field of representation to reality' (16). Such naturalising discourses of voice mask the effects and technologies of power at work in the inscription of identities. The voices that are thus produced are never unexpected (Carey, 1999), and the selves that speak are too easily 'read' ('without interruption'): their voices lack cultural and contextual specificity and they offer themselves to be read *literally*.

The repulsion of voice: Dangers on the dark side

This 'literalisation' of voice – the erasure of ambiguity, complexity, power, history and specificity – renders voice research more vulnerable than it might otherwise be to periods of backlash, when the apparent insufficiencies of voice become so troubling to some critics as to provoke a more thorough-going repudiation (cf. MacLure, 2003: ch 8). Periodically voices speak up to say that voice research has gone wrong or gone too far – that it is insular, parochial, partial, idiomatic, context-bound or weak. The affinity of voice with story, anecdote, performance and point of view seems to confound the serious business of analysis or theorising. Repair work is proposed by some critics: what is needed are better socio-political theories, or stronger contextual frames, or broader historical perspectives, to circumscribe, explain or augment the limited purview of 'voice research'. Goodson, for instance, finds that narrative methods in educational research, with their valourising of 'silenced voices', have 'remained ensconced in the particular and the specific' (1995: 97). Stories 'need to be closely interrogated and analysed in their social context' (95) – a task that will require the 'active collaboration' of the academic researcher with the 'story-giver', to 'allow us to locate and interrogate the social world in which [such stories] are embedded' (98). Hargreaves, noting that it has become 'fashionable' to attend to teachers' voices, and commending this as 'a useful emphasis', nevertheless worries that its commitments are 'parochial', and finds that advocates have 'moved beyond humanistic understanding to uncritical celebration and endorsement'. Such work needs, he argues, 'to embrace a broader social and moral perspective' (1994: 147). Moore and Muller (1999), speaking for a properly scientific method, and indeed the health of the whole field of sociology of education, judge 'voice research' to be beyond repair. The offences of voice research have persisted, they argue, from the New Sociology of Education, through feminist standpoint epistemologies, multiculturalism, postcolonialism and 'postmodernist approaches'. These offences include reductionism, relativism, 'perspectivalism', insularity, incoherence, nihilism and a simplistic critique of science.

Voice research is accordingly judged inadequate to the task of producing 'knowledge in the strong sense' (191). Having a 'weak' rather than a 'strong internal language of description', it lacks a 'stable, explicit and rigorous methodology of production' (202). Young (2000) agrees with the critique by Moore and Muller, adding a range of further offences, discussed below; however, he wants to 'rescue' the sociology of educational knowledge from the ravages of voice research.

Such criticisms seek to put voice back in its (subordinate) place – to contain it ('locate', 'embed', 'embrace' it) within wider contexts, stronger theories or broader perspectives. Or else they seek to repudiate it entirely – to eject it from the body proper of scientific research. It is interesting how the adjectives line up in the binary logic of these critiques. Voice research is weak, insular, parochial, specific, unstable, irrational, and irresponsible. It needs, or needs to be replaced by the strong, broad, stable, rigorous, rational, universal arguments of science and theory. Lined up against the manly adjectives of theory and science, voice research assumes a distinctly feminine demeanour.[9]

As well as appearing weak and powerless, and therefore lacking something, voice is also apprehended simultaneously as *excessive*. These critiques betray a noticeable strain of anxiety about the incontinence of voice. Hargreaves fears 'a world of voice without vision' – 'a world reduced to chaotic babble where there are no means of arbitrating between voices, reconciling them or drawing them together' (1994: 251). Young is preoccupied with 'the relativist *excesses* of voice discourses' (2000: 526, my emphasis), and indeed spells out his anxiety in the title of his article: 'Rescuing the Sociology of Educational Knowledge from the Extremes of Voice Discourse' (2000: 524).

It may come as no surprise to find that much of the blame for these excesses is attributed to postmodernism. '*This is the dark side of the postmodern world*', Hargreaves warns, 'where the authority of voice has supplanted the voice of authority to an excessive degree' (1994: 251; my emphasis). Young's comments on 'voice discourse approaches', which he takes to be based on 'postmodernist theories', are worth quoting at some length.

> [T]he intellectual dishonesty and potential harm that can be caused by voice discourse theorists need to be pointed out loudly and clearly [. . .]. 'Voice discourse' theorists are often clever and, in appearing to be democratic both in their deference to the experience of so-called 'real people' and in their critique of expertise, they are also seductive. In rejecting the claims for any kind of objective knowledge, the logic of their position is nihilist and leads to the cynicism of social scientists who reject the grounds of their own practice or, as in the case of Baudrillard, give up social science altogether. If taken seriously, as some in Germany and elsewhere took Nietszche, the rejection of any grounds for knowledge can lead to the view that the only question is who has the power to impose their view of the world.
>
> (2000: 534)

There is something excessive about Young's critique of the excesses of postmodernism and its accomplices, the 'voice discourse theorists'. This tendency for critique to bite its own tail is a recurring feature of critical responses to postmodernism. Young's anathema has many of the characteristics identified by Stronach and MacLure (1997) as typical of the repulsion of postmodernism: the distinctly personal flavour of the critique (directed toward theorists whose approaches are rejected precisely because of their alleged privilege of the 'personal'); the familiar litany of offences – nihilism, dishonesty, deviousness, seductiveness and cleverness; the hyperbolic apprehension of the 'harm' that postmodernism supposedly has the power to inflict (escalating, here, to the threat of totalitarianism).

Like postmodernism, voice seems therefore to repel. Its insufficiencies, apprehended as simultaneously lack and excess, produce anxiety. Something threatening inhabits voice, blocking analysis or elevation to universality, yet also falling short of that impossible fullness that would relieve researchers of the burden of mastery and afford us the moral relief of surrender to the authenticity of the other. How then could research be responsive, and responsible, to voices that must always be partial and marked by loss? I want to suggest that it might attend to those properties of voice that resist both surrender and mastery – properties such as laughter, mimicry, mockery, irony, secrets, masks, inconsistencies and silence. These supplementary, profane, mischief-making, analysis-blocking properties may be intimately connected with whatever is distinctive about a person's voice.

Humour, voice and the discourse of deficit

I want to consider the case of humour as one such troublesome property of voice. Humour seldom seems to be a good thing for the serious business of research. This was noticeable during a project that was investigating health practices and attitudes amongst a group of disaffected and socially disadvantaged young men (see MacLure et al., 2006). Like other researchers who have worked with young men, we found that humour was a pervasive feature of the boys' interactions, both amongst themselves, and with the researchers. The boys' interactions typically involved a good deal of collective fooling around; not giving a 'straight' answer to a question, especially if a sexual connotation could be found; and mocking each other's sexual orientation and making outrageous allegations of bad behaviour. ('Damien's gay!' 'Frank sucks bum-hole. Wanna hear him scream like a girl?' 'Dom's an alkie' (alcoholic)). Questions about personal problems or feelings were often met with sexual banter.

As noted above, humour is almost always represented (when it is acknowledged) as a *problem* for research and intervention. It may be read as a sign of faulty research design and a failure to get at young men's 'real' feelings – a result of interview effects associated with age, unequal power relations or gender antagonisms; or a failure to put the participants at ease; or intentional resistance to the inquiry (Allen, 2005; Sixsmith and Griffiths, nd). Humour is also often seen as a negative, or even dysfunctional feature of young men's culture itself. Noticing how humour is used to patrol the boundaries of masculine identity, and to perpetuate sexist stereotypes, some researchers conclude that it is inevitably conservative (Billig,

2002; Sixsmith and Griffiths, nd), and therefore an impediment to social interventions. Sixsmith, attempting to involve young men in 'participatory research'
about health, found that their 'black humour stifled any informative discussion and
precluded the development of health expertise' (2004: 16).

Humour is generally read therefore as *resistance* – to self-reflection, social
amelioration and indeed to analysis. And despite its noisy clamour, humour is also
associated with *silence*: It is taken as filling a space where something meaningful
and serious should have been said. 'Humour was also an effective way of *silencing*
talk about health, as well as policing the boundaries of accepted masculine behaviour', Sixsmith and Griffiths report (nd: 34; my italics). Humour is thus taken as an
offence against 'presence' – as a mark of inauthenticity, displacement and conceal-
ment. In research contexts it becomes a resistance to be overcome so that the truly
authentic voice – 'speech as it should have been', to requote Derrida – can be heard.

Derrida (1980) identifies frivolity with the economy of the supplement: as
différance that frustrates the desire of presence. He notes philosophy's long-
standing fear of contamination by literature – of being poisoned by the frivolity
of its stylistic pretensions and thus losing its access to truth or generality. Smith,
discussing Derrida's reading, spells out the resistant character of frivolity.

> The comedy or baseness of frivolity lies in the fact that unlike tragedy it cannot
> easily be generalised out into statements on the 'human condition' as it used
> to be called. Frivolity is light and unserious, and yet it is base, heavy, leaden or
> bathetic because it resists elevation to generality; not enough of the Hegelian
> spirit, the spirit of reason, lightens it (in both senses).
>
> (Smith, 1995: 27)

Comedy blocks generalisation and empathy (mastery and surrender). It resists
analysis. The task of method is, precisely, to get rid of frivolity. 'The method for
reducing the frivolous is method itself. In order not to be the least frivolous, being
methodic suffices' (Derrida, 1980: 125).

Perhaps method could find other ways of handling humour. Rather than seeing
it only as a problem, and keeping silent about it, trying to 'cure' it, or reading
beneath or through it, we might try to understand more about how humour works
in the fabrication of interactions, including research encounters. One advantage of
moving away from a view of humour as an offence against presence is that this
might disturb the discourse of *deficit* that surrounds the topic. In its flight from
humour, method always ends up finding someone, or something, lacking. In the
case of research with young men, the usual suspects are the young men themselves, or their masculine 'culture'. A more nuanced and less forensic attitude to
humour might allow us to recognise its productive role in maintaining solidarity
and identity and to respect its value for marginalised groups as a form of resistance
to power and inequality – even where this resistance manifests itself uncomfortably in the research/intervention situation as also a resistance to analysis. It is not
surprising that humour, silence and the ambivalent respect of mimicry have been
identified as strategies of subaltern resistance to disciplinary power (cf. Bhabha,

1994). This would not mean endorsing or overlooking the misogyny and prejudice that is often coded into such humour, nor denying that its appearance may well attest to defensiveness or uncooperativeness. But it would mean *also* considering the positive qualities that humour involves – such as skill, timing, collaboration and quick-wittedness. Tom and Joe, participants in the young men's health project, describe their relationship as one in which they can talk to each other about anything. 'Joe knows everything', says Tom, 'But I can still beat him up!'

Humour relies on a kind of 'double vision' – the ability to see the absurdity, irony or double meanings in social situations and roles. Tom, like other boys in the project, is capable of conveying affection, deference and dominance to his friend, while keeping an eye on how this is all going down with the researcher, without spelling out those propositions one at a time. When Joe says, 'Cover your faces lads', as Charlotte, the researcher, gets her camera out, he conjures a moment of solidarity with his mates, positions Charlotte on the 'other side' of the lens, and insinuates that her surveillance is comparable to the policing work of CCTV cameras. Everyone grins, including Charlotte. Noone covers his face. Charlotte does not need to decide whether she is being counted in or counted out by the joking for the interaction to proceed. The boys do not have to have reached a definite sense of whether they 'are' good or bad interviewees, resistant or compliant participants.

Humour often appears, as with Joe's remark, right at the point where the stage machinery of interaction suddenly comes into focus, momentarily revealing the shaky nature of the selves that this machinery supports. You can see this in the following fragment from the start of a life history interview with David, a primary school teacher, during a project carried out many years ago.

DAVID: Right – question one.
M MACLURE: Question one [disconcerted] – oh yes – I haven't got a check-list fortunately.
D: Jolly good –
MM: Perhaps the best way is to go backwards – right? How did you get here?
D: By car.

The illusion of interpretive depth suddenly evaporates as David subverts the normal rules of precedence of interview protocol. Performing a kind of impersonation of an interviewee, he mocks the faintly nauseous rapport of the interview relation and its pretensions to 'meaningful' talk – a performance that momentarily unsettles my self-assurance as interviewer, and calls attention to the necessary illusion involved in attempting access to 'inner' things such as a person's thoughts or his authentic self. A moment like this, when humour cracks the precarious order of the research encounter, would likely be edited out of research accounts (as indeed it was at the time of writing the report of the project), or 'interpreted' as the sign of something else – a false start, recalcitrance, unease, poor interview technique or gender influences. But such moments also point to the delirious nature of the distance between self and other on which interpretive penetration or analytic mastery depend.

The preferred speech genre of qualitative method is still that of the idealised, Habermasian space of open dialogue, shared perspectives, equal collaboration, solemn self-disclosure, the free exchange of meaning and information and 'in-depth conversational engagement' (Sixsmith, 2004: 17). Where these fail to transpire, doubts are cast on the authenticity of subjects' voices. Participants who remain silent or make jokes (and not only young men) may be judged incompetent as communicators and ineffectual as agents of their own well-being. Sixsmith's participatory method was intended to be democratic and 'empowering for the men in that they could benefit from the research (e.g. via a sense of well-being, having their voices heard, understanding themselves and how they lived their lives)'. However the young men's refusal/inability to fit themselves to the ortho-paedic structure of democratic dialogue led the researcher to consider them unable to engage in 'meaningful health talk' or 'informative discussion', or to develop 'health expertise'. Participatory research, the author concludes, had in this case 'gone wrong'[10] (Sixsmith, 2004: 16, 17).

Conclusion

Voice, if taken 'seriously', poses serious difficulties for the humanist and scientific discourses of research. Voices are idiomatic and capricious. Lodged in locality and specificity, and inclined to frivolity in the form of jokes, double meanings, pique and posturing, voices complicate their own transparency and authenticity. At the same time, they confound the usual business of analysis and generalisation, which can only deal with speech as it should have been – levelled out into the supposedly meaning-full, propositional economy of a dispassionate, interest-free dialogue. Measured against such an impossibly full, yet strangely empty, idealised speech, voices run the risk of being heard, if they are heard at all, as meaning-*less*, as in the case of the men's health project participants.

This tendency, to hear the voice of the other as meaningless, may be a spe-cific inflection of a deeper and more pervasive attitude toward aspects of voice. There is a long and dishonourable tradition in the United Kingdom, for instance, of hostility toward the accents and dialects of the urban working classes, on the part of those who take it upon themselves to speak for the status quo in the supposedly unaccented tones of 'standard English' (cf. Crowley, 1996). 'Non-standard' speech is often dismissed by such custodians of the language as not only meaningless outside its 'restricted' locale, but as semantically and cultur-ally 'impoverished', and even as sub-human. Class antipathy issues forth in a 'discourse of disgust' (MacLure, 2003) that describes non-standard accents in terms of animal noises and bodily emissions – as in these remarks by a newspa-per columnist, supporting a government-sponsored 'war' on 'communication by grunt':

> The grunters [. . .] swarm noisily past my windows between 11 and half past on Fridays and Saturdays after an evening in the nearby pub. They shout, gurgle and gobble in a largely consonant-free stream of noisy and incomprehensible

> dipthongs, among which the only recognisable – and oft-repeated – word invariably begins with the letter 'f'. (Elkin, quoted in MacLure, 2003: 32)

Voices are voided of meaning, broken down into fake-phonetic fragments and apprehended as a 'stream' of gurgling emissions and animal grunts from a swarming mob.

The hyperbolically visceral nature of such a recoil from voice, as stuff that issues from internal organs or the non-human insides of animals, suggests that the disruptive logic of voice is related to the materiality of speech, and its intimate and fraught implication in the *body*. Gurevitch (1999) notes the double meaning of 'tongue' – as both a body-part and a word for the language itself. The tongue, and the voice that it agitates, is the place where 'dumb matter' and the symbolic order meet, yet inevitably also miss. Voice remains tied to the body while also giving itself up to the incorporeality of 'the word' as meaning, truth or idea. Located both 'in' and 'outside' the body, there will always be something in voice that resists elevation to immateriality or universality. Yet voice never reaches a comfortable accommodation with the body, which is itself 'part of language and yet out of it' (Gurevitch, 1999: 527). The bodily complications of voice can be seen most clearly in those phenomena whose status as linguistic/non-linguistic is ambiguous, such as laughter, tears, cries, shouts, gesticulations and silences. These acts lie at the limits of language, interfering with its boundaries.

Voice – even when vigorously policed or suppressed – will always return to haunt Writing, and Method. The promise of voice seems always to be undone by something excessive or insufficient, prompting attempts to expel it from the body proper of research, or to domesticate its unsettling energies. I have argued for methodologies that would instead engage with these interruptive energies, which introduce difference and complication into writing and method. Such methodologies would need to handle with care the intimate association of voice with fear of difference and otherness, and the social and theoretical antagonisms that such fear produces. The work of developing such methodologies has, I think, barely begun.

Acknowledgements

Thanks are due to Charlotte Dean for fieldwork on the Young Men's Health Project, and her insightful commentaries on the 'data'. I am also grateful to Alecia Jackson and Lisa Mazzei for pointing me in the direction of some interesting and relevant literature on voice.

Notes

1 'Voice research' is the catch-all term used by Moore and Muller (1999) in their scathing attack on research that appeals to voice. The term is temporarily useful here, as it allows me to do introductory work without making a detour into definitions and positions in a 'field' that may be more than one, and is necessarily blurred around the edges.
2 This chapter, and this book, is not exempt of course from those circuits of repudiation and reclamation of 'voice'.

3 I am not arguing therefore 'against' such practices. They may offer useful and powerful resources for research. But they cannot, I suggest, bridge the gap or erase the difference between speech and writing, self and other, or indeed self and self.

4 The loss is not an 'empirical one', in the sense of some linguistic material (e.g. phonic, syntactic) failing to be carried over into the written mode. Following Derrida, I argue that it is the loss of something that was never there in the first place, the trace that is the movement of *différance*.

5 Derrida (1976: 167).

6 Ibid.: 141.

7 Ibid.: 114.

8 I am assuming, possibly wrongly, that, as the 'Jean' referred to in the text, Clandinin was the main writer of this particular segment of the co-authored book. My reading here also does a disservice to the textual complexity that unfolds subsequent to this extract, when the account begins to move across different time periods – Clandinin's own re-reading of the transcript 'some months later', and the recall that this prompted of a scene from her own school days in the 1950s, and then back to 'that January day of the conversation' and Karen's act of taking the other participants back to the moment of the anecdote and 'pull[ing] them forward into the future'. I would argue however that despite these temporal dislocations, the rhetorical integrity of Karen's teacher voice, and Jean's authorial one, is preserved.

9 The gendered inflection of the critique is also hinted at in Moore's and Muller's repeated use of 'woman' as their example of the shortcomings of 'voice'. Carey detects a similar masculinist tendency in Goodson's 'rather authoritative and patriarchal standpoint' (1999: 412). The textual workings of the 'male-theoretic' voice are discussed in MacLure (2003: Ch 8).

10 Barbara Johnson (1998: 101), writing of 'femininity' refers to it as 'an orthopedic notion (*orthopedic:* from *ortho*-"straight, correct, right", and *paideia*, "education")'.

References

Allen, L. (2005) Managing masculinity: young men's identity work in focus groups. *Qualitative Research*, 5, 1: 35–57.

Atkinson, P. (1990) *The Ethnographic Imagination: Textual Constructions of Reality.* London: Routledge.

Bhabha, H. (1994) *The Location of Culture*. London: Routledge.

Billig, M. (2002) Freud and the language of humour. *The Psychologist*, 15, 9: 452–455.

Butt, R., Raymond, D., McCue, G. and Yamagishi, L. (1992) Collaborative autobiography and the teacher's voice, in I. Goodson (ed.) *Studying Teachers' Lives*. London: Routledge.

Carey, L. (1999) Unexpected stories: life history and the limits of representation. *Qualitative Inquiry*, 5, 3: 411–427.

Carspecken, P. F. (1996) *Critical Ethnography in Educational Research*. London & NY: Routledge.

Clandinin, D. J. and Connolly, F. M. (1999) *Narrative Inquiry: Experience and Story in Qualitative Research*. New York: Jossey Bass.

Clifford, J. (1986). Introduction: Partial Truths. In J. Clifford & G. Marcus (Eds.), *Writing Culture: The Poetics and Politics of Ethnography*. Berkeley, CA: UCLA Press.

Clifford, J. (1990) Notes on field (notes), in R. Sanjek (ed.) *Fieldnotes: The Makings of Anthropology*. Ithaca: Cornell.

Clifford, J. and Marcus, G. (eds) (1986) *Writing Culture: The Poetics and Politics of Ethnography*. Berkeley, CA: UCLA Press.

Crowley, T. (1996) *Language in History: Theories and Texts*. London: Routledge.

Derrida, J. (1976) *Of Grammatology*, Trans., with a Preface by G. C. Spivak. Baltimore: Johns Hopkins.

Derrida, J. (1980) *The Archaeology of the Frivolous. Reading Condillac*. Pittsburgh: Duquesne University Press.

Derrida, J. (1998) *Resistances of Psychoanalysis* (Trans. P. Kamuf, P-A. Briault and M. Naas). Stanford, CA: Stanford University Press.

Fuller, G. (2000) The textual politics of good intentions: critical theory and semiotics, in A. Lee and C. Poynton (eds) *Culture and Text. Discourse and Methodology in Social Research and Cultural Studies*. Lanham, MD: Rowman & Littlefield.

Geertz, C. (1988) *Works and Lives: The Anthropologist as Author*. Cambridge: Polity Press.

Goodson, I. (1995) The story so far: personal knowledge and the political, in J. A. Hatch and R. Wisniewsky (eds) *Life History and Narrative*. London: Falmer.

Gurevitch, Z. (1999) The tongue's break dance: theory, poetry, and the critical body, *Sociological Quarterly*, 40, 3: 525–540.

Haraway, D. (1992) Ecce homo, ain't (ar'n't) I a woman, and inappropriate/d others: the human in a post-humanist landscape, in J. Butler and J. Scott (eds) *Feminists Theorize the Political*. London: Routledge.

Hargreaves, A. (1994) *Changing Teachers, Changing Times*. London: Cassell.

Johnson, B. (1987) *A World of Difference*. Baltimore: Johns Hopkins.

Johnson, B. (1998) *The Feminist Difference*. Cambridge, MA: Harvard University Press.

Lather, P. (1996) Troubling clarity: the politics of accessible language, *Harvard Educational Review*, 66, 3: 525–554.

Lather, P. and Smithies, C. (1997) *Troubling the Angels: Women Living With HIV/AIDS*. Colorado: Westview Press.

MacLure, M. (2003) *Discourse in Educational and Social Research*. Buckingham: Open University Press.

MacLure, M., Frankham, J., Dean, C., Falola, G. and Stark, S. (2006) *Young Men's Health Project*. Manchester: Manchester Metropolitan University, mimeo.

Marker, M. (2003) Indigenous voice, community, and epistemic violence: the ethnographer's 'interests' and what 'interests' the ethnographer. *International Journal of Qualitative Studies in Education*, 16, 3: 361–375.

Moore, R. and Muller, J. (1999) The discourse of 'voice' and the problem of knowledge and identity in the sociology of education. *British Journal of Sociology of Education*, 20, 2: 189–206.

Popkewitz, T. S. (1998) The culture of redemption and the administration of freedom as research. *Review of Educational Research*, 68, 1: 1–34.

Pratt, M. L. (1986) Fieldwork in common places, in J. Clifford and G. E. Marcus (eds) *Writing Culture*. Berkeley, CA: University of California Press.

Shostak, M. (1983) *Nisa: The Life and words of a !Kung Woman*. New York: Random House.

Sixsmith, J. (2004) Young men's health and group participation: participatory research gone wrong? *Clinical Psychology*, 43: 13–18.

Sixsmith, J. and Griffiths, J. (nd) *Men Talking Health*. A Report for the Health Development Agency. Manchester: Manchester Metropolitan University.

Smith, R. (1995) *Derrida and Autobiography*. Cambridge: Cambridge University Press.

Stronach, I. and MacLure, M. (1997) *Educational Research Undone: The Postmodern Embrace*. Buckingham: Open University Press.

Woods, P. (1985) Conversations with teachers: some aspects of life history method, *British Educational Research Journal*, 11 (1): 13–26.

Young, M. F. D. (2000) Rescuing the sociology of educational knowledge from the extremes of voice discourse: towards a new theoretical basis for the sociology of education. *British Journal of Sociology of Education*, 21, 4: 523–536.

Part II

Transgressive voices: Productive practices

Chapter 7

The problem of speaking for others

Linda Martín Alcoff

Consider the following true stories:

1   Anne Cameron, a very gifted white Canadian author, writes several first person accounts of the lives of Native Canadian women. At the 1988 International Feminist Book Fair in Montreal, a group of Native Canadian writers ask Cameron to, in their words, 'move over' on the grounds that her writings are disempowering for Native authors. She agrees.[1]
2   After the 1989 elections in Panama are overturned by Manuel Noriega, U.S. President George Bush declares in a public address that Noriega's actions constitute an 'outrageous fraud' and that 'the voice of the Panamanian people have spoken.' 'The Panamanian people,' he tells us, 'want democracy and not tyranny, and want Noriega out.' He proceeds to plan the invasion of Panama.
3   At a recent symposium at my university, a prestigious theorist is invited to give a lecture on the political problems of post-modernism. Those of us in the audience, including many white women and people of oppressed nationalities and races, wait in eager anticipation for what he has to contribute to this important discussion. To our disappointment, he introduces his lecture by explaining that he cannot cover the assigned topic, because as a white male he does not feel that he can speak for the feminist and post-colonial perspectives which have launched the critical interrogation of post-modernism's politics. He lectures instead on architecture.

These examples demonstrate the range of current practices of speaking for others in our society. While the prerogative of speaking for others remains unquestioned in the citadels of colonial administration, among activists, and in the academy, it elicits a growing unease and, in some communities of discourse, it is being rejected. There is a strong, albeit contested, current within feminism that holds that speaking for others – even for other women – is arrogant, vain, unethical, and politically illegitimate. Feminist scholarship has a liberatory agenda that almost requires that women scholars speak on behalf of other women, and yet the dangers of speaking across differences of race, culture, sexuality, and power are becoming increasingly clear to all. In feminist magazines such as *Sojourner*, it is common to find articles and letters in which the author states that she can only speak for herself.

In her important paper, 'Dyke Methods,' Joyce Trebilcot offers a philosophical articulation of this view. She renounces for herself the practice of speaking for others within a lesbian feminist community, arguing that she 'will not try to get other wimmin to accept my beliefs in place of their own' on the grounds that to do so would be to practice a kind of discursive coercion and even a violence.[2]

Feminist discourse is not the only site in which the problem of speaking for others has been acknowledged and addressed. In anthropology there is similar discussion about whether it is possible to speak for others either adequately or justifiably. Trinh T. Minh-ha explains the grounds for skepticism when she says that anthropology is 'mainly a conversation of "us" with "us" about "them," of the white man with the white man about the primitive-nature man . . . in which "them" is silenced. "Them" always stands on the other side of the hill, naked and speechless . . . "them" is only admitted among "us," the discussing subjects, when accompanied or introduced by an "us" . . . '[3] Given this analysis, even ethnographies written by progressive anthropologists are *a priori* regressive because of the structural features of anthropological discursive practice.

The recognition that there is a problem in speaking for others has followed from the widespread acceptance of two claims. First, there has been a growing awareness that where one speaks from affects both the meaning and truth of what one says, and hence that one cannot assume an ability to transcend one's location. In other words, a speaker's location (which I take here to refer to her *social* location or social identity) has an epistemically significant impact on that speaker's claims and can serve either to authorize or dis-authorize her speech. The creation of Women's Studies and African American Studies departments were founded on this very belief that both the study of and the advocacy for the oppressed must come to be done principally by the oppressed themselves and that we must finally acknowledge that systematic divergences in social location between speakers and those spoken for will have a significant effect on the content of what is said. The unspoken premise here is simply that a speaker's location is epistemically salient. I shall explore this issue further in the next section.

The second claim holds that not only is location epistemically salient, but certain privileged locations are discursively dangerous.[4] In particular, the practice of privileged persons speaking for or on behalf of less privileged persons has actually resulted (in many cases) in increasing or re-enforcing the oppression of the group spoken for. This was part of the argument made against Anne Cameron's speaking for Native women: Cameron's intentions were never in question, but the effects of her writing were argued to be harmful to the needs of Native authors because it is Cameron rather than they who will be listened to and whose books will be bought by readers interested in Native women. Persons from dominant groups who speak for others are often treated as authenticating presences that confer legitimacy and credibility on the demands of subjugated speakers; such speaking for others does nothing to disrupt the discursive hierarchies that operate in public spaces. For this reason, the work of privileged authors who speak on behalf of the oppressed is becoming increasingly criticized by members of those oppressed groups themselves.[5]

As social theorists, we are authorized by virtue of our academic positions to develop theories that express and encompass the ideas, needs, and goals of others. However, we must begin to ask ourselves whether this is ever a legitimate authority, and if so, what are the criteria for legitimacy? In particular, is it ever valid to speak for others who are unlike I or who are less privileged than I?

We might try to delimit this problem as only arising when a more privileged person speaks for a less privileged one. In this case, we might say that I should only speak for groups of which I am a member. But this does not tell us how groups themselves should be delimited. For example, can a white woman speak for all women simply by virtue of being a woman? If not, how narrowly should we draw the categories? The complexity and multiplicity of group identifications could result in 'communities' composed of single individuals. Moreover, the concept of groups assumes specious notions about clear-cut boundaries and 'pure' identities. I am a Panamanian-American and a person of mixed ethnicity and race: half white/Angla and half Panamanian mestiza. The criterion of group identity leaves many unanswered questions for a person such as myself, since I have membership in many conflicting groups but my membership in all of them is problematic. Group identities and boundaries are ambiguous and permeable, and decisions about demarcating identity are always partly arbitrary. Another problem concerns how specific an identity needs to be to confer epistemic authority. Reflection on such problems quickly reveals that no easy solution to the problem of speaking for others can be found by simply restricting the practice to speaking for groups of which one is a member.

Adopting the position that one should only speak for oneself raises similarly difficult questions. If I do not speak for those less privileged than myself, am I abandoning my political responsibility to speak out against oppression, a responsibility incurred by the very fact of my privilege? If I should not speak for others, should I restrict myself to following their lead uncritically? Is my greatest contribution to *move over and get out of the way*? And if so, what is the best way to do this – to keep silent or to deconstruct my own discourse?

The answers to these questions will certainly depend on who is asking. While some of us may want to undermine, for example, the U.S. government's practice of speaking for the 'third world,' we may *not* want to undermine someone such as Rigoberta Menchú's ability to speak for Guatemalan Indians.[6] So the question arises about whether all instances of speaking for should be condemned and, if not, how we can justify a position that would repudiate some speakers while accepting others.

To answer these questions we need to become clearer on the epistemological and metaphysical issues which are involved in the articulation of the problem of speaking for others, issues which most often remain implicit. I will attempt to make these issues clear before turning to discuss some of the possible responses to the problem and advancing a provisional, procedural solution of my own. But first I need to explain further my framing of the problem.

In the examples used above, there may appear to be a conflation between the issue of speaking for others and the issue of speaking about others. This conflation was intentional on my part, because it is difficult to distinguish speaking about from speaking for in all cases. There is an ambiguity in the two phrases: when one is speaking for another, one may be describing their situation and thus also speaking about them. In fact, it may be impossible to speak for another without simultaneously conferring information about them. Similarly, when one is speaking about another, or simply trying to describe their situation or some aspect of it, one may also be speaking in place of them, that is, speaking for them. One may be speaking about another as an advocate or a messenger if the person cannot speak for herself. Thus I would maintain that if the practice of speaking for others is problematic, so too must be the practice of speaking about others.[7] This is partly the case because of what has been called the 'crisis of representation.' For in both the practice of speaking for as well as the practice of speaking about others, I am engaging in the act of representing the other's needs, goals, situation, and in fact, *who they are*, based on my own situated interpretation. In post-structuralist terms, I am participating in the construction of their subject-positions rather than simply discovering their true selves.

Once we pose it as a problem of representation, we see that, not only are speaking for and speaking about analytically close, so too are the practices of speaking for others and speaking for myself. For, in speaking for myself, I am also representing my self in a certain way, as occupying a specific subject-position, having certain characteristics and not others, and so on. In speaking for myself, I (momentarily) create my self – just as much as when I speak for others I create them as a public, discursive self, a self that is more unified than any subjective experience can support. And this public self will in most cases have an effect on the self experienced as interiority.

The point here is that the problem of representation underlies all cases of speaking for, whether I am speaking for myself or for others. This is not to suggest that all representations are fictions: they have very real material effects, as well as material origins, but they are always mediated in complex ways by discourse, power, and location. However, the problem of speaking for others is more specific than the problem of representation generally and requires its own particular analysis.

There is one final point I want to make before we can pursue this analysis. The way I have articulated this problem may imply that individuals make conscious choices about their discursive practice free of ideology and the constraints of material reality. This is not what I wish to imply. The problem of speaking for others is a social one, the options available to us are socially constructed, and the practices we engage in cannot be understood as simply the results of autonomous individual choice. Yet to replace both 'I' and 'we' with a passive voice that erases agency results in an erasure of responsibility and accountability for one's speech, an erasure I would strenuously argue against (there is too little responsibility-taking already in Western practice!). When we sit down to write, or get up to speak, we experience ourselves as making choices. We may experience hesitation from fear of being criticized or from fear of exacerbating a problem we would like to remedy, or we may experience a resolve to speak despite existing obstacles, but in many cases we experience having the possibility to speak or not to speak. On the one hand, a theory that explains this experience as involving autonomous choices free of material structures would be false and ideological, but on the other hand, if we do not acknowledge the activity of choice and the experience of individual doubt, we are denying a reality of our experiential lives.'[8] So I see the argument of this paper as addressing that small space of discursive agency we all experience, however multi-layered, fictional, and constrained it in fact is.

Ultimately, the question of speaking for others bears crucially on the possibility of political effectivity. Both collective action and coalitions would seem to require the possibility of speaking for. Yet influential post-modernists such as Gilles Deleuze have characterized as 'absolutely fundamental the indignity of speaking for others,'[9] and important feminist theorists have renounced the practice as irretrievably harmful. What is at stake in rejecting or validating speaking for others as a discursive practice? To answer this, we must become clearer on the epistemological and metaphysical claims that are implicit in the articulation of the problem.

I

A plethora of sources have argued in this century that the neutrality of the theorizer can no longer, can never again, be sustained, even for a moment. Critical theory, discourses of empowerment, psychoanalytic theory, post-structuralism, feminist and anti-colonialist theories have all concurred on this point. Who is speaking to whom turns out to be as important for meaning and truth as what is said; in fact what is said turns out to change according to who is speaking and who is listening. Following Foucault, I will call these 'rituals of speaking' to identify discursive practices of speaking or writing that involve not only the text or utterance but its position within a social space which includes the persons involved in, acting upon, and/or affected by the words. Two elements within these rituals will deserve our attention: the positionality or location of the speaker and the discursive context. We can take the latter to refer to the connections and relations of involvement between the utterance/text and other utterances and texts as well as the material practices in the relevant environment, which should not be confused with an environment spatially adjacent to the particular discursive event.

Rituals of speaking are constitutive of meaning, the meaning of the words spoken as well as the meaning of the event. This claim requires us to shift the ontology of meaning from its location in a text or utterance to a larger space, a space which includes the text or utterance but which also includes the discursive context. And an important implication of this claim is that meaning must be understood as plural and shifting, since a single text can engender diverse meanings given diverse contexts. Not only what is emphasized, noticed, and how it is understood will be affected by the location of both speaker and hearer, but the truth-value or epistemic status will also be affected.

For example, in many situations when a woman speaks the presumption is against her; when a man speaks he is usually taken seriously (unless his speech patterns mark him as socially inferior by dominant standards). When writers from oppressed races and nationalities have insisted that all writing is political, the claim has been dismissed as foolish or grounded in *ressentiment* or it is simply ignored; when prestigious European philosophers say that all writing is political, it is taken up as a new and original 'truth' (Judith Wilson calls this 'the intellectual equivalent of the "cover record"').[10] The rituals of speaking which involve the location of speaker and listeners affect whether a claim is taken as true, well-reasoned, a compelling argument, or a significant idea. Thus, how what is said gets heard depends on who says it, and who says it will affect the style and language in which it is stated. The discursive style in which some European post-structuralists have made the claim that all writing is political marks it as important and likely to be true for a certain (powerful) milieu; whereas the style in which African American writers made the same claim marked their speech as dismissible in the eyes of the same milieu.

This point might be conceded by those who admit to the political mutability of *interpretation*, but they might continue to maintain that *truth* is a different matter altogether. And they would be right that acknowledging the effect of location on meaning and even on whether something is *taken* as true within a particular discursive context does not entail that the 'actual' truth of the claim is contingent upon its context. However, this objection presupposes a particular conception of truth, one in which the truth of a statement can be distinguished from its interpretation and its acceptance. Such a concept would require truth to be independent of the speakers' or listeners' embodied and perspectival location. Thus, the question of whether location bears simply on what is taken to be true or what is really true, and whether such a distinction can be upheld, involves the very difficult problem of the meaning of truth. In the history of Western philosophy, there have existed multiple, competing definitions and ontologies of truth: correspondence, idealist, pragmatist, coherentist, and consensual notions. The dominant modernist view has been that truth represents a relationship of correspondence between a proposition and an extra-discursive reality. On this view, truth is about a realm completely independent of human action and expresses things 'as they are in themselves,' that is, free of human interpretation.

Arguably since Kant, more obviously since Hegel, it has been widely accepted that an understanding of truth which requires it to be free of human interpretation leads inexorably to skepticism, as it makes truth inaccessible by definition. This created an impetus to reconfigure the ontology of truth, from a locus outside human interpretation to one within it. Hegel, for example, understood truth as an 'identity in difference' between subjective and objective elements. Thus, in the Hegelian aftermath, so-called subjective elements, or the historically specific conditions in which human knowledge occurs, are no longer rendered irrelevant or even obstacles to truth.

On a coherentist account of truth, which is held by such philosophers as Rorty, Donald Davidson, Quine, and (I would argue) Gadamer and Foucault, it is defined as an emergent property of converging discursive and non-discursive elements, when there exists a specific form of integration among these elements in a particular event. Such a view has no necessary relationship to idealism, but it allows us to understand how the social location of the speaker can be said to bear on truth. The speaker's location is one of the elements that converge to produce meaning and thus to determine epistemic validity.[11]

Let me return now to the formulation of the problem of speaking for others. There are two premises implied by the articulation of the problem, and unpacking these should advance our understanding of the issues involved. Premise 1: The 'ritual of speaking' (as defined above) in which an utterance is located always bears on meaning and truth such that there is no possibility of rendering positionality, location, or context irrelevant to content. The phrase 'bears on' here should indicate some variable amount of influence short of determination or fixing.

One important implication of this first premise is that we can no longer determine the validity of a given instance of speaking for others simply by asking whether or not the speaker has done sufficient research to justify her claims. Adequate research will be a necessary but insufficient criterion of evaluation.

Now let us look at the second premise.

Premise (2): All contexts and locations are differentially related in complex ways to structures of oppression. Given that truth is connected to politics, these political differences between locations will produce epistemic differences as well. The claim here that 'truth is connected to politics' follows necessarily from Premise (1). Rituals of speaking are politically constituted by power relations of domination, exploitation, and subordination. Who is speaking, who is spoken of, and who listens is a result, as well as an act, of political struggle. Simply put, the discursive context is a political arena. To the extent that this context bears on meaning, and meaning is in some sense the object of truth, we cannot make an epistemic evaluation of the claim without simultaneously assessing the politics of the situation.

Although we cannot maintain a neutral voice, according to the first premise we may at least all claim the right and legitimacy to speak. But the second premise suggests that some voices may be dis-authorized on grounds that are simultaneously political and epistemic. Any statement will invoke the structures of power allied with the social location of the speaker, despite the speaker's intentions or attempts to avoid such invocations.

The conjunction of Premises (1) and (2) suggests that the speaker loses some portion of control over the meaning and truth of her utterance. Given that the context of hearers is partially determinant, the speaker is not the master or mistress of the situation. Speakers may seek to regain control here by taking into account the context of their speech, but they can never know everything about this context, and with written and electronic communication it is becoming increasingly difficult to know anything at all about the context of reception.

This loss of control may be taken by some speakers to mean that no speaker can be held accountable for her discursive actions. The meaning of any discursive event will be shifting and plural, fragmented, and even inconsistent. As it ranges over diverse spaces and transforms in the mind of its recipients according to their different horizons of interpretation, the effective control of the speaker over the meanings which she puts in motion may seem negligible. However, a *partial* loss of control does not entail a *complete* loss of accountability. And moreover, the better we understand the trajectories by which meanings proliferate, the more likely we can increase, though always only partially, our ability to direct the interpretations and transformations our speech undergoes. When I acknowledge that the listener's social location will affect the meaning of my words, I can more effectively generate the meaning I intend. Paradoxically, the view that holds the speaker or author of a speech act as solely responsible for its meanings ensures the speaker's least effective determinacy over the meanings that are produced.

We do not need to posit the existence of fully conscious acts or containable, fixed meanings to hold that speakers can alter their discursive practices and be held accountable for at least some of the effects of these practices. It is a false dilemma to pose the choice here as one between no accountability or complete causal power. In the next section I shall consider some of the principal responses offered to the problem of speaking for others.

II

First I want to consider the argument that the very formulation of the problem with speaking for others involves a retrograde, metaphysically insupportable essentialism that assumes one can read off the truth and meaning of *what* one says straight from the discursive context. Let us call this response the 'Charge of Reductionism,' because it argues that a sort of reductionist theory of justification (or evaluation) is entailed by premises (1) and (2). Such a reductionist theory might, for example, reduce evaluation to a political assessment of the speaker's location where that location is seen as an insurmountable essence that fixes one, as if one's feet are superglued to a spot on the sidewalk.

For instance, after I vehemently defended Barbara Christian's article, 'The Race for Theory,' a male friend who had a different evaluation of the piece could not help raising the possibility of whether a sort of apologetics structured my response, motivated by a desire to valorize African American writing against all odds. His question in effect raised the issue of the reductionist/essentialist theory of justification I just described.

I, too, would reject reductionist theories of justification and essentialist accounts of what it means to have a location. To say that location *bears* on meaning and truth is not the same as saying that location *determines* meaning and truth. And location is not a fixed essence absolutely authorizing one's speech in the way that God's favor absolutely authorized the speech of Moses. Location and positionality should not be conceived as one-dimensional or static, but as multi-dimensional and with varying degrees of mobility.[12] What it means, then, to speak from or within a group and/or a location is immensely complex. To the extent that location is not a fixed essence, and to the extent that there is an uneasy, underdetermined, and contested relationship between location on the one hand and meaning and truth on the other, we cannot reduce evaluation of meaning and truth to a simple identification of the speaker's location. Neither Premise (1) nor Premise (2) entails reductionism or essentialism. They argue for the relevance of location, not its singular power of determination, and they are non-committal on how to construe the metaphysics of location.

While the 'Charge of Reductionism' response has been popular among academic theorists, what I call the 'Retreat' response has been popular among some sections of the U.S. feminist movement. This response is simply to retreat from all practices of speaking for; it asserts that one can only know one's own narrow individual experience and one's 'own truth,' and thus that one can never make claims beyond this. This response is motivated in part by the desire to recognize difference and different priorities, without organizing these differences into hierarchies.

Now, sometimes I think this is the proper response to the problem of speaking for others, depending on who is making it. We certainly want to encourage a more receptive listening on the part of the discursively privileged and to discourage presumptuous and oppressive practices of speaking for. And the desire to retreat sometimes results from the desire to engage in political work but without practicing what might be called discursive imperialism. But a retreat from speaking for will not result in an increase in receptive listening in all cases; it may result merely in a retreat into a narcissistic yuppie lifestyle in which a privileged person takes no responsibility whatsoever for her society. She may even feel justified in exploiting her privileged capacity for personal happiness at the expense of others on the grounds that she has no alternative.

The major problem with such a retreat is that it significantly undercuts the possibility of political effectivity. There are numerous examples of the practice of speaking for others that have been politically efficacious in advancing the needs of those spoken for, from Rigoberta Menchú to Edward Said and Steven Biko. Menchú's efforts to speak for the 33 Indian communities facing genocide in Guatemala have helped to raise money for the revolution and bring pressure against the Guatemalan and U.S. governments who have committed the massacres in collusion. The point is not that for some speakers the danger of speaking for others does not arise, but that in some cases certain political effects can be garnered in no other way.

Joyce Trebilcot's version of the retreat response, which I mentioned at the outset of this essay, raises other issues. She agrees that an absolute prohibition of speaking for would undermine political effectiveness, and therefore says that she will avoid speaking for others only within her lesbian feminist community. So it might be argued that the retreat from speaking for others can be maintained without sacrificing political effectivity if it is restricted to particular discursive spaces. Why might one advocate such a partial retreat? Given that interpretations and meanings are discursive constructions made by embodied speakers, Trebilcot worries that attempting to persuade or speak for another will cut off that person's ability or willingness to engage in the constructive act of developing meaning. As no embodied speaker can produce more than a partial account, and as the process of producing meaning is necessarily collective, everyone's account within a specified community needs to be encouraged.

I agree with a great deal of Trebilcot's argument. I certainly agree that in some instances speaking for others constitutes a violence and should be stopped. But Trebilcot's position, as well as a more general retreat position, presumes an onto-logical configuration of the discursive context that it simply does not obtain. In particular, it assumes that one *can* retreat into one's discrete location and make claims entirely and singularly within that location that does not range over oth-ers, and therefore that one can disentangle oneself from the implicating networks between one's discursive practices and others' locations, situations, and practices. In other words, the claim that I can speak only for myself assumes the autonomous conception of the self in Classical Liberal theory – that I am unconnected to others in my authentic self or that I can achieve an autonomy from others given certain conditions. But there is no neutral place to stand free and clear in which one's words do not prescriptively affect or mediate the experience of others, nor is there a way to demarcate decisively a boundary between one's location and that of all others. Even a complete retreat from speech is of course not neutral, as it allows the continued dominance of current discourses and acts by omission to re-enforce their dominance.

As my practices are made possible by events spatially far away from my body, so too my own practices make possible or impossible practices of others. The declaration that I 'speak only for myself' has the sole effect of allowing me to avoid responsibility and accountability for effects of my speech on others; it cannot literally erase those effects.

Let me offer an illustration of this. The feminist movement in the United States has spawned many kinds of support groups for women with various needs: rape victims, incest survivors, battered wives, and so forth, and some of these groups have been structured around the view that each survivor must come to her own 'truth' which ranges only over herself and has no bearing on others. Thus, one woman's experience of sexual assault, its effect on her and her interpretation of it, should not be taken as a universal generalization to which others must subsume or conform their experience. This view works only up to a point. To the extent it recognizes irreducible differences in the way people respond to various traumas and is sensitive to the genuinely variable way in which women can heal themselves, it represents real progress beyond the homogeneous, universalizing approach that sets out one road for all to follow. However, it is an illusion to think that even in the safe space of a support group, a member of the group can, for example, trivialize brother–sister incest as 'sex play' without profoundly harming someone else in the group who is trying to maintain her realistic assessment of her brother's sexual activities with her as a harmful assault against his adult rationalization that 'well, for me it was just harmless fun.' Even if the speaker offers a dozen caveats about her views as restricted to her location, she will still affect the other woman's ability to conceptualize and interpret her experience and her response to it. And this is simply because we cannot neatly separate off our mediating praxis which interprets and constructs our experiences from the praxis of others. We are collectively caught in an intricate, delicate web in which each action I take, discursive or otherwise, pulls on, breaks off, or maintains the tension in many strands of the web in which others find themselves moving also. When I speak for myself, I am constructing a possible self, a way to be in the world, and am offering that, whether I intend to or not, to others, as one possible way to be.

Thus, the attempt to avoid the problematic of speaking for by retreating into an individualist realm is based on an illusion, well supported in the individualist ideology of the West, that a self is not constituted by multiple intersecting discourses but consists of a unified whole capable of autonomy from others. It is an illusion that I can separate from others to such an extent that I can avoid affecting them. This may be the intention of my speech, and even its meaning if we take that to be the formal entailments of the sentences, but it will not be the effect of the speech, and therefore cannot capture the speech in its reality as a discursive practice. When I 'speak for myself,' I am participating in the creation and reproduction of discourses through which my own and other selves are constituted.

A further problem with the 'Retreat' response is that it may be motivated by a desire to find a method or practice immune from criticism. If I speak only for myself it may appear that I am immune from criticism because I am not making any claims that describe others or prescribe actions for them. If I am only speaking for myself I have no responsibility for being true to your experience or needs.

But surely it is both morally and politically objectionable to structure one's actions around the desire to avoid criticism, especially if this outweighs other questions of effectivity. In some cases, the motivation is perhaps not so much to avoid criticism as to avoid errors, and the person believes that the only way to avoid errors is to avoid all speaking for others. However, errors are unavoidable in theoretical inquiry as well as political struggle, and they usually make contributions. The pursuit of an absolute means to avoid making errors comes perhaps not from a desire to advance collective goals but a desire for personal mastery, to establish a privileged discursive position wherein one cannot be undermined or challenged and thus is master of the situation. From such a position one's own location and positionality would not require constant interrogation and critical reflection; one would not have to constantly engage in this emotionally troublesome endeavor and would be immune from the interrogation of others. Such a desire for mastery and immunity must be resisted.

The final response to the problem of speaking for others that I will consider occurs in Gayatri Chakravorty Spivak's rich essay 'Can the Subaltern Speak?'[13] Spivak rejects a total retreat from speaking for others, and she criticizes the 'self-abnegating intellectual' pose that Foucault and Deleuze adopt when they reject speaking for others on the grounds that their position assumes the oppressed can transparently represent their own true interests. According to Spivak, Foucault's and Deleuze's self-abnegation serves only to conceal the actual authorizing power of the retreating intellectuals, who in their very retreat help to consolidate a particular conception of experience (as transparent and self-knowing). Thus, to promote 'listening to,' as opposed to speaking for, essentializes the oppressed as non-ideologically constructed subjects. But Spivak is also critical of speaking for, which engages in dangerous re-presentations. In the end Spivak prefers a 'speaking to,' in which the intellectual neither abnegates his or her discursive role nor presumes an authenticity of the oppressed, but still allows for the possibility that the oppressed will produce a 'countersentence' that can then suggest a new historical narrative. Spivak's arguments show that a simple solution cannot be found in the oppressed or less privileged being able to speak for themselves, since their speech will not necessarily be either liberatory or reflective of their 'true interests,' if such exist. I agree with her on this point, but I would emphasize also that ignoring the subaltern's or oppressed person's speech is, as she herself notes, 'to continue the imperialist project.'[14] Even if the oppressed person's speech is not liberatory in its content, it remains the case that the very act of speaking itself constitutes a subject that challenges and subverts the opposition between the knowing agent and the object of knowledge, an opposition which has served as a key player in the reproduction of imperialist modes of discourse. Thus, the problem with speaking for others exists in the very structure of discursive practice, irrespective of its content, and subverting the hierarchical rituals of speaking will always have some liberatory effects.

I agree, then, that we should strive to create wherever possible the conditions for dialogue and the practice of speaking with and to rather than speaking for others. Often the possibility of dialogue is left unexplored or inadequately pursued by more privileged persons. Spaces in which it may seem as if it is impossible to engage in dialogic encounters need to be transformed in order to do so, such as classrooms, hospitals, workplaces, welfare agencies, universities, institutions for international development and aid, and governments. It has long been noted that existing communication technologies have the potential to produce these kinds of interaction even though research and development teams have not found it advantageous under capitalism to do so.

However, while there is much theoretical and practical work to be done to develop such alternatives, the practice of speaking for others remains the best option in some existing situations. An absolute retreat weakens political effectivity, is based on a metaphysical illusion, and often effects only an obscuring of the intellectual's power. There can be no complete or definitive solution to the problem of speaking for others, but there is a possibility that its dangers can be decreased. The remainder of this paper will try to contribute toward developing that possibility.

III

In rejecting a general retreat from speaking for, I am not advocating a return to an unself-conscious appropriation of the other, but rather that anyone who speaks for others should only do so out of a concrete analysis of the particular power relations and discursive effects involved. I want to develop this point by elucidating four sets of interrogatory practices that are meant to help evaluate possible and actual instances of speaking for. In list form they may appear to resemble an algorithm, as if we could plug in an instance of speaking for and factor out an analysis and evaluation. However, they are meant only to suggest the questions that should be asked concerning any such discursive practice. These are by no means original: they have been learned and practiced by many activists and theorists.

(1) The impetus to speak must be carefully analyzed and, in many cases (certainly for academics!), fought against. This may seem an odd way to begin discussing how to speak for, but the point is that the impetus to *always* be the speaker and to speak in all situations must be seen for what it is: a desire for mastery and domination. If one's immediate impulse is to teach rather than listen to a less-privileged speaker, one should resist that impulse long enough to interrogate it carefully. Some of us have been taught that by right of having the dominant gender, class, race, letters after our name, or some other criterion, we are more likely to have the truth. Others have been taught the opposite and will speak haltingly, with apologies, if they speak at all.[15]

At the same time, we have to acknowledge that the very decision to 'move over' or retreat can occur only from a position of privilege. Those who are not in a position of speaking at all cannot retreat from an action they do not employ. Moreover, making the decision for oneself whether or not to retreat is an extension or application of privilege, not an abdication of it. Still, it is sometimes called for.

(2) We must also interrogate the bearing of our location and context on what it is we are saying, and this should be an explicit part of every serious discursive practice we engage in. Constructing hypotheses about the possible connections between our location and our words is one way to begin. This procedure would be most successful if engaged in collectively with others, by which aspects of our location less obvious to us might be revealed.[16]

One deformed way in which this is too often carried out is when speakers offer up in the spirit of 'honesty' autobiographical information about themselves, usually at the beginning of their discourse as a kind of disclaimer. This is meant to acknowledge their own understanding that they are speaking from a specified, embodied location without pretense to a transcendental truth. But as Maria Lugones and others have forcefully argued, such an act serves no good end when it is used as a disclaimer against one's ignorance or errors and is made without critical interrogation of the bearing of such an autobiography on what is about to be said. It leaves for the listeners all the real work that needs to be done. For example, if a middle-class white man were to begin a speech by sharing with us this autobiographical information and then using it as a kind of apologetics for any limitations of his speech, this would leave to those of us in the audience who do not share his social location all the work of translating his terms into our own, apprising the applicability of his analysis to our diverse situation, and determining the substantive relevance of his location on his claims. This is simply what less-privileged persons have always had to do for themselves when reading the history of philosophy, literature, etc., which makes the task of appropriating these discourses more difficult and time-consuming (and alienation more likely to result). Simple unanalyzed disclaimers do not improve on this familiar situation and may even make it worse to the extent that by offering such information the speaker may feel even more authorized to speak and be accorded more authority by his peers.

(3) Speaking should always carry with it an accountability and responsibility for what one says. To whom one is accountable is a political/epistemological choice contestable, contingent and, as Donna Haraway says, constructed through the process of discursive action. What this entails in practice is a serious commitment to remain open to criticism and to attempt actively, attentively, and sensitively to 'hear' the criticism (understand it). A quick impulse to reject criticism must make one wary.

(4) Here is my central point. In order to evaluate attempts to speak for others in particular instances, we need to analyze the probable or actual effects of the words on the discursive and material context. One cannot simply look at the location of the speaker or her credentials to speak; nor can one look merely at the propositional content of the speech; one must also look at where the speech goes and what it does there.

Looking merely at the content of a set of claims without looking at their effects cannot produce an adequate or even meaningful evaluation of it, and this is partly because the notion of a content separate from effects does not hold up. The content of the claim, or its meaning, emerges in interaction between words and hearers within a very specific historical situation. Given this, we have to pay careful attention to the discursive arrangement in order to understand the full meaning of any given discursive event. For example, in a situation where a well-meaning first-world person is speaking for a person or group in the third world, the very discursive arrangement may reinscribe the 'hierarchy of civilizations' view where the United States lands squarely at the top. This effect occurs because the speaker is positioned as authoritative and empowered, as the knowledgeable subject, while the group in the third world is reduced, merely because of the structure of the speaking practice, to an object and victim that must be championed from afar. Though the speaker may be trying to materially improve the situation of some lesser-privileged group, one of the effects of her discourse is to re-enforce racist, imperialist conceptions and perhaps also to further silence the lesser-privileged group's own ability to speak and be heard.[17] This shows us why it is so important to reconceptualize discourse, as Foucault recommends, as an *event*, which includes speaker, words, hearers, location, language, and so on.

All such evaluations produced in this way will be of necessity *indexed*. That is, they will obtain for a very specific location and cannot be taken as universal. This simply follows from the fact that the evaluations will be based on the specific elements of historical discursive context, location of speakers and hearers, and so forth. When any of these elements is changed, a new evaluation is called for.

Our ability to assess the effects of a given discursive event is limited; our ability to predict these effects is even more so. When meaning is plural and deferred, we can never hope to know the totality of effects. Still, we can know some of the effects our speech generates: I can find out, for example, that the people I spoke for are angry that I did so, or appreciative. By learning as much as possible about the context of reception I can increase my ability to discern at least some of the possible effects. This mandates incorporating a more dialogic approach to speaking, that would include learning from and about the domains of discourse my words will affect.

I want to illustrate the implications of this fourth point by applying it to the examples I gave at the beginning. In the case of Anne Cameron, if the effects of her books are truly disempowering for Native women, they are counterproductive to Cameron's own stated intentions, and she should indeed 'move over.' In the case of the white male theorist who discussed architecture instead of the politics of post-modernism, the effect of his refusal was that he offered no contribution to an important issue and all of us there lost an opportunity to discuss and explore it.

Now let me turn to the example of George Bush. When Bush claimed that Noriega is a corrupt dictator who stands in the way of democracy in Panama, he repeated a claim which has been made almost word for word by the Opposition movement in Panama. Yet the effects of the two statements are vastly different because the meaning of the claim changes radically depending on who states it. When the president of the United States stands before the world passing judgement on a third-world government, and criticizing it on the basis of corruption and a lack of democracy, the immediate effect of *this* statement, as opposed to the Opposition's, is to re-enforce the prominent Anglo view that Latin American corruption is the primary cause of the region's poverty and lack of democracy, that the United States is on the side of democracy in the region, and that the United States opposes corruption and tyranny. Thus, the effect of a U.S. president's speaking for Latin America in this way is to re-consolidate U.S. imperialism by obscuring its true role in the region in torturing and murdering hundreds and thousands of people who have tried to bring democratic and progressive governments into existence. And this effect will continue until the U.S. government admits its history of international mass murder and radically alters its foreign policy.

Conclusion

This issue is complicated by the variable way in which the importance of the source, or location of the author, can be understood, a topic alluded to earlier. On one view, the author of a text is its 'owner' and 'originator' credited with creating its ideas and with being their authoritative interpreter. On another view, the original speaker or writer is no more privileged than any other person who articulates these views, and in fact the 'author' cannot be identified in a strict sense because the concept of author is an ideological construction many abstractions removed from the way in which ideas emerge and become material forces.[18] Now, does this latter position mean that the source or locatedness of the author is irrelevant?

It need not entail this conclusion, though it might in some formulations. We can de-privilege the 'original' author and reconceptualize ideas as traversing (almost) freely in a discursive space, available from many locations, and without a clearly identifiable originary track, and yet retain our sense that source remains relevant to effect. Our meta-theory of authorship does not preclude the material reality that in discursive spaces there is a speaker or writer credited as the author of her utterances, or that, for example, the feminist appropriation of the concept 'patriarchy' gets tied to Kate Millett, a white Anglo feminist, or that the term feminism itself has been and is associated with a Western origin. These associations have an effect, an effect of producing distrust on the part of some third-world nationalists, an effect of reinscribing semi-conscious imperialist attitudes on the part of some first-world feminists. These are not the only possible effects, and some of the effects may not be pernicious, but all the effects must be taken into account when evaluating the discourse of 'patriarchy.'

The emphasis on effects should not imply, therefore, that an examination of the speaker's location is any less crucial. This latter examination might be called a kind of genealogy. In this sense, a genealogy involves asking how a position or view is mediated and constituted through and within the conjunction and conflict of historical, cultural, economic, psychological, and sexual practices. But it seems to me that the importance of the source of a view, and the importance of doing a genealogy, should be subsumed within an overall analysis of effects, making the central question what the effects are of the view on material and discursive practices through which it traverses and the particular configuration of power relations emergent from these. Source is relevant only to the extent that it has an impact on effect. As Gayatri Spivak likes to say, the invention of the telephone by a European upper class male in no way preempts its being put to the use of an anti-imperialist revolution.

In conclusion, I would stress that the practice of speaking for others is often born of a desire for mastery, to privilege oneself as the one who more correctly understands the truth about another's situation or as one who can champion a just cause and thus achieve glory and praise. And the effect of the practice of speaking for others is often, though not always, erasure and a reinscription of sexual, national, and other kinds of hierarchies. I hope that this analysis will contribute toward rather than diminish the importance of the discussion going on today about how to develop strategies for a more equitable, just distribution of the ability to speak and be heard. But this development should not be taken as an absolute dis-authorization of all practices of speaking for. It is not *always* the case that when others unlike me speak for me I have ended up worse off, or that when we speak for others they end up worse off. Sometimes, as Loyce Stewart has argued, we do need a 'messenger' to advocate for our needs.

The source of a claim or discursive practice in suspect motives or maneuvers or in privileged social locations, I have argued, though it is always relevant, cannot be sufficient to repudiate it. We must ask further questions about its effects, questions that amount to the following: will it enable the empowerment of oppressed peoples?

Notes

This essay was originally published in *Cultural Critique* (Winter 1991–1992), pp. 5–32; revised and reprinted in *Who Can Speak? Authority and Critical Identity* edited by Judith Roof and Robyn Wiegman (Urbana, IL: University of Illinois Press, 1996); and in *Feminist Nightmares: Women at Odds* edited by Susan Weisser and Jennifer Fleischner (New York: New York University Press, 1994); and also in *Racism and Sexism: Differences and Connections* edited by David Blumenfeld and Linda Bell, Lanham, MD: Rowman and Littlefield, 1995.

1 See Lee Maracle, 'Moving Over,' in *Trivia* 14 (Spring 89): 9–10.
2 Joyce Trebilcot, 'Dyke Methods,' *Hypatia* 3.2 (Summer 1988): 1. Trebilcot is explaining here her own reasoning for rejecting these practices, but she is not advocating that other women join her in this. Thus, her argument does not fall into a self-referential incoherence.
3 Trinh T. Minh-ha, *Woman, Native, Other: Writing Postcoloniality and Feminism* (Bloomington: Indiana University Press, 1989), pp. 65 and 67. For examples of anthropologist's concern with this issue see *Writing Culture: The Poetics and Politics of Ethnography* edited by James Clifford and George E. Marcus (Berkeley: University of California Press, 1986); James Clifford 'On Ethnographic Authority' *Representations* 1.2: 118–146; *Anthropology as Cultural Critique* edited by George Marcus and Michael Fischer (Chicago: University of Chicago Press, 1986); Paul Rabinow 'Discourse and Power: On the Limits of Ethnographic Texts' *Dialectical Anthropology*, 10.1 and 2 (July 85): 1–14.
4 To be privileged here will mean to be in a more favorable, mobile, and dominant position vis-a-vis the structures of power/knowledge in a society. Thus privilege carries with it, e.g., presumption in one's favor when one speaks. Certain races, nationalities, genders, sexualities, and classes confer privilege, but a single individual (perhaps most individuals) may enjoy privilege in respect to some parts of his or her identity and a lack of privilege in respect to other parts. Therefore, privilege must always be indexed to specific relationships as well as to specific locations. The term privilege is not meant to include positions of discursive power achieved through merit, but in any case these are rarely pure. In other words, some persons are accorded discursive authority because they are respected leaders or because they are teachers in a classroom and know more about the material at hand. So often, of course, the authority of such persons based on their merit combines with the authority they may enjoy by virtue of their having the dominant gender, race, class, or sexuality. It is the latter sources of authority that I am referring to by the term 'privilege.'
5 See also Maria Lugones and Elizabeth Spelman, 'Have We Got a Theory for You! Cultural Imperialism, Feminist Theory and the Demand for the Women's Voice' *Women's Studies International Forum* 6.6 (1983): 573–581. In their paper Lugones and Spelman explore the way in which the 'demand for the women's voice' dis-empowered women of color by not attending to the differences in privilege within the category of women, resulting in a privileging of white women's voices only. They explore the effects this has had on the making of theory within feminism, and attempt to find 'ways of talking or being talked about that are helpful, illuminating, empowering, respectful.' (p. 25) This essay takes inspiration from theirs and is meant to continue their discussion.
6 See her *I . . . Rigoberta Menchú*, edited by Elisabeth Burgos-Debray, Trans. Ann Wright (London: Verso, 1984). (The use of the term 'Indian' here follows Menchú's use.)

7 For example, if it is the case that no 'descriptive' discourse is normative – or value-free – then no discourse is free of some kind of advocacy, and all speaking about will involve speaking for someone, ones, or something.

8 Another distinction that might be made is between different material practices of speaking for: giving a speech, writing an essay or book, making a movie or TV program, as well as hearing, reading, watching, and so on. I will not address the possible differences that arise from these different practices, and will address myself to the (fictional) 'generic' practice of speaking for.

9 Deleuze in a conversation with Foucault, 'Intellectuals and Power' in *Language, Counter-Memory, Practice*, edited by Donald Bouchard, Trans. Donald Bouchard and Sherry Simon (Ithaca: Cornell University Press, 1977): p. 209.

10 See her 'Down to the Crossroads: The Art of Alison Saar,' *Third Text* 10 (Spring 90), for a discussion of this phenomenon in the artworld, esp. page 36. See also Barbara Christian 'The Race for Theory' *Feminist Studies* 14.1 (Spring 88): 67–79; and Henry Louis Gates, Jr. 'Authority, (White) Power and the (Black) Critic; It's All Greek To Me' *Cultural Critique* 7 (Fall 87): 19–46.

11 I know that my insistence on using the word 'truth' swims upstream of current postmodernist orthodoxies. This insistence is not based on a commitment to transparent accounts of representation or a correspondence theory of truth, but on my belief that the demarcation between epistemically better and worse claims continues to operate (indeed, it is inevitable) and that what happens when we eschew all epistemological issues of truth is that the terms upon which those demarcations are made go unseen and uncontested. A very radical revision of what we mean by truth is in order, but if we ignore the ways in which our discourses appeal to some version of truth for their persuasiveness we are in danger of remaining blind to the operations of legitimation that function within our own texts. The task is therefore to explicate the relations between politics and knowledge rather than pronounce the death of truth. See my *Real Knowing*, with Cornell University Press.

12 Compare with my 'Cultural Feminism versus Post-Structuralism: The Identity Crisis in Feminist Theory' *SIGNS: A Journal of Women in Culture and Society* 13.3 (Spring 1988): 405–436. For more discussions on the multi-dimensionality of social identity see Maria Lugones 'Playfulness, 'World'-Travelling, and Loving Perception' *Hypatia* 2.2: 3–19; and Gloria Anzaldua, *Borderlands/La Frontera* (San Francisco: Spinsters/Aunt Lute Book Company, 1987).

13 This can be found in *Marxism and the Interpretation of Culture*, edited by Cary Nelson and Lawrence Grossberg (Chicago: University of Illinois Press, 1988): pp. 271–313.

14 Ibid., p. 298.

15 See Edward Said, 'Representing the Colonized: Anthropology's Interlocutors' *Critical Inquiry* 15.2 (Winter 1989), p. 219, on this point, where he shows how the 'dialogue' between Western anthropology and colonized people have been non-reciprocal and supports the need for the Westerners to begin to *stop talking*.

16 See again Said, 'Representing the Colonized' p. 212, where he encourages in particular the self-interrogation of privileged speakers. This seems to be a running theme in what are sometimes called 'minority discourses' these days: asserting the need for whites to study whiteness, for example. The need for an interrogation of one's location exists with every discursive event by any speaker, but given the lopsidedness of current 'dialogues' it seems especially important to push for this among the privileged, who sometimes seem to want to study everybody's social and cultural construction but their own.

17 To argue for the relevance of effects for evaluation does not entail that there is only one way to do such an accounting or what kind of effects will be deemed desirable. How one evaluates a particular effect is left open; (4) argues simply that effects must always be taken into account.

18 I like the way Susan Bordo makes this point. In speaking about theories or ideas that gain prominence, she says: ' . . . all cultural formations . . . [are] complexly constructed out

of diverse elements – intellectual, psychological, institutional, and sociological. Arising not from monolithic design but from an interplay of factors and forces, it is best understood not as a discrete, definable position which can be adopted or rejected, but as an emerging coherence which is being fed by a variety of currents, sometimes overlapping, sometimes quite distinct.' See her 'Feminism, Postmodernism, and Gender-Skepticism' in *Feminism/Postmodernism*, edited by Linda Nicholson (New York, Routledge, 1989), p. 135. If ideas arise in such a configuration of forces, does it make sense to ask for an author?

Chapter 8

Forays into the mist

Violences,[1] voices, vignettes

Lubna Nazir Chaudhry

Red . . . yeah, red . . . I am writing with a red pen . . .

Writing . . . yeah, writing myself . . . writing myself for myself . . . writing myself for myself for that/those not myself . . . for I don't need to write myself for myself . . . for myself does not need to be written for myself . . . so I write myself for myself for that/those not myself . . .

Red . . . yeah, red . . . I've a red pen, a red bag, a red purse, a red toothbrush . . . I even chose a red case for my new glasses . . . I also have red, dark spots on my pad . . .

Menstruating on my birthday, giving birth to myself? My mother was unclean for 40 days afterwards . . . She bathed officially on . . . (addition/subtraction) whatever . . . Did that mean I was born then? The blood I was born with was impure, 40 days the soul takes to get to the other world, 40 days it takes to get here?

Blood and me, me and blood . . . my blood . . . my brother . . . my sister . . . my parents . . . my flesh and blood . . .

Flesh . . . flesh and the soul . . . flesh and the spirit???

The flesh can connect, blood can not . . .

(Or blood connects, flesh can not . . .)

Or may be no connection . . .

> A shapeless amoeba with a thousand pores,
> Breathing in at times,
> Mostly gasping for air,
> Drowning in blood,
> Waving its projections wildly,
> 'The nucleus is not there!'
> 'They destroyed it to make the atom bomb.'

Creativity and destruction, Coleridge and Kubla Khan,

Appropriating the Orient to make a point,

The Orient where (somewhere in it) red is the color of mourning . . .

I bleed, I'm fertile, I can breed,

I can be clean again.

> 'I still can't find the nucleus.'
> (Chaudhry, 1992)

... the more I wrote the more I entered into the stories I was telling ... I was already having trouble distinguishing past from present: what had happened was happening, happening all around me, and writing was my way of striking out and embracing. . . . in (my) writing, however you look at it, backwards or forwards, in the light or against it, my loves and quarrels can be seen at a glance. Why does one write if not to put the pieces together? The fishermen of the Colombian coast must be learned doctors of ethics and morality, for they invented the word sentipensante, feeling and thinking, to define language that speaks the truth.

(Galeano, 1989/1991)

Preamble

This preamble is a protective measure, a pre-emptive strategy, in this day and age of 'good Muslim, bad Muslim'[2] and disaster fatigue. In recent years, in academic and other contexts in the US, my stories and insights from my fieldwork in Pakistan as a feminist ethnographer of Pakistani origins are mostly received with disinterest once people realize that the violence I am talking about has no direct relevance to their war on terror. What is even more disturbing is when people latch on to minute, even passing, references to either issues they think are worthy of attention with respect to Pakistan, or details they can understand only by using their lives as gauges to make some kind of specific connection. The bigger picture, the relationships between seemingly disparate and remote spaces, get lost, as I fumble to explain that my own brother was not a terrorist, that the codes of Islam cannot explain away the entire worldview of an individual, and that poverty cannot be merely measured through the number of things owned by people. So while the poststructuralist in me abhors this move to pin down meaning in any way, here I briefly underline the intellectual context, intent, and method delimiting my feminist ethnographic project of using three vignettes[3] to voice my researching of violence in different contexts within Pakistan, just in case they are filtered out in quests for significance and relevance.

This paper receives its impetus from the idea of writing as feminist practice, the impulse to speak subjectivities into existence in order to voice that which has been forbidden, repressed, or pushed to the margins by patriarchal codes of thinking, language, and representation (DuPlessis, 1990). From such a perspective, writing by positing women (and others oppressed by the patriarchal order) as subjects of consciousness can be used to enact a critical agency, linking textuality to emancipatory action by generating possibilities for transgressive discourse positions (Rhodes, 2005).

My adherence to the feminist notion of textual performativity, however, is qualified by an understanding of subjectivity as multiple, intersectional, and differential (Sandoval, 1991), an awareness of the Eurocentrism inherent in conceptions of the bounded individual and her unitary consciousness promoted by much of Western feminism, including its radical strands (Lazreg, 2000), and a drive to work towards the dismantling of Eurocentric thoughts and structures (Smith, 1999). As a feminist who claims a transnational Third-World[4] positionality, my subjectivity and consciousness is not just 'a site of struggle' (DuPlessis, 1990, p. 4) but also a 'site of multiple voicings,' voicings that originate from the differential discourses interpellating my layered consciousness (Alarcon, 1990, p. 365). I write through and from within not merely a woman's body, but a woman's body that is read in specific ways in particular contexts across her life-worlds: as a Pakistani; as a Pakistani woman; as a Pakistani woman in the post-9/11 global scenario; as a Pakistani woman with a doctorate; as a Pakistani now living in the United States; as a fellow Pakistani; as someone who says she is Pakistani; as someone who says she is a Pakistani woman like me; and so forth, just to conjugate one of my axes of identification. My writing is a space to voice my negotiations with competing demands on my selfhood, as well as my attempts to perform a multi-faceted resistant subjectivity in response to some of these demands that can only be spoken into existence through recognition of affiliation and solidarity with individuals, communities, and peoples across the disparate contexts of my life-worlds. My politics of decolonization remains inextricably intertwined with the cacophony of voices inhabiting me, and with my struggles to foreground the dynamic, and, at times, contradictory systems of meanings erased, invalidated, or distorted by historical and contemporary global relations of power.

The aspect of my decolonial project that is perhaps the most salient in the context of this particular piece, and which adds yet another layer to my deployment of a multiply voiced subjectivity, is the work of listening to the dead among us and acknowledging how they continue to impact the constitution of our subjectivities in this so-called postcolonial world. To use Holland's (2000, p. 1) words, 'raising the dead,' the recovery and mourning of the loss and trauma incurred, and then denied, through colonial processes of dispossession, enslavement, and apartheid, is a central objective for many aspiring to a decolonizing agenda. Technically, most of the world has been declared independent; however, colonial legacies persist through violent cultures, structures, and economies that operate at multiple levels, ranging from the local to the global (Punter, 2000). I write of violences that can be directly seen as aftermaths of coloniality and neo-coloniality, but also of violences that might apparently seem merely local, if we elide the issue of how the local, from its conception of who counted as human to its systems of justice (or injustice!), was and is shaped by geopolitics. While my attempts to raise the dead that I describe in this chapter are barely successful, and I do agree with Punter (2000) that perhaps fiction is the only way in which we can even begin to do justice to the depiction of the mist generated by centuries of European colonialism, I do hope the writing evokes not only the ghosts amidst us, but also how the dead live through us, articulating a vitality that blurs the boundaries between life and the afterworld as well as the past and the present.

This chapter continues my earlier efforts to render ethnographic insights into written products (see, for instance, Chaudhry, 1997), whereby the discursiveness[5] of the fieldwork process, the polyvocality of the encounters that generated those insights, is recreated in a bid to emphasize the relationality and intersubjectivity underlying our knowledge generation as qualitative researchers. (Such an under-taking vis-à-vis the voicing of fieldwork, according to those highly cognizant and critical of the colonial genealogy of anthropological methods,[6] is a central facet of the larger project of decolonizing and democraticizing research processes and representations.) While the voice in the vignettes that ultimately relates the insights and the story of the encounters is mine, I subvert my ethnographic authority in two key related, albeit distinct, ways.

Firstly, I strive for a dialogic fabric in the vignettes, extensively incorporating direct quotes and indirect retelling of what people say to me, thus interrupting, perhaps even fracturing, any tendency towards an omniscient narrative.[7] I try not to flatten the voices of my research participants and do so by paying attention to the specificity of peoples' experiences, delineating the multivocality evidenced even in the context of one particular interaction with one particular individual, and situating the voices in the field squarely within the context of the fieldwork encounter, rather than as frozen in time and space, or as the transparent and authentic voices of the native informant.[8] Secondly, I attempt to write reflexively about my own shifting subjectivity during and right after the fieldwork, recording my reactions, intellectual and those deemed emotional, as they are elicited during my meetings with my research participants, my memories of those meetings, and through evocative and mental linkages with parts of my life in other temporal and spatial contexts. The point of this exercise in self-reflexivity, this situating of myself as a multi-voiced social subject impacting the fieldwork process, even as she is being impacted by it, is to deconstruct my roles in the field and the desire behind those roles (Lather, 1991), to chart the power dynamics circumscribing the fieldwork process even when a supposed insider is the researcher (Narayan, 1993), and to at least begin to dissolve the object–subject dichotomy in order to trouble the fiction of the researcher as a bounded entity (Abu-Lughod, 1993; Rosaldo, 1987). In other words, I choose to insert my voice beyond the time-sanctioned role of analytical narrator to highlight the limits of that role. As Trinh (1989, p. 2) writes:

> *A writing for the people, by the people, and from the people is, liter-ally, a multipolar reflecting reflection that remains free from the conditions of subjectivity and objectivity, yet reveals them both. I write to show myself showing people who show me my own showing. I-You, not one, not two.*

While my feminist ethnographer voice, despite its differential deployment in dif-ferent contexts and its intersections with my other subject positions, does give some semblance of cohesion to the paper, each vignette exhibits in a particularly distinct manner, utilizing different modes of narration, the intricate interplay of my reflexive multiply subjective voice, the voices of the research participants, and my foray into the mist that holds the voices of the dead. The genre of the first vignette can perhaps be best described as a blend of investigative journalism and detective fiction. Here I attempt to reconstruct my discovery of an incident of exceptional violence, a murder, that I stumbled upon during fieldwork related to a study designed to understand peoples' experiences of structural violence,[9] 'the unequal life chances . . . needlessly limiting peoples' physical, social and psychological well-being' (Uvin, 1998, p. 145). I work closely with my field-notes, undertaking a processual analysis of the sequence of events whereby we obtained the information about the murder, although the gaps in our information and the lack of closure in the story about the murdered woman are almost anti-climactic in the wake of the meticulously linear rendering of the narrative. The second vignette is an intensive exploration of one interview with a survivor in an urban context of armed conflict that is in one way an antithesis of the opening vignette: I went in to record my research participants' experience with bloodshed and physical violence and emerged with some understanding of the complex ways in which direct violence in a situation of armed combat intersects with forms of structural violence framing everyday lives. Here the linearity of the narrative, what could have been a straightforward reporting of one interview, is continually disrupted by the 'breaking into' voice of my subjectivity as the privileged researcher confronted by the limits of her own understanding as well as the strength of the convictions voiced by one of the quietest research participants I have ever known. The final vignette is the most self-reflexive narrative, in a mode that is almost stream-of-consciousness. It is also the narrative where the rootedness of my own subjectivity within histories of violence and relationships of domination and subjugation as well as my envisaging of an alternative is made the most explicit. Again, any tendencies towards a linear narrative are foreclosed by irruptions from different quarters: my own shifting subject positions, the voices of interlocutors in the field, and the linkages I make between the different kinds and levels of violence, past and present, with which I am confronted in the different domains of my life.

Taken together, the vignettes signify an experiment in the presentation of qualitative data on postcolonial violence through the utilization of a critical feminist lens that privileges the imperative to work reflexively with the voices of the researcher, the research participants, and the dead, as they conjoin with each other in the hovering mist, rather than positing any meta-theories about the origins, emergences, and classifications of these different kinds of violence.[10] The presence of violence infuses the narratives, and as Jeganathan (2000, p. 113) writes, 'There will be no "getting beyond" violence; no explaining it away.' However, the vignettes are as much an affirmation of life as they are about the recurrent violence symptomatic of the contexts deemed postcolonial: the voices inhabiting them are insistent, if not always vibrant; layered, if not always complex; and, definitive, if not always transparent in the way that fulfils our needs as social scientists. While at one level, my experiment might indicate the tensions between the realist mode of representation favored by ethnography and the decolonial project of reinscribing loss; at another level, it does effectively locate the multiple voices of the postcolonial subject and the relationships circumscribing that subjectivity between the polarities of life and death, pointing to the possibility of an agency that can perhaps transcend both, even if it is just in a vision for a decolonized future.

Vignette 1

Saadia,[11] a 15-year-old young woman, from a *Mochi*[12] (shoemaker) family is the first person to tell us the story of the young woman from the landlord family who was killed by her brother-in-law two years before our fieldwork in Dhamyal,[13] a village in the North West of the Pakistani province of Punjab. We are visiting the village in relation to our research for the Pakistan Poverty Assessment.[14] The day before, during our preliminary interview, what we call a 'site mapping,' with a group of women in the house of a local landlord, we were directed to this *Mochi* household in the *Kammi Kameen*[15] part of the village. Saadia's grandmother was mentioned as one of the poorest in the village, since she is a widow, has major health problems, and has the additional responsibility of looking after a married daughter and her children. Saadia joins us in the room where her grandmother is convalescing, as Nadia, my research assistant, and I go back and forth between getting in-depth information about her grandmother's experiences with the health-care system, and painstakingly filling out two pre-devised questionnaires meant to solicit more structured household-level information and a *Kammi Kameen* perspective on larger village dynamics (we have discovered that adhering to only one questionnaire in a linear, meticulous fashion is the best way to lose the interest of our research participants).

We go off-task for a while. Nadia and I are struck by the vibrant beauty of the newcomer. The older woman introduces her granddaughter as the oldest child of her married daughter. She tells us that Saadia's father abandoned his family, so now Saadia, her mother, and her siblings live with her. Occasionally, Saadia goes to live with her uncles, her mother's brothers, in Rawalpindi, one of the bigger cities in Pakistan. Saadia is quite well-dressed compared to the other young women we have met in Dhamyal. Her clothes are simple and quite old, but well-cut, in accordance with the current trends (later we find out that she alters her clothes every few months). Her beautiful long hair is artfully pulled together in a braid that hangs down her back. Saadia tells us that she is technically in school, but she has been unable to pass the eighth standard examination for quite a few years now. She tells us that it gets difficult to study around the time of the examinations because they are so near to the harvest period, the period when she gets to work in the fields. She has worked in the fields. She is paid in kind by the landlords with peanuts and wheat, the two chief crops of the region. Saadia's family uses the wheat themselves and sells off the peanuts.

Saadia's detailed reporting of her work in the fields brings us back to our questionnaires. We wrap up the household-level questionnaire and the in-depth exploration of the healthcare system and focus exclusively on the village-level analysis. Saadia joins in the conversation and soon becomes a bona fide respondent, supplementing the information her grandmother provides us about Dhamyal, freely sharing her perspectives and opinions about the village and its inhabitants. She talks about the upcoming elections and the voters' demands for accessible drinking water. She is supportive of the demand, but she does not seem very fond of her fellow villagers. She complains that they are always criticizing her for moving around too freely within and outside the village. Evidently, her grand-mother, mother, and maternal uncles have always allowed her a good deal of freedom, especially since she has contributed to the household income from such a young age.[16] Still, she avoids going out alone as much as possible since she feels harassed.

The murder pops up when we ask if there are any disputes over land and prop-erty in Dhamyal. 'A girl even got murdered two years ago because of a land issue,' Saadia announces. Her grandmother tries to stop Saadia from giving us the story of the murder but then proceeds to fill in the details that Saadia leaves out. They tell us that the girl from the landlord family was murdered because she was sup-posedly having an affair with a young man from a *Kammi Kameen* family. The man was allowed to escape. The police came to investigate the matter. However, the murderer was not arrested. Saadia and her grandmother are adamant that the business of the love affair was cooked up, an '*ilzaam*' (an accusation). They insist the murder is somehow connected to a dispute over land and property, although they are not sure of the particulars in the situation. Saadia is especially vehement in her defense of the murdered young woman's virtue, although when I ask her if she had known the woman well, she shakes her head.

When we finish the session, Saadia offers to accompany us to our next destination in the village. Her grandmother, however, frowns and says something to the effect that she needs to be careful. Saadia appears not to listen, but I interrupt the old woman and reassure her that we will ask the younger children to accompany us instead. Later I wonder about my deference toward the grandmother's wishes and my choice to collude in her attempt to control Saadia's movements.

The same day the men in our team[17] hear from some men in the village about the alleged love affair and the subsequent killing of the young woman by her brother-in-law, her sister's husband. The *Kammi Kameen* young man was only beaten up, and he and his family told to leave the village. The men also seem to imply what Saadia claims: the boy was deliberately not killed because his killing, the murder of a young man, and especially of one who is not a family member, can turn into a bigger issue. According to the men as well, the police did not make an arrest, although they did look into the matter. Neither the *Mochi* women nor the men knew if any formal reports were registered with the police.

For the most part, till the last day of our fieldwork in Dhamyal we hear very little about the murder from other women. When we bring up the murder during interviews with women from landlord households, our questions are met with tense silence, followed by attempts to change the topic. In other contexts, like interviews with *Kammi Kameen* women, and during our interview in the state-run primary school for girls, women confirm the fact of the murder, but then say they do not know much about it. In the schoolteacher's case, the professed lack of knowledge about the murder seems to be part of the teacher's general detachment, indifference, and even disdain toward the 'backward' people whose children she has to teach. One of the teachers commutes every day from a nearby small town and laments her rural appointment through most of the interview. The other teacher moved to

Dhamyal from Rawalpindi after her marriage to a teacher in the local government school for boys and holds her parents responsible for her comedown in life.

Evidently, the men continue to talk about the murder during the course of the fieldwork, but only if they are asked direct questions. Their representation of the incident is, for the most part, quite bland and matter-of-fact, although some of them do frame the murder in terms of a measure taken to protect the integrity of the landlord family.

On the last afternoon of our fieldwork in Dhamyal, Nadia and I pay a visit to a private school run by the only Syed[18] family in the village. The principal turns out to be Majida, a woman in her fifties or so. Majida, her son, his wife, and two of Majida's former students teach the 135 students, girls and boys, most of them in grades below five, although the school is a middle school.[19] The school was set up through money Majida's husband earned in the Middle East. Now, Majida's husband has a religious healing practice in Dhamyal. Villagers hold Majida's family in high regard, and they receive gifts of wheat from the landlords in the village as well as free service from *Kammi Kameen* families.

Majida appears to be very committed to the formal education of girls, even though she seems to be overly harsh toward the little girls when it comes to enforcing a dress code that emphasizes covering their heads (she uses corporal punishment). We are especially inspired by her attempts to increase the enrollment of girls from *Kammi Kameen* backgrounds. She tells us that the landlords are not in favor of these girls getting educated because they fear that once the *Kammi Kameen* get educated, they will no longer want to work for them. Majida put up a fight to set up this school. She now offers discounted education to girls of poor families, despite threats from her adversaries. Another interesting aspect of the school is that while the common impression among the villagers we talk to is that the Syed school separates the boys' space from the girls' with a partition, in actuality we see no such partition. Girls and boys sit together in the same room, albeit in separate rows.

After filling out our 'school visit questionnaire' we switch to a general discussion of the village and its sociopolitics. We have been so comprehensive in our efforts to get different standpoints: why miss out on the opportunity to get an analysis from a Syed perspective? Majida's attitude toward the women in the village is laudatory. She thinks the women in the village are '*jaffakash*' (very hardworking), while the men tend to be lazy. Even little girls work in the field and carry water from a long distance to their homes. There are no very rich people in the village, since no one owns a huge plot of land, but the *Kammi Kameen* are the poorest.

Nadia then abruptly brings up the question that has preoccupied us since our conversation with Saadia. 'What is the story about the killing of the young woman?' Majida pauses. Looking at us rather secretively, she asks, 'So you know about it?' We both nod our heads. When she does not say anything, I ask insistently, 'Was she killed because of a land dispute?' She shakes her head, and responds, 'No, it was *an izzat ki baat* (a matter of respect). What else could they have done? They are after all respectable people.' Majida tells us that the girl belonged to a landlord family, and the boy was a *Jolaha* (weaver), a *Kammi Kameen*. The police got involved, but since it was a '*ghar kaa mamla*' (a household matter), they did not arrest anyone. Majida becomes increasingly more animated, and she goes on to express her approval of the message this murder has communicated to the other young people in the village. Majida's repeated and vociferous commendation of the *izzatdaar* (respectable) people, and the service that they have done to the community through the killing of the young woman goes on for a few minutes.

I feel my temper rising, but it is Nadia's rather white face (she just keeps on taking diligent notes through it all) that makes me change the topic rather rudely by posing an abrupt question to Majida about the general law and order situation in the village. We both leave the school premises in a little while after that, shaken, but unable to stop talking about Majida's perspective on the murder. Given the vein of the initial part of our interview where Majida espoused rather revolutionary beliefs in education (and my theoretical understanding of contradictory subject positions notwithstanding), her unequivocal support, and even glorification, of the young woman's murder came as a shock.

Later that afternoon as we walk to our van parked on the outskirts of the village, we see Saadia, her head covered but her back straight, looking stylish in yet another worn-out but well-stitched outfit, walking purposefully toward the fields beyond the village residential boundary. 'How are you, Saadia? Where are you off to?' I hail her as the other team members start getting into the vehicle. 'I have to get some vegetables from someone's field,' she shouts back. After a mutual exchange of '*Khuda Hafiz*' (May God protect you), we are both on our way. As the van makes its way on the dirt path that connects the village to the highway, I continue to look at Saadia till she disappears from my sight into the now darkening fields. I surprise myself by worrying about where she is going. I sense within myself an urge to somehow protect her. Her independence is endearing, but in light of what we have found out during our fieldwork, also frightening. How will she be punished for it? While earlier on I had attributed her fashion sense to her excursions into city life, I now think it is somehow inherent in her, this instinct to escape, to transcend dinginess.

I admonish myself for my tendency to cast Saadia as the heroine of my story in Dhamyal. She *is* brave and honest, but she is also rather naïve and foolhardy. She is only 15, and given her visits to the city, most probably looks up to the kind of modern womanhood I represent. Her frankness during our conversation was possibly also a bid to impress Nadia and me. My thoughts turn to Majida, the other research participant who was open with me, also possibly because she was trying to connect with other educated women. While I find it difficult to accept Majida's perspectives on the murder, I have to admit to myself that I identify with the kind of resistance I perceive Saadia is enacting against her oppressive conditions – I have my own history of violating codes of behavior upheld by my family and community. Although my resistance and rebellion predates my exposure to feminism, Western and otherwise, my training as a researcher is grounded in ontological and epistemological underpinnings that have its origins in larger histories of colonialism and neo-colonialism, privileging certain ways of being over others.[20] In my final writing up of this fieldwork, if I simplistically romanticize Saadia and demonize Majida I would be undermining my own decolonizing agenda.

My grappling with the politics of representing Saadia and Majida further exhausts my overburdened mind, so instead I begin to reflect on the multiple forms of violence we encountered in Dhamyal. The women in the village live their lives at specific intersections of class and caste,[21] yet the violence against them, whether it is the murder of the woman from the landlord household, the constant surveillance to which young women like Saadia are subjected, or the rigid enforcement of a dress code at school, has a definite gendered character. This is not to take away from the atrocity of the murder. This is also not to assert that Saadia's challenges in a household beset by food insecurity, partially a consequence of their landless status, are the same as the relatively privileged lifestyle of a young woman growing up in a landlord's household. The point is that the *Jolaha* young man was probably spared because the repercussions of killing a man might have been greater; the brother-in-law had no qualms killing the young woman, and his crime was actually lauded by some in the village, women as well as men. The man's life was deemed more valuable, or at least his death entailed more danger to the murderer or the stability of village life. If we agree with the concept of the 'continuum of violence,'[22] then the young woman's murder was made possible precisely because it is ideologically permissible to exercise the kind of control over women's bodies that Saadia complains about or Nadia and I witnessed in the Syed School. Of course, the material fact of the murder taking place, and the murderer going free could not have taken place without the complicity of the state institutions, a complicity born of a colonial legacy that set out to make the rule of law remote from the lives of ordinary people, thus serving the needs of the feudal landlords that were needed to maintain control of the lands.[23]

I open my notebook to jot down my thoughts. I realize for the first time that I do not know the name of the young woman who was murdered. No one mentioned her name, and somehow I had not asked for it. I try to imagine what she looked like. I close my book with a snap when Saadia's vivacious face appears in my mind's eye.

Vignette II

I spend the first half an hour or so (it seems much longer) in Mehr-un-Nisa's[24] home in Orangi, Karachi's largest *basti* (squatter settlement), struggling with the wires of the sophisticated recording equipment I borrowed from my co-researcher, acutely conscious of the gaze of my intended research participant, her mother, and two sisters. I did dutifully test everything before I started off for the interview, but somehow I am unable to switch on the microphone after Mehr-un-Nisa and I make ourselves comfortable on the straw mat covering the floor.

Although I personally think taperecorders are potentially detrimental to the goal of establishing trust with research participants, I am accountable to the collectivity governing the research project[25] – we have decided to taperecord interviews for a reliable archive.[26] Our objective is to record women's perspectives on the Karachi context of conflict,[27] and we are especially interested in interviewing women who have faced the death of a family member due to the violence. Since Mohajirs – the group that moved to Karachi during and after the 1947 Partition, from parts of the sub-continent that were given to India – have been at the center of what, from some perspectives,[28] has been a civil war situation in the working-class and lower middle-class areas of Karachi, our research participants are mostly Mohajir. Mehr-un-Nisa, whose family does claim a Mohajir identity, has lost a brother.

'*Click!*' The record button finally stays in place, and the red light indicates that the microphone is working. We all get settled again, and the formal interview is set in motion, but I never quite get over my dismay at appearing incompetent in the eyes of those trusting me with their life stories.

Still, it is most probably to my perceived vulnerability that I owe Mehr-un-Nisa's relative openness during the course of the interview. During the preliminary round of introductions, Mehr-un-Nisa's father was the only member of the family who expressed some degree of friendliness, although he appeared rather embarrassed (I later find out that this was because he cannot offer me tea since that day there is no money to buy milk). Mehr-un-Nisa and her mother muttered civilities, but without meeting my eyes or smiling, and her two younger sisters just stared at me. I suppose my anxiety at the breaking down of my equipment makes me appear less remote, and both Mehr-un-Nisa and her mother visibly thaw toward me. Later on, Mehr-un-Nisa tells me that she had been hesitant to welcome me because she was afraid that I was here to make fun of their poverty. She had consented to the interview because she respects the man who is helping me find research participants.

We sit in one of two rooms in a house that is made of a mixture of baked and unbaked bricks. The only two articles in the room are the straw mat and a brass glass. While Mehr-un-Nisa and I talk, her mother lies on the side, a newspaper rolled into a pillow underneath her head, occasionally fanning herself with another newspaper. At times, she interjects into the conversation, but Mehr-un-Nisa is my primary respondent. Mehr-un-Nisa assiduously answers all my questions, but her answers, even to my broadly framed queries, are brief and to the point. I am struck, however, by her wisdom, for her somewhat terse responses are uttered after careful deliberation. I also note a deep sadness in her eyes, which is in contrast to the haziness I see in her mother's gaze. Mehr-un-Nisa tells me, in the course of the interview, that the doctor gives her mother sleeping pills to help her with the psychological illness that has set in after her brother's death. When I inquire if there are any side effects from taking the medicine, Mehr-un-Nisa replies matter-of-factly, 'She gets a lot of relief from it,' confirming my impression of her quiet independence.

Mehr-un-Nisa dropped out of school when she was 15, four years before this interview in August of 2000, right after her older brother, 19-year-old Iqbal, was killed. Iqbal had quit school after his matriculation (tenth standard) since their father's health did not allow him to work everyday. Her father, who is 70 at the time of the interview, had worked in a lawyer's office, but for the past ten years has been working for a salary of 100 rupees per day (approximately

$2.00) at the Nimco Center, a store where they sold savory snacks. Her mother has never worked outside the home. Her other brother, who is a year younger than Mehr-un-Nisa, dropped out of school after their older brother died as well but has not been able to find any sustainable employment. Three of the four younger sisters go to school, but the fourth 'cannot learn anything' after the death of her brother, so she has stopped going to school. Mehr-un-Nisa and her sisters contribute to the household income by sewing clothes for people in the neighborhood, but sewing jobs are only available intermittently, usually around the times of festivals.

The reports I have received so far from neighbors and others in Karachi of the events surrounding Iqbal's death are confusing and even contradictory. Although everyone agrees on the apolitical nature of Iqbal's life – he was not involved with any of the warring factions in Karachi, there is no agreement about either the killers or their motivation. Some people said that his disengagement from Mohajir politics was what annoyed the more militant Mohajirs. A few said that the police or the paramilitary forces killed Iqbal because they mistook him for someone else or because he was friends with someone who was involved in the conflict. Others said that his death was the result of a random killing by either the Mohajir militants or the law-enforcing authorities, since both groups went on occasional rampages to spread terror in Orangi Town.

Mehr-un-Nisa simply states that '*dahshatgurd*' (literally meaning those who spread terror) shot him. Children from the neighborhood came running into their home to tell them when Iqbal was kidnapped outside their house one afternoon. No one really saw who the kidnappers were. A few hours later a neighbor brought in the body that he said he found near a mosque a short distance away from their home. The rest of the interview primarily focuses on the aftermath of her brother's death. Unlike some of my other interviewees, Mehr-un-Nisa lets me decide the direction of the interview. While I try to elicit the overall women-centered picture[29] expected by the research collectivity, my specific concern with issues around agency[30] and reconstitution of selves[31] in the wake of violence does circumscribe the conversation to quite an extent. I am particularly interested in the different kinds of selves enacted as survivors share their accounts of forging new lives within and against their violent worlds.[32]

For Mehr-un-Nisa I find that right after her brother's death there is a sense of selves being swallowed by nothingness:

LUBNA: What were your feelings at your brother's sudden death?
MEHR-UN-NISA: I fainted. I had no consciousness.
LUBNA: What happened after you gained consciousness?
MEHR-UN-NISA: I was very sad after seeing my brother's face. Just now our brother had gone out after eating food . . . 11 o'clock at night we saw his dead face.

Mehr-un-Nisa was under a doctor's care for a few weeks after her brother was buried. She had to terminate the treatment since the medicines were too expensive, and her mother's cure was the priority. Her mother, however, has barely recovered since then. Since Iqbal's death she has not been able to continue the job of running the household. Mehr-un-Nisa and her older sister took on the responsibility for household chores, while her sister had the additional task of taking care of their mother. After her sister's wedding, which took place a month before the interview, Mehr-un-Nisa has been in-charge of the home and her mother's care.

Mehr-un-Nisa, the sister and the daughter, eclipse the other selves enacted during the course of the interview. Although the presence of Mehr-un-Nisa, the sister and daughter, is felt during Mehr-un-Nisa's representation of her life before her brother died, it is in the post-violent context of her life that these selves, and hence her relationships with her immediate family, seem to become all-consuming. When asked if she has any friends, Mehr-un-Nisa replied, 'After my brother's death, we ended contact with everybody.'

Mehr-un-Nisa's reconstitution of her sister and daughter selves following her brother's death seems to be shadowed by emptiness, which is perhaps an attenuated strain of the nothingness that engulfed her earlier:

LUBNA: . . . you cannot go to college on your father's income. Did you think about working for the exam as a private student who could study at home?
MEHR-UN-NISA: I have thought about it a lot of times, but they say leave it.
LUBNA: Who says leave it?
MEHR-UN-NISA: The heart and mind say that. The rest of the sisters should study, and we should try to get them educated.

Here Mehr-un-Nisa, the sister, reasserts herself in the face of emptiness and an aborted desire. That the reconstituted selves as sister and daughter, who seem to leave very little room for the enactment of other selves, are also sites of loss is highlighted in the following segment of the interview:

LUBNA: When you left school, did anyone, a teacher, come to find out why?
MEHR-UN-NISA: Give the fee, then study. Otherwise not.
LUBNA: Was there a way for you to get a scholarship?
MEHR-UN-NISA: No, nobody said anything.
LUBNA: Did anyone advise you to sit for the exams privately?
MEHR-UN-NISA: My uncle says that.
LUBNA: But you do not feel like it?
MEHR-UN-NISA: If we had lived in a good way, then I would have wanted to. I wanted to become a doctor. It was not fated to happen.
LUBNA: Were you studying science?
MEHR-UN-NISA: Yes.
LUBNA: Why did you want to become a doctor?
MEHR-UN-NISA: When I used to see Dr Khurshid, I would get that desire.
LUBNA: What was it about Dr Khurshid that you liked?
MEHR-UN-NISA: He talks very wisely. His words are very good. That is why I thought I should become a doctor. Then one of our teachers was becoming a doctor. She has become a doctor. She used to live in this block. Now she has gone to the city.

For Mehr-un-Nisa, the desire to become a doctor had represented attaining wisdom and the chance to move to the city, a move symbolizing upward mobility and perhaps freedom from class- and gender-based constraints. Education, and its inaccessibility for her, and others like her, is a prominent theme in the interview with Mehr-un-Nisa. She talks about the high fee in private schools and the impossibility of getting admission in the overcrowded government schools. Toward the end of the interview, when I ask if it is possible to bring peace to Karachi, she answers, 'If we get good education and good jobs, then maybe all this will end.' Very early in the conversation, when I ask her for an analysis of who is responsible for the violence, she replies succinctly, 'It is the whole society's fault. We should give our children pens, not guns.'

In identifying with both Dr Khurshid and her former teacher, Mehr-un-Nisa posits schooling as a transgendered space of opportunity and possibility, a direct contrast to the gendered sphere of her domestic existence. 'I do not go out of the house,' is Mehr-un-Nisa's laconic response to an inquiry involving her assessment of what different people were saying about the violence. Later on, she elaborates that she does step out at times to buy groceries or medicines for her mother. Evidently, her family conforms to quite rigid gendered norms that restrict women's mobility in public spaces, although the women do not observe *purdah* (veiling). The reigning fear in a climate of violence coupled with inadequate public transportation facilities serves to tighten the restrictions.

Mehr-un-Nisa's selves as sister and daughter are fundamentally relational selves, deriving their agency through identification with various family members, but hierarchical power relations structure the parameters of relationality as well the agency it enables.[33] Mehr-un-Nisa's reminiscences about her brother, Iqbal, as the one who 'was very humorous,' and without whom 'the evenings do not seem like evenings anymore,' for 'when he used to come home, it was great,' point to the joy he brought her. However, the relationship with Iqbal is imbued with meanings drawn from specific patriarchal constructions of what it means to be a good brother or a good sister in Mehr-un-Nisa's family.[34] Iqbal worked outside the home in order to provide for the family. He was also the one to escort his sisters to school or wherever the girls went. For Mehr-un-Nisa, he was also a window to that other world of seeming openness and liberty, and listening to his stories about work, and the people he met, afforded a vicarious pleasure. In her turn, although her mother was at that time managing the home, Mehr-un-Nisa, as would have behooved a good sister, reciprocated by personally taking care of Iqbal's needs at home. Mehr-un-Nisa's relationships with other members of the family are similarly demarcated. Thus, while Mehr-un-Nisa's role as the sister and daughter, who ran the household, granted her a certain authority within her family, that authority remains circumscribed by codes of gender-appropriate behavior.

Although Mehr-un-Nisa identifies herself as ethnically Mohajir, it is the classed and gendered dimensions of her selves that come to the forefront in the interview. She does inhabit an ethnicized space, for all her neighbors are Mohajir, and her family is strict about finding matches within the Mohajir community.

Her friends at school, however, used to be Mohajir, Punjabi, and Pathan. When I push her further in order to elicit a more detailed analysis of the sociopolitical context around her, she tells me that she prefers to remain immersed in her housework and not engage with the world around her. 'Sometimes, when I think then my mind goes crazy, that why are there so many killings in the last three four years. Why is this happening?' While Mehr-un-Nisa's relative isolation, in physical and mental terms, is the outcome of circumstances interfacing with structures, it is also, to a certain degree, a preference, representing a coping mechanism in a life-world rendered unfamiliar and chaotic by violence: 'It did not seem like this was Orangi Town anymore. Everyday, all the time, we heard the noise of firing.'

Mehr-un-Nisa also appeared disinterested in her family's history. She knows very little about her parents' migration to Karachi around the time when East Pakistan declared its independence as Bangladesh and knows nothing at all about her family's first migration from the Indian state of Bihar to East Pakistan in 1947 (her mother tells me they are from Bihar). When I ask her if she ever asks her parents about their lives before they moved to Karachi, she simply states, 'We have got everything here, so what is the point in asking about it?' Her mother responds in a comparable, though slightly more definitive, tone when I ask her if she shares stories from her previous homes with her children, 'They do not want to hear about it. I do not want to talk about. We are here now.' A pact seems to exist, across generations, whereby the past is deemed redundant, irrelevant, or taboo. Perhaps the agony of the present and the imperative to survive in the midst of that agony leaves no room for memories from what would seem like the remote past. Alternatively, memories from a painful past could only add to suffering in the present.

I take leave of Mehr-un-Nisa and her family feeling rather overwhelmed by the starkness of it all: Mehr-un-Nisa's unembellished words; her mother's uncompromising grief and letting go of life after her son's death; the unqualified sadness in Mehr-un-Nisa's eyes; the austerity of the room where the interview takes place; the harshness of the physical violence that can ravage a family; and the unmitigated burden of continuing an existence in an unjust, unfair, and inequitable world. Mehr-un-Nisa comes across as a determined young woman, but her determination manifests itself in striving toward the absolute acceptance of the limits in her life. Mehr-un-Nisa prays only occasionally, and says she is not a very good Muslim, but she does draw strength through her faith in God and destiny. However, her resignation to her perceived lot in life is not just a consequence of religious beliefs. It is based on a realistic appraisal from the vantage point of her knowledge and social positionality, of the gendered, classed, and violent world around her.

Even in the short time I spent with her, I see glimpses of Mehr-un-Nisa's interesting inner life. Her intelligence is evident from the manner she chose to frame her perspectives and couch her thoughts. If consciousness can be simply equated with agency, then Mehr-un-Nisa is an agent, not just in her role as sister and daughter or through her assumption of a self-contained persona, but also in her attempt to make sense of her place in the world she inhabits. However, from Mehr-un-Nisa's perspective, these particular exercises of agency – the diligent realization of house-hold responsibilities, the self-imposed isolation, and the consciousness of limits – are the aftermath of a brother's untimely death in an unjust system which not only allowed that death, but then makes no provisions to support the healing and financial stability of her family.

On the rather long ride back to my co-researcher's lovely home in the Karachi populated by the upper classes (the contrast between that Karachi and the peripheral Karachi never ceases to amaze me), I have ample time to continue my ruminations on the relationships between death, agency, and social stratification. In the context of the Karachi that Mehr-un-Nisa inhabits, lower middle-class young men of a certain ethnicity are more likely to be killed; their family's fortunes, given their lack of resources and the gendered nature of livelihoods, are most likely to be tied to their earnings; and their sisters are most likely to give up their dreams in the light of gendered norms that define women's life paths, even if these young men manage to survive.

I recall a dream I had a few months after my little brother, Chand, died:[35] one of my aunts is holding me in her arms telling me not to cry over the loss of the house that he was going to build me because my other brother, Noman, could still do that for me. I remember waking up startled – in my conscious life I did not ever remember having any financial expectation from these boys so much younger than me; my earliest memories are of spending my pocket money on them. Then I realized that at some deep subconscious level I did see my brothers as guarantors of security in a world that was patriarchal[36] across societies, even if the patriarchies manifested themselves differentially. Yet, despite this parallel to Mehr-un-Nisa's sense of losing a protector and a closely connected family member, in contrast to Mehr-un-Nisa's truncated dream of education, I had managed to actualize the goals I had set myself. I mourned my brother intensely, even thought of dropping out of graduate school, but eventually wrote the dissertation and got a job.

I begin to question my efficacy as a feminist, and my dreams of an inclusive women's movement in Pakistan: Why would women like Mehr-un-Nisa, for whom agency in the best of circumstances translates into mere survival, even consider alliances with the likes of us, with our habitats in the lap of luxury and our foreign degrees, as useful, given the strong possibility that we can never understand their realities? I doze off as I meditate on the inadequacy of feminist initiatives, scholarly and otherwise, in the face of lives ravaged by the totalizing effects of multiple forms of violence, structural and physical.

Vignette III

I sit beside my little brother's grave in my father's ancestral village, Gorala,[37] located almost on the border between the Pakistani and Indian Punjabs, trying to explain to a 70 plus old man, who is somehow related to me, why there were pictures of policemen trying to get me off a bus in the newspapers. I fumble in my attempts to do so, my explanation to this man I call *Taya Jee*, which means father's older brother, punctuated by pauses where I desperately try to conjure up Punjabi equivalents of words and phrases that I throw around thoughtlessly in my other life in the city: 'resistance,' 'symbolic protest,' 'discriminatory legislation,' and so forth. I had been part of a peaceful protest against the stone-to-death sentence awarded to a woman named Zaafran Bibi. Some of us had also demanded the repeal of the piece of legislation, the Hadood Ordinance, on which the sentence was based.[38]

Daughters of my village do not usually go around marching in demonstrations. Neither do they allow strange men to touch them, let alone pull and push them till they are bruised. And if for some reason that does happen, *Taya Jee* points out, they make sure they are not being photographed or that their photographs are not being splashed all over the country. Furthermore, daughter or son notwithstanding, the spiritual heritage of my family entails subscription to codes of faith, peace, and acceptance, which rules out any kind of overt protest or expression of discontent. I cringe at this implication of being such a multi-leveled disgrace to my ancestors.

Taya Jee proceeds to remind me how my paternal family lives under the shadow of a centuries-old curse from a *sufi*. One of my ancestors had shot at the *sufi's* lion with an arrow. The lion died, and the good man had prayed that my family never enjoy any worldly success. As a result, through the generations, members of our family who have tried to engage too much with 'the world' have only created more misery in their lives.

I give up trying to make *Taya Jee* understand the imperative of resisting power relations and dwell instead on the two-pronged myth defining my family's place in this village. On the one hand, there is the mystic legacy symbolized by my great grandfather's mausoleum in the courtyard of the mosque; on the other, the consequences of an ancestor's violence against the lion intersect with this history of spirituality. My brother is buried right outside the mausoleum, and even as I am sitting here trying to tune out *Taya Jee's* relentless lecture, people of all ages, mostly men, are passing by with their offerings of flowers. An *urs* (a spiritual gathering of sorts) is held every year at this site, and my family continues to benefit from the respect and devotion bestowed upon us by people in and around the village, despite my father's rejection of his role as the heir to this mystic legacy. I wonder what came first, my ancestors' embracing of the spiritual path or the internalization of the *sufi's* curse? It is so much easier to reject the 'world,' when one is convinced that its gifts are not available anyway.

My train of thought is interrupted by yet another loving pat on my *dopatta*-covered[39] head. As I respond appropriately to the greetings from yet another Taya, the idea of arranging a focus group with all these *Taya Jees* pops into my head. I am in the village after all to wrap up my piece of the study on memories of the 1947 partition of the Indian sub-continent.[40] The researcher in me always seems to have the last word.

After successfully vanquishing my activist as well as daughter-of-the-village selves, I turn to *Taya Jee* and remind him that we need to continue our interview. *Taya Jee* tells me that he is too tired now but will try to find other research participants. As he gets up sighing and walks away, I turn to my notebook, jotting down my reflections on the last two interviews.

Before *Taya Jee*, I had interviewed another old man, Deen Mohammed, who was a Sikh before Partition. I also addressed him as *Taya Jee*, although he is not a biological relative. Unlike my other strident *Taya*, *Taya* Deen's voice and hands shook throughout the interview, and he spoke in whispers. He told me that he had converted to Islam after he elected to stay on in Pakistan, despite persuasions from both sides to migrate to India. I had tried my best to uncover some dire story of coercion, but it appeared that Deen Mohammed had been compelled by his own need to stay in Gorala (he could not imagine living elsewhere), which in turn had translated into the need to embrace Islam. Deen Mohammed's entire immediate family, with the exception of himself and his sister, were killed when Deen and his family were hiding in the fields one night in August 1947. 'Who killed them, *Taya Jee*?' I had asked relentlessly. 'Them . . . the Mus . . . Muslims,' he had muttered, without making eye contact. *Taya* Deen's conversion to Islam had not erased his non-*Jat*, lower/server caste origins.[41] Although he refers to Gorala and the surrounding 24 villages as our 'Lalli' villages, he is not a Lalli, which is a Jat clan.[42] Deen Mohammed, like all the other interviewees, male and female, insists that no one from the 25 Lalli villages in the region killed a Sikh or Muslim from the *Lalli* clan or the supporting (lower/server) castes living in the 25 villages. Outsiders were responsible for killings from all religions and castes.

My father's side is Lalli. In 1947, Gorala was predominantly Sikh Lalli. The Muslim Lallis, which include my grandfather's family, were in the minority.[43] While none of my interviewees have painted an idyllic tale of co-existence – the Sikh majority did control most of the resources in the village, and religious distinctions and lines were quite strictly drawn during community gatherings, including weddings and funerals, where food for Sikhs and Muslim guests was cooked, and, at times, even served, separately; there were no ongoing historical conflicts between the Sikh and the Muslim Lallis. In fact, men and women spoke of close nuclear family ties and individual friendships. At that time, the village was situated in District Gurdaspur, which, given its status as an overall Muslim majority district, was expected to be part of Pakistan in its totality. However, the district's fate was only decided after India and Pakistan were declared independent,[44] and only one of its sub-administrative units, Tehsil Shakargarh, the tehsil in which Gorala was located, eventually became part of Pakistan.

With the splitting of the district into segments that were now clearly marked as Pakistani or Indian, and with the areas now clearly demarcated as Muslim or Sikh majority, rumors of violence on both sides of the border began to carry a lot more significance for the inhabitants of my father's village.[45] Earlier, those incidents were and could happen only to other people in other villages. The Sikh Lallis especially felt vulnerable since in Pakistani Shakargarh they were unmistakably a minority group. Before the division of District Gurdaspur, the Muslims had been a marginal majority, and there were areas, like the Lalli villages, where the non-Muslims were numerically stronger. In addition to this rather even distribution of power among the two key religious groups of the district, identities based on histories of shared ancestry and kinship groups had worked together with identities based on religion to interpellate relationships within Gorala, across the other Lalli villages, and with other nearby villages. For instance, most of my research participants in their accounts of 1947 refer to the neighboring non-*Lalli* villages, almost exclusively populated by Muslims, who might have migrated from Afghanistan centuries ago, as *Pathan* villages. In this case, genealogy in terms of ethnic origin remains more salient as an identity marker than religion.

Even after the partition of Gurdaspur, and the more insistent circulation of a discourse that mapped religion to national territory and identity,[46] the Sikhs and Muslim Lallis in Gorala were not afraid of each other. They were cousins, and shared the same bloodline. A pact was written out. If a Sikh group came to attack the village, the Sikhs would take the brunt. If there were a Muslim attack, the Muslim villagers would be the protectors. Eventually, through the impetuousness of a group of young men from different religious backgrounds in the village who proceeded to attack a nearby Pathan village to abduct a girl one of them liked, the Sikhs had to flee to protect themselves from the wrath of the Pathans. Deen Mohammed's family was killed as they were hiding in the sugarcane crop on their way to the nearby bridge over the river Ravi that connected both sides of the newly declared border.

Even if I am beginning to be convinced that perhaps familial ties were not violated during that phase of senseless violence, that most of the perpetrators were indeed outsiders, and that most of my relatives were not involved in any massacres at all, the story of the three Sikh Lalli old men who were left behind haunts me. These old men remained in their houses in the villages, ostensibly as guards, when the rest of the village fled into the fields. They were even spared when the 'outsiders' swept through the fields. They were killed later on when the Muslims returned to their homes. No one tells me who killed them. The responses to a direct query remain vague. My question as to why they were not protected when they were being killed is also shrugged away. Only one of my *Tayas*, *Taya* Akbar, who now lives in Lahore, the capital city of the province of Punjab, met my gaze and said, '*Clear karna thaa naa . . . ?*' I guess that roughly translates into 'it had to be cleared, don't you get it?' When I asked for clarification, clearly showing I did not get it, he turned his head away mumbling something about Pakistan and shouted for his daughter to bring us more tea.

My family, my blood, is not just cursed because of the killing of a lion. Somewhere in me is a part that is guilty of being complicit in the death of three elderly kinsmen. My Sikh relatives left them behind, deemed them redundant. My Muslim relatives either killed them directly, or let them die. I cannot write any more. The guilt in my blood, the violence in my blood, pounds in my head, blocking further thoughts from breaking through.

Later in the day, as I am making my way to the car that will take me back to my routine in the city, I am surprised to see Deen Mohammad, the old man I have interviewed earlier, purposefully walking toward me. But, no, this is not the same trembling person who earlier on shed tears and closed his eyes as he talked about his massacred family. He looks at me squarely and says, 'You were right to get on that bus. Absolutely right! Don't listen to anyone. These people do not know. I still shake when I think of the Indian and Pakistani soldiers coming after me (in order to take me to the other side of the border), but I never gave in to them. The case went on for five years after 1947, and I stood my ground. Also, remember it was one of your uncles who got my sister back when a Muslim in this village sold her off. And ask your father about Bimla, the Hindu girl your grandparents saved from those hooligans. Your family was attacked, but they never gave up the girl. Acceptance of God's will does not mean saying yes to cruelty.'

Is Deen Mohammed telepathic? Or is the gossip going around the village so intense that he feels he has to reassure me? I do not get a chance to probe because Deen Mohammed turns around and walks away as soon as he finishes his words. He is shaking quite uncontrollably, so I just resume my journey to the car, bemused by the necessity of modifying my brooding to make space for a history of resistance in my blood.

The two-hour car journey to the city with my parents is spent co-analyzing my 'data' and mourning my brother's loss from our lives. My father tells me Bimla's story again. He has actually written it down for me a couple of years ago, but I need to listen to it right now. I try to share with my parents the overwhelming sense of guilt and despair that engulfed me earlier. My mother does not help by telling us how soon after the 1971 war[47] she overheard two second cousins of mine, now retired from the Pakistani military and living in the village, boasting about the number of women they raped in East Pakistan.

I sleep fitfully that night. In my dreams I am in my village, which for some reason is in Bangladesh, and I am running after buses that are taking all the women from the village away. I know that these women are going to be raped and then sentenced to death by stoning. At first, I am running alone, but then a group of old men, led by Deen Mohammed, follow me. I wake up just before I manage to touch one of the buses.

I get out of bed, grab a notebook, and begin to write points I want to make in an article on violence and resistance. I write about the presence of violence at many levels in our everyday lives, as the powers-that-be around us use borders and legislation to 'clear out' those seen as surplus, as not belonging, or as not conforming: the old Sikh Lalli men; the lower-caste families in my village; Zaafran Bibi; and the women raped by the Pakistani army in 1971, and before, in what is now Bangladesh – because they were deemed as '*kaafir*,' non-believers. In addition to the direct violence that injures or kills us physically through wars and conflicts, there is the indirect structural and linguistic violence as well as the violence we do to our own selves by conforming to what is expected by the powers-that-be. I put down my tendency to let my researcher self override my other selves as an example. How many times have I not taken a stand in the name of safeguarding my livelihood or remaining true to my role as a detached academic?

When I was trying to get on that bus in May 2002, my initial intent was twofold. Firstly, I was following instructions being shouted out by experienced activists that we should not let the police haul off our male colleagues without the protection of our female presence. Evidently, men arrested on their own are vulnerable to a greater degree of violence and humiliation. Secondly, I did not want the law-enforcing institutions of this country to erase the resistance enacted by the women protesting against the Hadood Ordinance. We were obviously not even worthy of an arrest. It was only when the policeman pushing me off the bus said, 'Do you think I as a man will let you get on this bus? You, a woman, think you can get on this bus?' – that getting on the bus took on the proportions of a life-and-death symbolic act.

My action/reaction in the moment was meaningful, and that is what I want to keep in mind. Otherwise, like the story of three old Sikh Lallis, I can let the negativity of the event co-opt my memory of resistance. The media had a hey-day with the photographs they took of the police pushing and pulling me. I did not even notice them photographing me. The next day at the press conference organized to protest the violence, the cameramen positioned themselves around me, their cameras aiming to shoot much in the same way their pictures from the day before captured the policemen and policewomen with their batons and guns aimed at me. The violence became threefold when even some so-called friends sarcastically labeled me 'the heroine.' For them, it was all about the pictures in the paper. I begin to digress in my notes as I ramble on about images superseding reality . . .

Notes

1 Following Kleinman (2000), I have opted to pluralize violence in order to highlight the multiplicity of the violence in peoples' lives.
2 Here I borrow from Mamdani's (2004) title.
3 In these vignettes, I draw from my field-notes, the scribbles I made while actually *in* the field, and the more systematic field-journal entries I made every night, where I still obediently follow what I learned in my first critical ethnography course: section out the more 'objective' rendering of field observations and conversations from my 'personal' reflections and analysis of field sites and interactions. In addition, I have interview transcripts for the studies excerpted in the second and third vignettes. For the first vignette, I also utilize the rigorous field documentation provided by my research assistant, Nadia Assad.
4 Following Sandoval (1991), I use the term 'Third World' as a political identity, rather than to merely indicate geographical location. While I am cognizant of critiques of the term 'Third World' – it does rank the West as first on the list and it lumps together diverse regions of this planet, I use it to signify an identity based on a political engagement with shared histories of dispossession, slavery, and other forms of colonial and neo-colonial violence.
5 My initial understanding of polyvocality owes a debt to Clifford (1988) and Behar (1993).
6 See, for instance, Narayan (1993).
7 See Rosaldo (1987) on the necessity to maintain a 'double vision' (p. 147), whereby the social analyst's narrative is held in creative tension with those of the research par-ticipants, since after all ' . . . each viewpoint is arguably incomplete . . . a mix of insight and blindness, reach and limitations, impartiality and bias – and taken together they achieve neither omniscience nor a unified master narrative but complex understandings of ever-changing, multifaceted social realities' (p. 128).

8 See Jacobs-Huey (2002) for a succinct analysis of the prevalent debates in this regard.

9 While we started off the study as a poverty assessment, the fieldwork led me to reject the paradigm of poverty in favor of a perspective that views peoples' suffering in contexts of inequalities, injustices, and discrimination within, across, and between countries as consequences of forms of violence that have become routinized, systematicized, and normalized as part of the status quo (Anglin, 1998; Uvin, 1998). Drawing on this study, Chaudhry (2005) details the multi-layered structural violence within which peoples' lives are embedded.

10 See Hall (1990) for a discussion on how to conceive of theories that do not seek to define or classify but work instead with the contingent and the contextual flow of realities, ideas, and images.

11 The names of all individuals in this particular vignette, with the exception of my research assistant Nadia, are fictitious.

12 I have italicized non-English words in the text. The data for the different studies on which this chapter is based was collected in a mixture of Urdu, Pakistan's national language, and local varieties of regional languages. I therefore work with translations of my fieldwork interactions and observations. In some instances, I have retained the usage of words, phrases, or sentences in their original language, if I felt the translations did not capture the connotations. English equivalents are provided in either footnotes or parentheses when these words appear for the first time in the chapter.

13 The name of the village has been changed, but particulars about its geography and physical features are factual.

14 The fieldwork on which this vignette is based was conducted in relation to a study (World Bank, 2002) jointly undertaken by the World Bank and the Sustainable Development Policy Institute (SDPI), Islamabad. The study aimed at understanding rural poverty with reference to more than just household income and expenses, and attempted to investigate the experience of those identified as the poor with reference to public services, the rule of the law, electoral processes, collective action within communities, conflicts, and disasters. I was one of the two senior researchers on the project. The data was collected in 2001, and we visited this particular village in June.

15 Literally meaning the lowly ones, who work and serve. *Kammi Kameen* refers to a group of castes or kinship groups designated as lower castes.

16 Overall, in the study we found that women from *Kammi Kameen* families in Punjab, including young unmarried women, enjoy greater mobility than their counterparts in landlord families, mainly because codes of respect tied to the control of women's bodies are relaxed when household economies rely on women's work outside the home. This mobility, however, comes with its own risks, as *Kammi Kameen* women are more likely to face sexual harassment. See Chaudhry (2004a) for details.

17 A research team of eight members, four of them women, visited each site in the study. Given the gender-segregated nature of the spaces we researched, most of the data with men was collected by the male members of our team.

18 Syeds claim to be the direct descendants of the Prophet Mohammed and are usually revered and treated with a lot of respect in Muslim communities in Pakistan.

19 A middle school offers eight grades of instruction.

20 For discussion on the colonial roots of research and the imperative to decolonize, see Smith (1999).

21 Caste refers to the kinship collectivity with which a household identifies. Research participants tended to use the term '*zaat*' meaning 'caste,' interchangeable with '*biradiri*' meaning kinship group. Class in the context of this study primarily refers to socioeconomic status that is a consequence of the possession or lack of assets and resources, including land and opportunities for employment. We met people who belonged to *Kammi Kameen* families who are faring better than some landlord families with small agricultural plots.

22 Scheper-Hughes and Bourgois (2004, p. 19).

23 See Ali (1988).

24 I have used Mehr-un-Nisa's first name as well as the first name of her brother with her permission.

25 The project, funded by the Ford Foundation, was developed as a contribution to feminist security scholarship about South Asia by South Asian scholars. I was one of six researchers who participated in the project. The data in Karachi was collected in 2000.

26 The archive, SDPI (2001), consists of interviews conducted with women in the Karachi context of conflict and Afghan women living in refugee camps in Pakistan.

27 The Karachi conflict, in its most recent phase, was generated after a riot in April 1985. Although the conflict played out in ethnic terms – initially, the Mohajirs, post-independence migrants from regions now in India, and the Pathans from Pakistan's North West Frontier Province were the key combatants – it was ultimately a battle over resources in the urban margins. As the violence progressed into the 1990s, it also became about state brutality and in-fighting among the Mohajirs. The violence in its earlier stages was actually supported by the Pakistani military state through the provision of arms and finances. Later on, the Indian government funneled funds into the armed conflict as retaliation for Pakistan's interference in Kashmir. In addition, the conflict also was augmented through a leakage from the US supply of arms that went through the Karachi port to the so-called Afghan Mujahideen fighting against the Soviet occupation. See Chaudhry (2004b) for a concise history of the Karachi conflict.

28 See Hussain (1990) for a perspective that puts forth the Karachi conflict as a crisis of the state and civil society.

29 Following Patai (1988), the emphasis was not on merely learning the facts of women's lives, but on comprehending 'how a person verbally constructs an image of her life, how she creates a character for herself, how she becomes the protagonist of her own story' (p. 150).

30 I work with a definition of agency based on my reading of feminist postructuralist thought (e.g., Davies, 1991; Sandoval, 1991). This definition does not presuppose a transcendent subject outside the context of her constitution but positions subjects as dynamic, located in particular societal times and spaces and yet active negotiators with power relations in these different times and spaces.

31 In accordance with my poststructuralist understanding of agency, I see selves as multiple, fluid, and contingent on power relations in disparate contexts. Selves are then constituted through powerful discourses that are mediated, contested, and even co-produced by people as they create their selves. Alarcon (1990) is one of the key influences on my thought in this regard.

32 See Chaudhry (2004b) for further details.

33 Joseph (1999, pp. 2–3) writes, 'Relational selfhood and patriarchy are not seen to be inimical to the coexistence of agency and the self. ... The agency of the self emerges experientially and existentially although it may not be the agency of the bounded, separate individual.'

34 Joseph (1994) presents an analysis of how patriarchy underwrites and infuses relationality between brothers and sisters in the context of Lebanon.

35 My brother, six years younger than me, died in a car accident in 1994 on the part of the Grand Trunk Road connecting Islamabad to Peshawar in what I perceive as an instance of road violence. At that time the highway was a single lane. My brother and his friend died when their car got caught between two buses coming from the opposite direction, whose bus drivers decided to relieve the monotony of their tedious jobs, often with no breaks for more than 24 hours, by racing each other.

36 I take patriarchies simply to be social systems premised on the superiority of men over women, predicated on a gendered division of labor, and generally based on the imperative to control women's bodies and sexuality.

37 Actual name of the village. The name of the people inhabiting this vignette are actual as well.

38 The Hadood Ordinance was passed during the US-backed military regime of Zia-ul-Haq, who ruled Pakistan from 1977 till 1988. Despite intensive protests by the women's movement and human rights activists in Pakistan and other countries, the Ordinance remains intact to this very day. Hadood is the plural of *Hudd*, literally meaning limits, and Hadood punishments are defined by the powers-that-be as being ordained by the Holy Quran or *Sunnah* (examples/precedence based on the Prophet Mohammed's life), and are, therefore, fixed, leaving no room for flexibility or discretion on the part of the judge. The Ordinance prescribes punishments against a variety of offences, but the punishments with respect to adultery, *Zina*, have particularly harsh and unjust implications for women in cases of adultery and rape. The testimony of four Muslim males is required in order to prove that a sexual encounter was a rape. If a woman cannot prove that she has been raped, a case of adultery can be filed against her, since she has 'confessed' to extra-marital sexual intercourse. Khan (2006) provides a comprehensive and insightful analysis of the implications of the Hadood Ordinance for the everyday lives of women in Pakistan.

39 A dopatta is a long scarf.

40 The project entitled *Constructions of violence and recovery of alternatives: Partition and memory in the Indian sub-continent* was partially funded by the Social Science Research Council Grant for Collaborative Research in Conflict Zones. Saba G. Khattak was my co-principal investigator for this particular grant. In addition, we collaborated intellectually on this project with a larger team of academicians from Pakistan, India, and Bangladesh as well. Ashis Nandy from the Center of the Study of Developing Societies, Delhi, was key in facilitating these intellectual exchanges.

41 *Taya* Deen came from a *Kammi Kameen* background.

42 Jat is a landlord caste. As in the case of Dhamyal, research participants used '*zaat*' (caste) and '*biradiri*' (kinship group) interchangeably. Lalli is a sub-caste or a particular clan within the larger Jan collectivity.

43 The history of religious conversion in Gorala remains contested. Since both Islam and Sikhism are relatively younger religions in the context of South Asia, the earlier ancestors of the Lallis probably practiced some form (or forms) of Buddhism or Hinduism. It is not clear whether the conversion to Islam in Gorala happened after or before the emergence of Sikhism as a religion in the fifteenth century. In other words, we are not sure for how long Lallis in the region existed as two distinct religious streams, or if the Sikhs came from the Muslims taking up Sikhism and vice versa. See Grewal (1998) for a concise history of Sikhism and its interface with other religions in Punjab.

44 See Khan (2007).

45 For analyses of the events that led to the violence related to the 1947 partition as well as discussions of the violence, including the partition of Punjab, see Butalia (2000), Khan (2007), and Zamindar (2007).

46 There is a significant body of literature that analyzes how the imposition of a Eurocentric nation-state structure with its emphasis on the idea of a unified identity and the mapping of this identity on to a piece of territory in a context where colonial powers had further entrenched, and at times even created, divisions between peoples based on ethnicity or religion, has led to ongoing violence in the formerly colonized nations. See, for instance, Bowen (2002), Chatterjee (1993), and Davidson (1993).

47 The 1971 war between India and Pakistan, which culminated in the birth of Bangladesh, was actually triggered by the Pakistan army's ruthless operation against an insurgency in what was then East Pakistan. According to Bangladeshi authorities, 3 million people were killed, and 200,000 women, including very young girls, were raped, although these figures remain under dispute (Rummel, 1997). See Beachler (2007) for a recent analysis of the genocide in Bangladesh.

References

Abu-Lughod, L. (1993). *Writing women's worlds: Bedoiun stories*. Berkeley and Los Angeles: University of California Press.

Alarcon, N. (1990). The theoretical subject of *This Bridge Called My Back* and Anglo-American feminism. In G. Anzaldua (Ed.), *Making face, making soul/hacienda caras: Creative and critical perspectives by women of color* (pp. 356–369). San Francisco: Aunt Lute.

Ali, I. (1988). *The Punjab under imperialism, 1885–1947*. Princeton, NJ: Princeton University Press.

Anglin, M. K. (1998). Feminist perspectives on structural violence. *Identities, 5*(2), 145–151.

Beachler, D. (2007). The politics of genocide scholarship: The case of Bangladesh. *Patterns of prejudice, 41*(5), 467–492.

Behar, R. (1993). *Translated woman: Crossing the border with Esperanza's story*. Boston: Beacon Press.

Bowen, J. (2002). The myth of global ethnic conflict. In A. L. Hinton (Ed.), *Genocide: An anthropological reader* (pp. 333–343). Maden, MA: Blackwell Publishers.

Butalia, U. (2000). *The other side of silence: Voices from the partition of India*. Durham, NC: Duke University Press.

Chatterjee, P. (1993). *The nation and its fragments*. Princeton, NJ: Princeton University Press.

Chaudhry, L. N. (1992). *Birthday thoughts*. Unpublished poem.

Chaudhry, L. N. (1997). Researching my people, researching myself: Fragments of a reflexive tale. *International Journal of Qualitative Studies in Education, 10*(4), 441–453.

Chaudhry, L. N. (2004a). *Women and poverty: Salient findings from a gendered analysis of a quasi-anthropological study in rural Punjab and Sindh*. Islamabad, Pakistan: Sustainable Development Policy Institute.

Chaudhry, L. N. (2004b). Reconstituting selves in the Karachi conflict: Mohajir women survivors and structural violence. *Cultural Dynamics, 16*(2/3), 259–290.

Chaudhry, L. N. (2005). Salient contours of structural violence in the lives of rural women: From field-work in Sindh and Punjab. In SDPI Staff (Eds.), *Troubled times: Sustainable development and governance in the age of extremes* (pp. 460–482). Islamabad & Karachi, Pakistan: Sustainable Development Policy Institute & Sama Editorial and Publishing Services.

Clifford, J. (1988). *The predicament of culture*. Cambridge, MA: Harvard University Press.

Davidson, B. (1993). *The black man's burden: Africa and the curse of the nation-state*. New York: Three Rivers Press.

Davies, B. (1991). The concept of agency: A feminist poststructuralist analysis. *Social Analysis, 30*, 42–53.

DuPlessis, R. B. (1990). *The pink guitar: Writing as feminist practice*. New York: Routledge.

Galeano, E. (1989/1991). *The book of embraces* (C. Blefrage, Trans.). New York: W. W. Norton.

Grewal, J. S. (1998). *The Sikhs of the Punjab*. Cambridge, UK: Cambridge University Press.

Hall, S. (1990). Cultural identity and diaspora. In J. Rutherford (Ed.), *Identity, community, culture, difference* (pp. 222–237). London: Laurence and Waishart.

Hussain, A. (1990). The Karachi riots of December 1986: Crisis of state and civil society in Pakistan. In V. Das (Ed.), *Mirrors of violence: Communities, riots, and survivors in South Asia* (pp. 185–193). Oxford: Oxford University Press.

Holland, S. P. (2000). *Raising the dead: Readings of death and (black) subjectivity*. Durham, NC: Duke University Press.

Jacobs-Huey, L. (2002). The natives are gazing and talking back: Reviewing the problematics of positionality, voice, and accountability among 'native' anthropologists. *American Anthropologist, 104*(3), 791–804.

Jeganathan, P. (2000). On the anticipation of violence: Modernity and identity in Southern Sri Lanka. In A. Arce & N. Long (Eds.), *Anthropology, development, and modernities: Exploring discourses, counter-tendencies and violence* (pp. 112–126). London, UK: Routledge.

Joseph, S. (1999). Introduction. In S. Joseph (Ed.), *Intimate selving in Arab families: Gender, self, and identity* (pp. 1–17). Syracuse, NY: Syracuse University Press.

Joseph, S. (1994). Brother/sister relationships: Connectivity, love, and power in the reproduction of patriarchy in Lebanon. *American Ethnologist, 21*(1), 50–73.

Khan, S. (2006). *Zina, transnational feminism, and the moral regulation of Pakistani women*. Vancouver, Canada: UBC Press.

Khan, Y. (2007). *The great partition: The making of India and Pakistan*. New Haven, CT: Yale University Press.

Kleinman, A. (2000). The violences of everyday life: The multiple forms and dynamics of social violence. In V. Das, A. Kleinman, M. Ramphele, & P. Reynolds (Eds.), *Violence and subjectivity* (pp. 226–241). Berkeley: University of California Press.

Lather, P. (1991). *Getting smart: Feminist research and pedagogy with/in the postmodern*. New York: Routledge.

Lazreg, M. (2000). The triumphant discourse of global feminism: Should other women be known? In A. Amireh & L. S. Majaj (Eds.), *Going global: The transnational reception of Third World women writers* (pp. 29–38). New York: Garland Publishing.

Mamdani, M. (2004). *Good Muslim, bad Muslim: America, the cold war, and the roots of terror*. New York: Doubleday.

Narayan, K. (1993). How native is a 'native' anthropologist? *American Anthropologist, 95*(3), 671–686.

Patai, D. (1988). Constructing a self: A Brazilian life story. *Feminist studies, 14*(1), 143–166.

Punter, D. (2000). *Postcolonial imaginings: Fictions of a new world order*. Lanham, MD: Rowman & Littlefield Publishers.

Rhodes, J. (2005). *Radical feminism, writing and critical agency: From manifesto to modern*. Albany, NY: State University of New York Press.

Rosaldo, R. (1987). *Culture and truth: The remaking of social analysis*. Boston: Beacon Press.

Rummel, R. J. (1997). *Death by government*. Edison, NJ: Transaction Publishers.

Sandoval, C. (1991). US Third World feminism: The theory and method of oppositional consciousness in the postmodern world. *Genders*, 10, 1–24.

Scheper-Hughes, N. & Bourgois, P. (2004). Introduction: Making sense of violence. In N. Scheper-Hughes & P. Bourgois (Eds.), *Violence in war and peace: An anthology* (pp. 1–31). Malden, MA: Blackwell Publishing.

SDPI (2001). *Archive on women, conflict, and security*. Islamabad: Sustainable Development Policy Institute.

Smith, L. T. (1999). *Decolonizing methodologies: Research and indigenous peoples*. London, UK & Dunedin, NZ: Zed Books & University of Otago Press.

Trinh, T. M. (1989). *Woman native other: Writing postcoloniality and feminism*. Bloomington: Indiana University Press.

Uvin, P. (1998). *Aiding violence: The development enterprise in Rwanda*. West Hartford, CT: Kumarian Press.

World Bank (2002). *Pakistan qualitative poverty survey, 2001*. Washington D.C.: World Bank.

Zamindar, V. F.-Y. (2007). *The long partition and the making of modern South Asia: Refugees, boundaries, histories*. New York: Columbia University.

Chapter 9

'What am I doing when I speak of this present?'

Voice, power, and desire in truth-telling

Alecia Youngblood Jackson

The title of this chapter comes from a question asked by Michel Foucault (1990) in his 1984 lecture entitled, 'The Art of Telling the Truth,' in which he interprets Kant's text, 'What is Enlightenment?' What is important for Foucault is how Kant's text offers a different way of questioning the present. Kant's questioning considers (in metaphysical fashion) the meanings, origins, and truth of the present, but in doing so leads this line of thought somewhere else. The first part of Kant's questioning has to do with what the present 'is'; the second, which Foucault finds exemplary, has to do with how subjectivity is fashioned from the process of telling the truth. Foucault (1990, p. 89) suggests that a new question of modernity is, 'What am I doing when I speak of this present?' This new question is one that 'problematizes its own discursive contemporaneity'; it becomes an interrogation of the thinking subject as both 'element and actor' in belonging *in a certain and particular way* to the present, of speaking a *certain and particular* truth about the present (p. 88).

My contribution to this collection is focused on how the contradictory subject positions taken up by research participants shape what they do when they speak of their present, or tell truths. Rather than going after a meaning of voice, I follow Foucault in an attempt to suspend the serious yet unavoidable imperative to locate meaning. 'We are condemned to meaning,' Foucault wrote (cited in Dreyfus and Rabinow, 1982), yet rather than stabilizing meaning once and for all, I want to play at the edges of what is going on when truth-telling appears to happen. In doing so I emphasize the entanglement of truth, power, desire, and the subject/voice in certain acts of speaking of the present. This may, I hope, gesture toward 'research as provoking, not representing, knowledge' (Britzman and Pitt, 2003). What is inevitably contained in this chapter are my efforts to reveal those provocations and to experiment with the discursive and performative accomplishments of voice by accentuating not the multiplicity or plurality of one research participant's voice but its effects. To do such is to delay a description of meaning (of data, of voice) by moving toward the *effects of attempting to represent meaning using data, using voice.*

Certainly, truth-tellers construct many things as they represent their selves to others (and to themselves). And, this truth-telling is often plentiful with much that confuses researchers and that does not make 'easy sense' (see Mazzei, Chapter 3, this book). However, to consider the function and effects of voice does not take it at face value but as a not-so-innocent product of 'giving an account of oneself' (Butler, 2005). To return to Foucault, these effects surface when we ask, 'What are research participants doing when they speak of their present?'

The interview

To examine the effects of truth-telling – or how desire, power, and voice coalesce to produce what might be said about the present – I use one interview, its transcript, and the subsequent member check and 'response data' (St.Pierre, 1999) of a woman, Amelia, narrating her present. Amelia's present consisted of her speaking (and subsequently writing) about staying in her place – about living out her adult life in her childhood hometown. Amelia and I had grown up together since the age of four, and we parted after high school graduation when I went to college and she remained in our hometown, married, raised a family, and worked as a secretary in our former elementary and high schools and then in the same school system's central office (a job that she still has today). The interview lasted about two hours, was conducted in her home, and I provided her with a transcription of our conversation within one week of the interview.

The interview with Amelia provides a potent site for examining what might be happening in the risky work of truth-telling. Amelia's spoken and written voice emerged as unstable and contradictory, exposing how power, subjectivity, and desire shaped the way she spoke of her present. The instability and contradictions in narrating the present occurred when Amelia's husband came home from work and began to participate in our interview, and when Amelia read our interview transcript and revised her data to the point of silencing (by actually erasing and marking out) many of her more negative remarks about her hometown. She requested that much of her criticism be omitted or changed and replaced her first words with more favorable ones. I use three specific examples from the interview data to illustrate these shaky moments of truth-telling.[1]

The first shift was made obvious as Amelia commented on the new Baptist preacher in her church; her husband came home from work and joined us in the kitchen as Amelia spoke, and she changed her characterization of the new preacher upon the arrival of her husband. Second, Amelia's transcript contained a disapproval of undesirable places in the town that she later revised to cast these places from a more positive stance. Third, Amelia omitted other disparaging remarks of leadership and change in her hometown to produce a more sanitized perception of place. 'What was Amelia doing?' This is not a question of intention but of how the subject is positioned and positions herself *as* she speaks about her present, about truths that she lives by. Amelia's truth-telling incited conflicting ways of thinking about her present, of situating and representing herself *in a particular way* within her present.

Some researchers might regard Amelia's interview as two versions of a truth. To do so, however, would be to put Amelia's voice in opposition to itself; such oppositional thinking inevitably entails a choice, a privileging of one over the other. For example, two versions might also require me to select one that I deemed more than something else: be it more desirous or more critically political. Furthermore, considering the data as two versions by virtue of one spoken voice and one written voice might lead to the decidability of one version as tied to a more privileged sign system; therefore, one is more true than the other. As Socrates, Plato, Aristotle, St. Paul, Rousseau, Hegel, Husserl, and Saussure exalted speech as the living present, the same oppositional trap is unavoidable in pitting the spoken voice against the written voice. To wiggle outside this trap, I detour momentarily to Derrida.

Speech is writing is speech; or, it's *all* voice

AMELIA: There are several places in Garner that I would change, but that's like it is anywhere. There are some places that are run down and have been let go, but the city has done a lot of restoration to the houses, and they look beautiful now. They've been working real hard on all those houses.

The above excerpt is Amelia's revised data, written on the transcript by her and sent back to me. She had crossed out her previous spoken voice and wanted her written voice to be used as her description of the 'bad places' in town. Amelia's unrevised data was less tolerant and therefore more bitterly critical of the abject areas of Garner. Together, both data contain Amelia's range of perspective and emotion about the pockets of drug communities, the numerous rental properties, and the scattered areas of low-income and public housing in Garner.

I preceded this section by mentioning the traditional epistemological approach to two opposing truths – privileging the spoken over the written. Of course, relying on the spoken in Amelia's case (because she subsequently refused her speech) conjures up ethical concerns for honoring the interests of the subject. But there is another problem here: one of even assuming that either data is fully true, which might seduce researchers into believing that both versions together offer a whole, inclusive, conscious truth. Working in a post-qualitative frame, the question of 'which data is true/full/complete' and can therefore exist as a foundation for meaning is no longer relevant. Derrida helps us to work through this dilemma of opposition through the *trace*.

Derrida is suspicious of Western metaphysics's obsession with consciousness because of what gets claimed as being fully present in language. For one, Derrida doubts that consciousness can be present to itself through language. He believes that privileging consciousness is privileging presence, especially if it is related to speech – the 'ether of metaphysics' (1968/1982, p. 16). If speech is the direct line to one's thinking, then writing interrupts that purity. If speech is consciousness and presence, then writing is death and absence. Writing cuts off speech, kills it, and therefore kills presence, consciousness, and self. Derrida (1967/1997) puts it forcefully:

What writing itself, in its nonphonetic moment, betrays, is life. It menaces at once the breath, the spirit, and history as the spirit's relationship with itself.
It is their end, their finitude, their paralysis. (p. 25)

Useless and dangerous, writing escapes control and robs speakers of their being. It replaces a living exchange of ideas with a vast network of circulated, reproduced, cited material that is vulnerable to abuse. Thoughts and language ought to be controlled by the conscious and present speaker, but writing precariously spins language out of control – as well as subjects.

In his critique of speech, Derrida does not reverse the binary to privilege writing. Derrida deconstructs presence and origin in writing to claim that these can also be the failures of speech. Utterances – either written or spoken – do not have presence or origin; they have both a partial presence and a partial absence. Under Derrida's deconstructive scrutiny, the speech/writing binary collapses into itself, and through what he calls 'arche-writing' (1967/1997, p. 70), he shows that speech is writing is speech.

Derrida confronts writing to expose that there is no inherent opposition between speech and writing in their 'narrow' definitions. 'Narrow' speech and writing are linear in that they attempt to unify experience; it is precisely this problem of narrowing voice, in both speech and writing, that qualitative researchers encounter. The work of narrowing refers to an 'originary presence' and an 'absolute past' of a lived experience (1967/1997, p. 66) – what we as qualitative researchers want as we collect the voices of others. We want the lived experience to be present to us through voice and then represented to others in how we write about those voices. However, Derrida's concept of the *trace* renders this type of writing an impossible task, 'since past has always signified present–past; the absolute past that is retained in the trace no longer rigorously merits the name "past" ' (p. 66). In other words, our memories and our 'present' significations always contain traces of what has happened before and since, belying consciousness. Amelia cannot speak of her present without inciting what had to be absent (or silenced) to make possible truth-telling about the present.[2]

Voice is not pure; voice cannot be adequately oppositional. 'Nothing is anywhere ever simply present or absent' (Derrida, 1972/1981, p. 26), and this point brings up the seduction of relying on one source of data as being more true – or more present – than another. Of wanting to 'find' foundational meaning in the voices of others. Of depending on the consciousness of truth-tellers to be aware of their present – as if that can be accomplished in either speech or writing (or voice). The real – the past, the present – can never be fully represented because of the trace, teaching us the futility of origins, of points of departure, of 'the full continuity of speech' (Derrida, 1967/1997, p. 70). The trace exposes the way meaning moves and plays along with the truth-teller's subjectivity. To the point, Amelia did not begin at the beginning, or even with the real fully present to her conscious; nor did she represent a stable self to me (or, I would argue, to herself).

If I follow Derrida to think about *all* of Amelia's data as voice, then I escape becoming ensnared in oppositional thinking and privileging spoken data over written data, or vice versa. Rather than separating and containing Amelia's voice – or simply pluralizing it or quantifying it as multiplicitous – I want to cast *none* of her voice as representing any stable kind of truth. Furthermore, the trace further muddies what is happening in Amelia's truth-telling as she voices her present. If the present is always already contaminated by absence, then absence will always haunt truth-telling. This is not a matter of making absence present – of pursuing absence. The point is that there is nothing really *there* for Amelia to retrieve. The telling *itself* produces truth and constitutes Amelia. Rather than Amelia existing outside of language with plans to tell a truth(s), her intentions and meanings are constituted during language as a performative act and are as contingent as herself. Neither speech nor writing nor Amelia can be fully expressive or representational – which distracts from metaphysical meanings and grounding, 'real' truths. Such a diversion draws attention, instead, to what Amelia is doing while inhabiting the trace, and how truths are constituted in, rather than outside, the trace.

Now that I have somewhat settled the dilemma of opposition and avoided narrowly defining what is voice, I turn again to consider what a voicing subject does when speaking of her present. In a 1983 interview, Foucault said,

> I wish to know how the reflexivity of the subject and the discourse of truth are linked – How can the subject tell the truth about itself? . . . If I tell the truth about myself, as I am now doing, it is in part across a number of power relations which are exerted over me and which I exert over others.
>
> (1990, pp. 38–39)

Specifically, I explore how a voicing subject is also a desiring subject as she grapples with truth-telling within relations of power. As Foucault (1976/1990) wrote, 'Where there is desire, the power relation is already present: an illusion, then . . . to go questing after a desire that is beyond the reach of power' (p. 82). In the following sections, I continue to engage Foucault's question of 'what am I doing when I speak of this present?' by attempting to understand how desire and power merge to provide conditions for the production of truth and subjectivity.

Truth and power

AMELIA: We went from Tommy to Steven. I'm not saying that Tommy is bad and Steven is great, but we went from one extreme to another. Tommy was very outgoing and very involved. His kids went to Garner and he was always at things. Steven is the complete opposite. His children are home-schooled, and he doesn't go to school events where people from the church would be. He's not visible at all. Outside the church, he's not visible. Our kids need that, especially in the youth department . . .

[Will, Amelia's husband and deacon at the church, enters the kitchen]

AMELIA (CONTINUES): Our new preacher Steven is a very Godly man. He's very close with God. He is a fine addition to our community. [Amelia pauses and looks at the interview guide] Do you want me to talk about what we do *after* church now?

Amelia's voiced data, bound to power, is an effect of her struggle to tell truth(s). The above excerpt from our interview is another example of unruly meaning that offers up Amelia's perspectives on the same present: her church life. I follow Foucault in wanting to know more about what *governs* Amelia's statements. What produces one truth, and what produces another? Again, I want to avoid declaring these truths as simply oppositional and incompatible but all as emerging from 'relations of power, not relations of meaning' (Foucault, 1990, p. 114).

It is not that Will had 'power over' Amelia. To think about how power works in this situation, I use Foucault's notion of power relations that are productive, forming a chain that relies on relations to advance, multiply, and branch out deeply into social networks. Foucault was very clear in his assertion that power relations exist only when the field of possibilities is open, and people may react to each other in various ways; that is, power becomes possible through the 'moving substrate' of unequal, yet unstable, local relations (Foucault, 2000). Power relations are specific and local to subjects who are in mutual relations with one another. Power, then, 'is everywhere; not because it embraces everything, but because it comes from everywhere'; it is not a consolidating and invincible unity or structure but a repetitious and self-producing effect of mobile, strategic practices and relations within particular social networks (Foucault, 1976/1978, p. 93).

With this view of power, I can interpret how, in the interview excerpt above, power relations shifted in response to contextual demands within a discursive field. If truth is 'produced by multiple forms of constraint' (Foucault, 1980, p. 131), then Amelia's truth is responsive to those constraints. The constraint, rather than simply being her husband as one person who 'holds' power, is in my view the intersection of the discursive fields of patriarchy and southern Baptist religion, which (as discourses) regulate certain acceptable rules and values that sanction what can be said, and what cannot be said, about the institution of the church. As Bové (1990) wrote, discourse creates specific ways of being and acting in the world, and it shapes institutions (such as churches) 'in which we largely make ourselves' (p. 58).

Amelia's church/religion is one of the discursive structures in which she constructs her subjectivity; many times in her interview, she returned to the topic of the importance of her church to her personal life and to her community's ethos. I am not southern Baptist and I am not a member of her church, so our power relation was not inevitably bound to the discursive rules of 'being' good southern Baptist women in conversation about religion. A crack, a slight opening enabled Amelia to produce a truth, to inhabit a structure in a different way. However, as power 'never ceases its interrogation, its inquisition, its registration of truth' (Foucault, 1980, p. 93), Amelia was positioned/subjected in relation with Will who did not *possess* power but who would only be able to *recognize* certain truths about a discourse in which they were both intimately embedded. This was one of many instances in which a desiring voice was produced by the discursive constraints in our interview. I elaborate this observation in the next section.

A stopping point: On desire

AMELIA: We've been very fortunate here in Garner to have Pete as our city commissioner for as long as we have. He's been in office since 1975! He's really
given us a sense of tradition that we need. With some new people moving into
the community, we need to keep that we are a small, close-knit community
where everyone is concerned about other people and their needs.

The above excerpt is the last example from Amelia's data that I will use to muse
about voice, power, and desire in truth-telling. Again, Amelia edited the above data
after she read the transcript; she requested to delete specific sentences that were
embedded within the paragraph. Without those sentences, the data appear to be a
positive, supportive description of leadership in the town as well as of the town's
'identity,' as Amelia perceived it. However, the deleted data troubled some of what
is visible here; she had been highly disapproving of Pete's long tenure as a city
commissioner, and she had been resentful of newcomers to the community. Her
purposeful deletions continue to beg the question, 'What is Amelia doing when
she speaks of her present?' I end this chapter by considering the force of desire
in truth-telling within relations of power to gesture toward what Amelia might be
doing.

Judith Butler (2004) provides some direction in the link between desire and
power; she writes,

> The Hegelian tradition links desire with recognition, claiming that desire
> is always a desire for recognition and that it is only through the experi-
> ence of recognition that any of us becomes constituted as socially viable
> beings. (p. 2)

Butler goes on to elaborate this idea, arguing that desire for recognition is in actuality a site of *power* where who gets to be recognized, and by whom, is governed
by social norms. Furthermore, Butler maintains, the choice to be recognized (or
not) within the constraints of normativity is a condition of agency in the doing,
and undoing, of subjectivity. Desiring subjects, wanting recognizability, always
exist in relations of power.

It may not have been necessary for me to recognize Amelia as an acceptable
version of a southern Baptist woman, the wife of a deacon, a lifelong community member who honors and practices the discursive values of her hometown.
That is, Amelia's truth-telling and subjectivity was bound to much more than her
relationship with me. As Deleuze and Guattari (1972/1983) maintained, 'Social
production is purely and simply desiring-production itself under determinate conditions' (p. 29). They go on to explain, similar to Butler, that desiring-production
is sometimes a political option, implying a sense of agency. Amelia's desire for
recognizability – produced within social relations of power – enabled her to position herself among various subject positions as she spoke about her present. Such
a nomadism allows Amelia to 'wander away from [herself], allowing something

else to be produced' (Goodchild, 1996, p. 3). This new production of herself and her truths, in their many forms, surfaced as she spoke of her present.

I remain with Deleuze and Guattari here because they provide an immanent account of desire, one that helps me to think about what Amelia attempted to do as she voiced her present. Deleuze and Guattari reject a psychoanalytic, transcendent desire that seeks a lack that is 'out there' to be gotten. Their combined thought is that psychoanalytic desire, caught in a field of transcendency, is characterized by two failures: (1) the delusion and illusion of pleasure as its final aim and (2) the unattainable lack or imaginary object that animates desire. Each of these failures refers to an exterior agency that promises desire to be either hollowed out or filled up, suggesting finality and completion.

A line of flight that irrupts from within is Deleuze's desire – 'not escaping from oneself, but allowing *something* to escape, like bursting a pipe' (Deleuze, 1990, p. 19). I do not see Amelia escaping from herself, via truth-telling, into some sort of fantasy or unattainable/outside self. Instead, as Amelia spoke of her present, desire brought into play '*all* [her] unconscious investments' (Deleuze, 1990, p. 20) – those that were social, cultural, historical, political, psychological, and so on, not simply those that were outside her histories. If desire connects to all manner of 'becomings' (Deleuze and Guattari, 1980/1987, p. 21), then desire produced certain ways for Amelia to 'become' in her present, to voice certain truths. Desire, as immanent, was embedded in her truth-telling to express a politics of desire and alternative practices of subjectivity: 'the production of desire is inseparable from the creation of new modes of social existence' (Goodchild, 1996, p. 41). Desire provided access for Amelia to become recognizable in all sorts of ways – for her to create existences for herself (through voice) that were at once constrained and enabled by discourse. A desiring voice, then too, is a discursive voice.

Deleuze and Guattari (1980/1987) wrote, 'It is always by rhizome that desire moves and produces' (p. 14). Now, as they warn, it's not easy to see things from the middle. Desire is 'never separable from complex assemblages . . . and interactions' (1980/1987, p. 215), and this intricacy is what makes everything look different from the middle. Mapping desire to see what it produces is what Deleuze and Guattari would have me do, and as I do that from the middle, I see how a desiring voice erupted within Amelia's social, cultural, and historical planes. All of Amelia's contexts in which she was immersed connected during the interview to produce how she spoke of her present. Her desire was a product of being caught up in relations: her relationship with me, her relationship with her husband, her position in the community and at work, her lifetime connection to her hometown, her subjectivities as a mother, sister, daughter, cousin, niece. All of these social relations, cultural meanings, and histories assembled together to create truths by a desiring voice, a discursive voice, a performative voice.

Last words

I began this chapter by posing a Foucauldian question to some data: 'What is Amelia doing when she speaks of her present?' I endeavored to avoid altogether, for this chapter anyway, the dilemma of determining what 'speaking' is to claim that voice is inclusive of all attempts to tell the truth. I wanted to be more concerned about what voice 'does' than what it 'is.'

What voice does – or its function, its effect – is neither simple nor conclusive. When Amelia spoke of her present, she did not innocently enact a narrative voice. As Butler (2005) wrote, 'In speaking the 'I,' I undergo something of what cannot be captured or assimilated by the 'I,' since I always arrive too late to myself' (p. 79). If we arrive too late to tell the truth(s) about ourselves – or arrive too late to capture a holistic, authentic narrative that tells it all – then there are other things happening in the moment of truth-telling. It is this 'other' that I have tried to trace – not to account for but to show its constitution and its effects.

An effect was a desiring voice that was not outside herself but immanent to, and a product of, relations. An effect was a discursive voice that was constrained and enabled by regulating rules and beliefs that arrange the possibilities of truth-telling. An effect was a performative voice, a doing that positions and elaborates the 'I' *through* the telling and that becomes a failure in itself because of the traces of the unaccountable in 'giving an account of oneself' (Butler, 2005). Voice as at once desiring, discursive, and performative sidesteps the simplicity of representing a multiplicity of voices and instead hones in on analyzing dimensions and textures of voice – especially the fragility and failure of voice to provide coherence, comfort, and presence.

While I have explored what Amelia does when she speaks of her present to consider how desire, power, and truth position her to belong to her present, I end with a fragment of a W. S. Graham (1979) poem that turns around Foucault's question and wonders what voice might do to us:

> *What is the language using us for?*
> *I don't know. Have the words ever*
> *Made anything of you, near a kind*
> *Of truth you thought you were? Me*
> *Neither.*

Notes

1 For ethical reasons, I do not re-produce Amelia's spoken (i.e., unrevised) data, except for her comments on the preacher. However, I do have her permission to describe her spoken data in broad strokes, for the purposes of illustration and argument in this chapter.
2 For a rigorous problematizing of silence in qualitative research, see Mazzei (2007).

References

Bové, P. A. (1990). Discourse. In: F. Lentricchia (Ed.) *Critical Terms for Literary Study*. Chicago: University of Chicago Press.

Britzman, D. and Pitt, A. (2003). Speculations on qualities of difficult knowledge in teaching and learning. *The International Journal of Qualitative Studies in Education*, *16* (6), 769.

Butler, J. (2004). *Undoing Gender*. New York: Routledge.

Butler, J. (2005). *Giving an Account of Oneself*. New York: Fordham University Press.

Deleuze, G. (1990). *Negotiations*. New York: Columbia University Press.

Deleuze, G. and Guattari, F. (1983). *Anti-Oedipus: Capitalism and Schizophrenia* (R. Hurley, M. Seem, and H. Lane, Trans.). Minneapolis: University of Minnesota Press (Original work published 1972).

Deleuze, G. and Guattari, F. (1987). *A Thousand Plateaus: Capitalism and Schizophrenia* (B. Massumi, Trans.). Minneapolis: University of Minnesota Press (Original work published 1980).

Derrida, J. (1981). *Positions* (A. Bass, Trans.). Chicago: University of Chicago Press (Original work published 1972).

Derrida, J. (1982). Différance. *Margins of Philosophy* (pp. 1–27) (A. Bass, Trans.). Chicago: University of Chicago Press (Original work published 1968).

Derrida, J. (1997). *Of Grammatology* (G. C. Spivak, Trans.). Baltimore, MD: The Johns Hopkins University Press (Original work published 1967).

Dreyfus, H. L. and Rabinow, P. (1982). *Michel Foucault: Beyond Structuralism and Hermeneutics* (2nd Edn). Chicago: University of Chicago Press.

Foucault, M. (1978). *The History of Sexuality. Volume 1: An Introduction* (R. Hurley, Trans.). New York: Vintage Books (Original work published 1976).

Foucault, M. (1980). *Power/Knowledge: Selected Interviews and Other Writings: 1972–1977* (L. Marshall, C. Gordon, J. Mepham, and K. Soper, Trans.). New York: Pantheon Books.

Foucault, M. (1990). *Politics, Philosophy, Culture: Interviews and Other Writings of Michel Foucault, 1977–1984* (A. Sheridan, Trans.). New York: Routledge.

Foucault, M. (2000). *Power. Volume III, Essential Works of Foucault 1954–1984* (P. Rabinow, Ed., R. Hurley et al., Trans.). New York: The New Press.

Goodchild, P. (1996). *Deleuze and Guattari: An Introduction to the Politics of Desire*. Thousand Oaks, CA: Sage Publications.

Graham, W. S. (1979). 'What is language using us for?'. *Collected Poems 1942–1977* (pp. 195–196). London: Faber and Faber.

Mazzei, L. A. (2007). *Inhabited Silence in Qualitative Research: Putting Poststructural Theory to Work*. New York: Peter Lang.

St.Pierre, E. A. (1999). The work of response in ethnography. *Journal of Contemporary Ethnography* 28(3), 266–287.

Chapter 10

Researching and representing teacher voice(s)

A reader response approach

Becky M. Atkinson and Jerry Rosiek

Introduction

The development of the field of teacher knowledge research was inspired and guided by a respect for teacher voice. Freema Elbaz (1991), an early scholar of teacher voice, commented, 'The notion of voice has been central to the development of research on teachers' knowledge and thinking' (p. 10). In the 1980s a consensus emerged in the field of teacher education that the exclusively positivist, process-product approach to research on teaching failed to take into account many important aspects of teaching practice. In the interest of finding teaching techniques whose effectiveness could be demonstrated across large populations of students and teachers, process-product research, also known as effective teaching research, had bracketed out the influences of individual classroom contexts in its inquiries (Gage, 1972; Good & Brophy, 1986; Rowe, 1974). Consequently, its prescriptions ignored the influence of those local contexts and the importance of teachers' reflection and adjustment to that context. Teachers' thinking about how to adjust and take advantage of the peculiar intersections of their subject matter content, students' lives and cultures, and their own individual talents and interests was devalued if not entirely erased.

The current emphasis on evidence-based decision making and 'scientifically based' research practices harkens back to effective teaching research and threatens to further marginalize teacher voice, as noted by Marilyn Cochran-Smith and Susan Lytle: 'Even though NCLB[1] rhetoric ostensibly elevates teachers and makes them the standard-bearers for high expectations for students, the discourse of teacher deficits, fueled by increased monitoring and surveillance of daily practice, has never been more prevalent' (2006, p. 680). Effective teaching research and the teacher education curriculum based on it ignores the possibility of knowledge being generated by teachers' inquiries and experiences into their own practical experience. The idea that the effective teaching movement attempts to create 'teacher proof' curriculum means that teachers are treated as piece workers, as opposed to professional decision makers. The consciousness and creative intelligence of teachers are removed from the pedagogical process. In our view, and those of us

in the teacher knowledge research tradition, this is a problem. It essentially elim-
inates teachers' lived experience as a possible source of knowledge without just
cause.

In response to these excesses, a community of scholars has forwarded a naturalistic conception of research on teaching in which, as Andy Hargreaves explained,
'The concern for *voice* has come to have special relevance . . . in how research
knowledge about teachers and their work is generated' (1996, p. 12). Instead
of looking for effective teaching behaviors that can be replicated and mandated
without regard for educational context, teacher knowledge researchers study the
ways teachers actually make professional judgments about representing the particulars of their subject matter while attending to the influence of school and
local culture, the relevance of student characteristics, pedagogical resources in
a teacher's professional or personal background, and ethical and political considerations (Rosiek & Atkinson, 2005). These multifaceted programs of research
indicate a move away from understanding teachers as expert technicians and well-
trained functionaries and toward an understanding of teaching as intellectually
complex work, requiring both foundational knowledge and the exercise of professional judgment.[2] Teacher knowledge researchers have objected to the way
the current emphasis on scientistic research has led to a loss of teacher voice in
educational decision making, despite the fact that the term 'voice' is not used
widely in this research field (though *Harvard Educational Review* uses it in their
series, 'Voices in Schools'). The knowledge of practice and experiences shaping
the interpretive context that only teachers possess are not counted as valuable or
informative in the current climate of reform. To counter this, teacher knowledge
researchers have argued for the need to bring teacher reflection, teacher first-hand
experience, teacher wisdom, and therefore teacher voice into the research conversation. The argument is primarily epistemic because these arguments can be
made more precisely. Research on teachers' processes of reflection and judgment
attends to teacher voice as a compelling point for developing epistemological
and methodological frameworks for teacher knowledge research. Teachers know
something important that cannot be discovered using effective teaching research
methods.

In the context of this concern, teacher voice takes on many meanings. Talking
about 'voice' in the singular is one of many rhetorical strategies used to resist
the hegemony of effective teaching research. Asserting the importance of teacher
voice in research about teaching champions more naturalistic alternatives to traditional process-product research, and makes it possible to demand a place in the
research process for collaboration with teachers and for teacher scholarship. This
use references the particular and collective positions and roles in which teachers
are situated and within which their knowledge of practice is both discursively and
experientially produced. But the valorizing of teacher voice also, as we will see,
sustains inadequate and naïve assumptions about the characteristics of teaching
that shape teacher voice. One of the consequences of those inadequate assumptions
is that there is a generic quality to what teachers know and how they talk about

their knowledge of practice, reinforced by the use of the singular 'teacher voice,' and that teachers agree on what that 'voice' says. We believe that the approach discussed in this chapter, reader response theory, makes it clear that teachers do not always agree, and that they speak in individualized and dissonant voices that have been shaped by immense variations in the contexts in which they teach. We will make use of the plural 'teacher voice(s)' to signify the highly contingent and localized construction of individual teacher's knowledge of practice that inflects their voices with unique interpretations forged in individual experiences that are at the same time mediated through social, cultural and professional discourses. So, our use of the singular 'voice' refers to the collective political entity and the plural 'voice(s)' refers to the polyvocal and dissonant meanings individual teachers make of their work.

Limitations to voice in teacher knowledge narratives

Teacher knowledge scholars' commitment to teacher voice compels them to grapple with the challenge of finding ways to listen to and represent teacher voice(s) in ways that both convey teacher thinking as it is lived and that makes this thinking available for critique and discussion. Engagement with these challenges by the various programs of teacher knowledge research as well as the desire to resist the hegemony of effective teaching research has led to debates about 'authentic' sources of teacher knowledge and possible distortions or silencing of teacher voice(s) in written representations (Clandinin & Connelly, 1995, 1996, 2000; Cochran-Smith & Lytle, 1993; Miller, 1990). In an effort to provide the means for teachers to be heard in the educational research community, some scholars have advocated for increased use of narrative representations by educational researchers (Barone, 2001a, 2001b, 2007; Clandinin & Connelly, 1995, 2000; Shulman & Mesa-Baines, 1993; Shulman, Lotan & Whitcomb, 1998). The argument is (a) that teachers think more through narratives than through nomothetic or paradigmatic modes of thinking; and relatedly, (b) that teachers can process information presented in narrative form more readily (Bruner, 1992; Clandinin, 2006; Clandinin & Connelley, 1995, 2000; Cochran-Smith & Lytle, 1993). Instead of an exclusive focus on the prescribed practices and principles based on experimental educational research, teacher knowledge scholars argue for a parallel tradition of research that documents the wisdom emerging from teachers' practice, wisdom that could be best expressed in narrative form. Narratives, it is argued, capture teacher voices and teacher knowledge better.

This is certainly commendable. However, respect for teacher knowledge and what teachers have to say about their work, of course, does not mean freedom from criticism. There are limitations to the reliance on using narrative as a way to privilege teacher voice and represent teacher knowledge in resistance to the hegemony of overly scientistic approaches to educational scholarship (e.g., the effective teaching research movement). First of all, at the level of representation, narrative forms (re)produce lived experience and so are not free of ideologically and semiotically mediated meanings; they are not pure reflections of experiences. This problematizes claims for greater authenticity attached to narrative as better vehicles for teacher voice. Second, the fact that these narratives are published in scholarly journals and/or books means that they cannot be considered separate from the interests and politics of the academic context in which they are published. How authentic are teacher voice(s) in narratives that come with such layers of packaging? Third, narratives are a re-signification of lived experiences and do not capture episodes like the shutter of a camera. Narrative is always already a re-telling, and as such functions as a meaning-making activity in itself. Because of that quality, narrative is dynamic and changeable.

At the epistemic level, the crippling limitation to the reliance on narrative and voice as strategies to counter the silencing effect of traditional research literature is that in an effort to defend a place for teacher voice(s), an oversimplified, essentialized, and even romanticized conception of teacher thinking might be forwarded. The interest in gaining political leverage for the inclusion of teachers' voice(s) may squelch rigorous questions about the sources for and singularity of teacher voice. Teachers may think in ways that cannot be 'voiced,' as conceptualizations of practical knowledge have suggested (Fenstermacher, 1994; Shulman, 1987, 2001). Ideological and discursive limits on teachers' ability to reflect can be ignored or suppressed in first-person teacher narratives. This is unfortunate for two reasons: (1) it fails to provide an account of the richness, drama, and difficulty (even failure) of teachers' reflections, and consequently this kind of teacher knowledge research often ends up producing representations of teachers' thinking that feels moralistic and preachy; and (2) it directs attention to individual teacher thought and away from the need to create and sustain teacher communities that can support critical reflection on the many assumptions that guide teaching practice.

Furthermore, there are epistemological limits to the regulative ideal that teacher narratives portray teachers' thinking as it actually happens or happened; that is, the meanings of the narratives are not completely controlled by the authors. Listening to teacher voice(s) or reading their narratives of practice turns out not to be a straightforward proposition. First, when listening to teacher voice(s) with an eye on the audience for those voices, whether other teachers in the hall or a grade level meeting, in professional organization conferences, in personal journal entries, in case studies written for other teachers' analysis, or Back to School Night, the context and medium for the expression of teacher voice constrain and enable what teachers can say about their teaching. In other words, the contexts in which teacher voice(s) are expressed act as discursive filters on their voices. Secondly, when the audience for these expressions is other teachers, meaning is interpreted through a variety of discursive lenses that listeners or readers bring with them. This array of interpretive frameworks problematizes the conception that there is an 'authentic voice' (Cochran-Smith & Lytle, 1993) for teachers and their experience, and challenges any naïve conception that authentic teacher voice(s) can be 'liberated' from the shadow of more formal academic research on education. Together, these concerns highlight the need for an approach to teacher knowledge research that treats all knowledge production both in the form of teacher narrative, as well as considerations of teacher voice, as socially mediated and historically and culturally contingent.

This chapter explores the utility of reader response theory as a tonic for the limitations of teacher narrative representations and teacher voice(s) in illuminating the fullness and richness not only of what teachers know, but also how they make meaning in their work. What has been missing from the conversations about teacher narratives is attention to the practitioner/consumer of these research texts who is reading about her field of practice. The teachers who read these narratives of practice are not passive recipients of messages from their authors. When teachers read teacher narratives of practice, their own knowledge produced in practice and the voice developed in that practice shape how the narratives are received and appropriated by the teachers. When teachers talk about these narratives, what they say is mediated through personal and professional experiences and discursive influences. The voice(s) produced in the reading and responding to the narratives are both emergent from and revelatory of knowledge that is multi-dimensional, socially mediated and historically contingent. The discrepancies between authors' portrayals of teaching in narratives and how teachers talk about those narratives offer rich insight and challenge to a research field advocating that we listen to the voice(s) of teachers.

We do this by using reader response theory to analyze how teachers read and talk about their interpretations of teacher narratives of practice. Teachers' varied reception and appropriation of teacher knowledge narratives demonstrate that readers' attention is editorial. The fact that teacher knowledge research narratives cannot be counted on to directly communicate messages into the mind of the readers of that research does not, we will argue, undermine the value of this research. To the contrary, studying teachers' responses to these narratives provides another way to listen to teacher voice(s) in this research. If teachers' conversations about research narratives are viewed with the same respect as the experiences of the teachers portrayed in those narratives, then these responses can be seen to be insightful and informative about the professional, social, and historical discourses shaping the communal production of teachers' knowledge. Teacher voice(s) generated from their engagement with teachers' narratives becomes a research tool that not only points to how interpretive resources foreclose some of their critical abilities and interests; it also illuminates how teacher narratives elicit unintended meanings from the teachers who read and talk about them. These benefits broaden the scope and responsibility of teacher knowledge research to include a necessary examination of the interpretive strategies teachers bring to research narratives and those shaping the narratives themselves, with implications for teacher education as well as narrative research.

We will begin our argument with an overview of contemporary reader response theory. We will articulate that theory with contemporary teacher knowledge scholarship. That will be followed with examples of how teachers read and talk about teacher knowledge narratives. Using these examples, we make the case that the engagement of teachers' critiques of narratives about teaching are bound to and bound by their own historical, social, and professional communities. These inevitable differences of interpretations that are shaped by competing professional and social discourses are discussed as evidence of the polyvocal, as opposed to monovocal, nature of teachers' voice(s). A polyvocal conception of teacher voice(s), we argue, recommends a variety of narrative genres, styles, and topics as means to offer more nuanced representations of teachers' work. This view of teacher voice(s) and teacher knowledge also indicates a need for more deliberate efforts to prepare teachers as critical readers and thinkers in communities of inquiry in both preservice and in-service teacher education.

Reader response theory: Meaning as transaction

Reader response theory refers to theories of literature, literary criticism, and reading that share a common emphasis on the readers' participation in creating meaning for a text. These theories emerged in response to more formalistic approaches to studying and teaching reading and literature that focused on the authority of the text as the determiner of its meaning. Disenchantment with the formalism and autocracy of the text pushed by the hegemony of the New Criticism (Empson, 1930; Brooks, 1947; Ransom, 1941; Richards, 1929) led to the exploration of critical and analytical approaches that were more oriented to the reader's reception of and response to the text (Tompkins, 1980). New Critics located the meaning of the text in the text as an independent autonomous object and the reader's role as an 'archeological' task of excavation and discovery (Iser, 1978). French poststructuralist work in literary criticism by Jacques Derrida (1974) and Roland Barthes (1975) challenged the archaeological relationship of the reader to the text, asserting the instability of the text and the unavailability of stable meanings in literary or cultural structures. They offered that the meaning of a text is not to be 'found' or excavated in the words or the form, but instead emerges during the reading of the text as the reader interacts with the words, echoing educator Louise Rosenblatt's theory proposed over forty years earlier.[3] In sum, meaning does not stem from the capacity of language to create, stabilize, or express it, but from the abilities and resources of the reader to co-construct it.

Within this context, Wolfgang Iser proposed a theory of literature and criticism he named 'Aesthetic Response' (1974, 1978), later re-named reader response theory in the writing of Stanley Fish (1980). Iser emphasized the individual reader's experience with the text as contributing to the construction of its meaning. He suggested that the act of reading evokes an aesthetic response as the reader draws on her interpretive resources to engage the text. The character of the interpretive resources – cultural, academic, historical, phonemic, linguistic, personal and/or experiential – and the degree to which the reader accesses them depends on the qualities and features of the text. Iser devoted much of his writing to exploring the processes and components that comprise a reader's response to a text as she engages with a text to produce what he described as a 'virtual text' (1978).

More currently, Tom Barone extends reader response theory to educational research. Two of his particular works (Barone, 2001a and 2001b) offer illustrations and explanation of how reader response theory can be applied to the production and analysis of representations of educational research and the goals and purposes of such inquiry. The following sections will offer a more detailed overview of the components of reader response theory as suggested in the individual work of Iser, Fish, and Barone, and their application to the project of this chapter.

Indeterminacy of the text

Iser, Fish, and Barone agree that the most important element of a text that shapes the reader's response is the 'indeterminacy of the text.' The indeterminacy of the text refers to the amount of interpretive space generated by the choices of the writer relative to topic, genre, word choice, imagery, allusions, linguistic structures, tone and sense of audience. Traditional research reports, newspaper articles, travel guides, how-to manuals (generally non-fiction texts) are written with more determinacy in the text. These texts, in general, are didactic, concrete, procedural, and generally can be described as monovocal, providing the writer's or researcher's conclusions and convergent meanings to readers who are expected to use conventional and compliant interpretation in appropriating responses to them.

On the other hand, other texts offer more ambiguous language, leave gaps or silences in explanations or arguments, and rely on allusions, inference, and/or imagery, requiring more effort on the part of the reader to make sense of what the writer is communicating. Many of these texts offer multiple and sometimes conflicting perspectives on an experience and are polyvocal in presenting an array of voices on a topic or experience, or create or evoke spaces for many voices. These texts exhibit indeterminacy, or what Barone (2001a, 2001b) calls textual ambiguity, offering readers the option to either forego engagement with the text altogether, or make sense of the text from their own supplies of interpretive resources (Iser, 1974). This indeterminacy results in multiple interpretations of a single narrative and less certainty of meaning.

Reception and reconstruction

Of course, every writer intends for her readers to possess the reading skills, dispositions, experiences, and background knowledge necessary to actualize the text in the way she intended when she wrote the text. However, in reading a text, the reader can only pay attention to, select, and understand – receive – those elements of the text made available to her (this point will become evident from the responses to teacher narratives presented later in this chapter). A reader's reception of the text is informed by her language abilities, her expectations of the text shaped by past experiences with reading this kind of literature, and the social, cultural, historical, and professional experience and understandings that enable and/or constrain her ability to access discreet elements of the text. In a first engagement with the author's text, the reader enters the world of the author, so to speak, in order to reconstruct what the author has composed. This initial effort is an attempt to make sense of the world assembled in the text. The received text – which is not a faithful duplicate of the written text on the page – is at the same time mediated through the reader's own referential background and interpretive strategies in the interface between reader and text to reconstruct the virtual text. That reconstruction, that virtual text, argues Iser, constitutes something new each time it is read; he wrote, 'Literary texts initiate performances of meaning rather than actually formulating meaning themselves . . . literary texts produce something they themselves are not' (1978, p. 27). The meaning of a text emerges when the sense that has been made of it is transformed through the readers' interpretive resources.

Interpretive resources are not only individual, as emphasized by Iser, but also collective, historical, and communal, as suggested by Stanley Fish (1980). Although Iser's theory of aesthetic response acknowledges the contingent nature of the relationship between the reader and the text, and therefore, also of that between the reader and the writer, Iser's analysis attended to meanings of texts as individual productions within specific social and historical contexts. Fish's concept of 'inter- pretive communities' broadens the scope of analysis to include the influence of membership in groups of people shaped by experiences and ways of viewing the world on individual interpretation of texts. Fish describes interpretive communi- ties as groups of people who share common historical, social, professional, and cultural experiences, traditions, habits, vocabulary, assumptions, practices, and attitudes that provide semiotic resources for interpretation of human activity. Spe- cifically, these interpretive resources mediate the work of writers in constructing texts as well as the work of readers in receiving, reconstructing, and appropriating texts. Along these same lines, as will become evident in this chapter, each of the eight members of the teacher focus group reflected membership in the interpretive community shaped by individual school culture and the educational philosophy of central office and school administrators. Those schooling communities were shaped by economic class, race, and location as urban or suburban. Additionally, racialized discourses shaped the teachers' comments about case studies focused on racial bias and equity in the form of color-blind language promoted by school leadership.

Appropriation

After receiving and reconstructing the text to make sense of it, the reader holds the reconstruction of the text up to her lived experience, constituted by personal exper- ience and interpretive resources shaped within professional, social, and cultural discourse communities. She makes interpretive decisions about how that recon- struction should be appropriated into her repertoire of practical knowledge and past experience; as Barone (2001b) explains, 'The reader takes the text home into the world of her daily experience to see what it might say about familiar conditions, conventional practices, and the values and ideologies that support them' (p. 178). This bringing together of the virtual text, with the reader's world of experiences and 'frameworks of knowledge' (Hall, 1980), shapes how the reader appropriates the meaning of the text into a response, reflecting what the text means for the reader. This process constitutes the reader's response to a text that often is further shaped when the reader talks or writes about the text.

Iser, Fish, and Barone all suggest categories for ways readers appropriate and talk about texts. Those we offer here reflect an adaptation of their suggestions. We propose three categories of appropriations: conventional, imaginary, and critical that apply to our work with teachers in this chapter. Readers can appropriate texts in conventional ways that confirm their own beliefs and reinforce their own experiences. Conventional appropriations of texts indicate that the reader accepts the text – writer's perspective, topic, language, genre, tone – uncritically and undisputedly. Imaginary appropriations are carried out by readers who, in Barone's words, 'pragmatize the imaginary' (2001a, p. 178), by responding to qualities in the text that generate a search for possibility or that challenge taken-for-granted assumptions. Readers who appropriate a text in this way find resonance with possibilities the text seems to suggest.

Critical appropriations take three forms. Some can offer a critique of the text based on issues of social justice and equity, drawing on critical theory and postmodern analysis to refute or challenge the author's propositions. Other appropriations focus on the silences, the voices and experiences not represented in the text, the 'surplus of meaning' (Derrida, 1974) that generates divergent meanings for texts by virtue of what is not said. A third form of critical appropriation includes those that dispute the premise of the text; readers may redefine terms, rename experiences described, or shift attention from the writer's interest to their own concerns, sometimes with the effect of trivializing or pathologizing the writer. Examples included in the following section draw on teachers' critical appropriations of narratives rather than on the other two forms of appropriation because the variations and occasions for divergent interpretations and voice(s) in response to teacher narratives accommodate our interest in how discursive communities constrain and enable teacher voice(s).

Teacher response theory: How teachers talk about teacher narratives

It is Iser's and Fish's work that is most immediately applicable to contemporary teacher education research. Iser's work succeeded in providing vocabulary and concepts for this literary approach, but his emphasis was on the individual reader and her interaction with the text. Stanley Fish's concept of 'interpretive communities' (1980) expanded the lens of Iser's approach by locating the reader as well as the writer in 'interpretive communities,' whose influence shape both the writing of text and its reception and interpretation by the reader. His work makes it possible to consider reader response analysis as a poststructural approach that can make visible the cultural, social, historical, and professional discourses that shape reading and interpretation as both individual and communal discursive practices.

More importantly for this essay, this mediation of meaning through interpretive communities problematizes claims about teacher knowledge or 'teacher voice' as original, identifiable, pure, individual, unique, or as vulnerable to distortion from university or academic influences, claims all offered at different points from the various programs in teacher knowledge research. Additionally, the conceptualization of interpretive communities offers another way to account for enhanced, divergent, alternative, and oppositional readings of the text, similar to the 'encoding/decoding' discrepancies noted in Stuart Hall's work (1980). This is an important point because often times teachers' divergent, critical, or resistant interpretations of teacher knowledge narratives are discounted as wrong or lazy. Reader response theory affirms teacher voice(s) as significant and informative in that they tell something about what communities of teachers know and think about the focus and topic of the narrative and also tell something about the features in the narrative that evoke certain responses. Differences and gaps between the narrative and its interpretations by teachers as individuals and as members of various interpretive communities are not 'mistakes,' but are insights into both the crafting of the text and the semiotic resources of the teachers.

Rosenblatt's (1938/1996) and Iser's (1974, 1978) assertions that the meaning of a text is not in the text but in the transactions carried out between the reader and the writer during the process of reading affirm the character of the differences between teachers' appropriations and author's intent as not misunderstandings or mistakes but as meaningful interpretations of the text. Hall's (1980) concept of various and differing 'frameworks of knowledge' that direct a writer's encoding of a message and a teacher's decoding of that message points to the inevitability of this gap and the influences that operate within it. Fish's (1980) notion of interpretive communities through which readers develop interpretive strategies for transacting meaning with texts elaborates Hall's concept, and it directs attention to the social, cultural, and professional discourses that work in the gap to mediate the meaning of texts. Reader response theory allows us to see these differences as inevitable, but also as rich with information to guide in designing new genres of narrative, for writing research representations that respond to nuances in teachers' understanding of their experience, and for examining how teachers learn to read and talk about their craft within a critical community of readers.

For research on teachers that aims to privilege the voices and experiences of teachers framed in epistemological considerations, what teachers have to say concerning research narratives about their work reveals the discursive influences that both bind and inspire how they read and talk about representations of their work. Examinations of how teachers talk about teacher narratives also show the limitations to assumptions about the capabilities of narratives of teachers' work to unproblematically represent and privilege teacher voice(s) and knowledge.

The examples presented in this section come from an empirical study of teachers' focus group conversations about several recently published case studies and narratives of teachers' practice. Eight teachers of diverse gender, racial, and educational backgrounds read 11 different teacher knowledge research narratives and met once a month for eight months to discuss them. Each meeting involved discussions of one or two of these narratives. A total of 12 individual interviews were conducted between group sessions to follow up on concerns or insights expressed during the group discussions.

We must state here that this particular group of teachers, despite individual differences of age, length of teaching experience, education, ethnicity, gender, school district and grade level, rarely expressed opinions or perspectives that dramatically diverged from each other. During most of the discussions, the teachers' comments indicated a monovocal resistance to what was suggested in many of the narratives. However, during several conversations, some teachers shared divergent experiences that contradicted their seeming agreement in earlier discussions, suggesting critical appropriations of polyvocal voices. This critical appropriation directed our attention to features of the narratives as well as the discursive influences and experiences shared by the teachers that evoked both the resistant monovocal voice of agreement to disagree with the narrative and self-contradicting polyvocal voices. The monovocal voice seemed to be influenced by dominant educational discourses of technocratic and color-blind approaches to student differences. Polyvocal voices emerged when teachers' stories of practice contradicted how they talked about the issues of gender and race raised in the narratives. Because the focus of this chapter is on how teachers talk about teacher narratives, a detailed analysis of the features of the narratives must be deferred to another project. The remaining discussion will examine teachers' critical appropriations of resistant responses to three teacher narratives.

Critical appropriation of the regulative ideal of the reflective practitioner

The text

Simon Hole's (1998) first-person narrative, 'Teacher as Rain Dancer,' uses the metaphor of the rain dancer to emphasize the importance of teachers' reflective thinking for student learning. The narrative describes a teaching dilemma in which the needs of an individual student compete with the need of the class and with the teacher's need to follow through on a decision she has already shared with the class. The teacher voice in the narrative suggests that such common classroom tensions call for reflective thinking on the influences shaping teacher decision making that can guide them to more satisfying decision making in the future. Hole proposes that teachers' exploration of the sources of their feelings of tension through reflection offers ways to resignify their negative feelings of discomfort to recognition of such tensions as a 'marker' (p. 420) of an opportunity for growth.

The teacher voice in the narrative promoted the regulative ideal of the reflective practitioner, a not unreasonable expectation, because reflective thinking by teachers is advocated by all professional teaching organizations as well as NCATE-accredited teacher preparation programs.[4] It has become something of a mantra in the field of teacher education. This is the only viewpoint offered in the narrative. Indeed, Hole recounts a colleague's experience, but her voice is not used to tell the story. It is clear that Hole's essay is framing teacher reflection as a normative ideal, and offers no alternative voices or perspectives on how to grapple with classroom tensions and dilemmas.

The teachers' voice(s)

As a group, the teachers' conversation converged on a critical appropriation of this narrative. They expressed viewpoints indicating that they felt that the teacher voice in the narrative had been glib and presumptuous in asserting the efficacy of reflective thinking to solve instructional and management issues. The essay was criticized for making little mention of the outside pressures that limit teachers' time to reflect. The focus group, all of them accomplished teachers in their own ways, shared frequently that their time for reflection on decision making was limited by the demands of high stakes testing, planning and implementing interventions, and reporting data to administrators. The teachers' comments also criticized Hole's essay for assuming that teachers have the autonomy to use their reflections to shape instruction. They did not see their experience of the constraining conditions that limited opportunities for reflection and marginalized their wisdom for decision making represented in the narrative, and that seriously compromised the narrative's ability to enlist the readers in support of teacher reflection as represented in the essay.

The teachers in the focus group also agreed that this narrative offered an unprofessional representation of the work of teachers. They believed that teachers who are anxious about their decisions and constantly second guess them do not display professional confidence in their own abilities. Hole's sharing of his own doubt, his 'touchy feely' expressions of anxiety, and his remarks about his 'sense of impending doom' were not received as honest and intellectual self-interrogation, but as expressions of unprofessional and inappropriate emotionalism that did not match the image of the professional educator valued by this particular group of teachers. Different professional teacher voice(s) were mediating this mismatch: the narrative's teacher voice of self-reflexive reflection and the focus group's teacher voice of assurance and self-confidence.

It is clear that the teachers' critique of the narrative did not come from the theoretical approach most often associated with the term 'critical,' but from their resistance to an account of teaching expressed in a teacher voice that did not acknowledge understanding of the demanding conditions in which they work, one that misrepresented teacher professionalism. Indeed, in the present era of accountability, representations of teachers who appear to be self-doubting and unsure of their decision making justify the 'discourse of teacher deficits' (Cochran-Smith & Lytle, 2006) seen in increasing demands for teacher accountability and regulation by external evaluators.

The predominance of the teachers' concerns with the pressures of accountability and testing provokes questions about the nature of and extent to which discourses surrounding current accountability policies contribute to constructing a monovocal voice within a diverse group of teachers. The ubiquity and power of accountability practices may act as a shared discourse inclusive of the majority of teachers, so that it enables a monovocal voice, and forecloses closer examinations of other influences and concerns that should compel teachers' more critical thinking. It certainly indicates a sufficient amount of similarities in experiences to enable a common perspective that flexes enough presence to emerge in these conversations as a competing narrative for the teachers' attention and subsume their individual voices.

Ironically, even as this group of teachers was rejecting the representation of teachers' reflective thinking as distracting from the demands of teaching and as unprofessional, they were engaged in reflective deliberations. This irony sheds light on the complexity of teacher voice(s). Despite the expression of a monovocal voice of agreement that disparaged reflective thinking in response to the teacher narrative, these teachers were enacting voices that engaged with reflective thinking in many individual ways, evidenced by the narratives of their own practice they shared with the group. Additionally, they had spent some time reading the narrative as part of their voluntary responsibility to participate in the study. They had given an hour of their time after a full day of teaching to come together to dialogue about their reading. Obviously, their voiced objections were not to the intellectual engagements of reflective thinking, but to the representation of teacher reflection expressed by the teacher voice in that particular narrative.

This is important information for those who craft these narratives of practice, not an illustration of teachers' laziness, provincialism, or anti-intellectualism. The teachers read a silence about the pressures and demands that shape daily decision making that come not just from internal tensions, as illustrated in Hole's narrative, but from increasingly intrusive external federal, state, and local mandates. This narrative was a simplification of the complexities and 'messiness' of everyday teaching practice, and thus reductive of teachers, their work, their knowledge, and the richness of their voice(s).

Critical appropriation of a case study on gender equity

The text

After a brief introduction to the problematics and history of gender equity for teachers and classrooms, Frances Maher and Janie Ward (2002) present a third-person narrative of a classroom teacher's attempt to promote the interests and leadership of the girls in her second-grade classroom titled 'Sexism in the Classroom.' Nina, the classroom teacher, is depicted as knowledgeable of the research findings that indicate that girls, although achieving academically, find less voice and space in classrooms as they grow older. The vignette illustrates how a group of boys in Nina's classroom challenge her attempt at validating girl's interests and abilities, and her response to their challenge. The final paragraphs of the narrative describe Nina in reflective consultation with other educators with interests in gender equity and beginning to make plans for changes in her classroom. The short narrative is

followed by comments from various educators who offer a variety of perspectives and theory on gender inequity in schools, from individual understandings to
community norms and expectations regarding gendered behavior and practices.

The teachers' voice(s)

The focus group teachers offered critical appropriations for this case-study narrative. Rather than attributing student behaviors exhibited in Nina's story to the
effects of sexism, as did the teacher commentators in the case study, the teachers
in the focus group interpreted the events in Nina's story to be the product of weak
teacher leadership, and a classroom climate that had not established respect as a
shared value. Although the teachers shared disagreement regarding the focus on
gender as the source of the problem, several teachers offered competing narratives
as to why gender equity was not a concern. For four of the teachers, their grade
level identities as elementary school teachers shaped voice(s) in conflict to the
assertions of the teacher voice in the narrative. They expressed a belief that the
elementary school curriculum and format did not allow for issues of gender to be
at play. Furthermore, they located issues of gender equity at the secondary school
level, one teacher stating that in secondary schools, subjects, especially math and
science, tend to become 'gendered.' Their perception was that because secondary
schools are more subject-specific, teachers at that level deal more with gender
issues. On the other hand, elementary teachers, who have the same students all
day and teach all the subjects, are not affected by that problem.

Several of the elementary school teachers challenged Sadker & Sadker's (1994)
findings, reported by Maher and Ward in the introduction to the vignette. One
teacher commented, 'It just doesn't seem like what they're saying research shows
is what I really saw.' This group of teachers emphatically rejected the American
Association of University Women's (AAUW) 1991 assertion that the research
findings indicated that boys rebel when classroom curriculum features more female
characters than male characters; their knowledge and experience of their students
did not support the AAUW assertion. The teachers claimed that elementary children
just don't think about those things; as one teacher puts it, 'Most elementary kids
just take it as face value. I can choose from these books, and grab one and go. They
don't sit there and analyze it.' One second-grade teacher commented that when
she read that part of the case study, she reflected on her reading series as well as
its supplemental books. She decided that both boys' and girls' experiences were
equally represented in those texts. She commented, 'And the boys don't say much
if the girl is the hero, and girls don't say much if the boy is the hero.'

The teachers shared viewpoints that if there is trust and respect modeled and
sustained by the teacher, problems related to gender will not arise. As one teacher
put it, ' ... Something's just not right with the environment when those kind of
words are being spoken to each other.' They obviously did not feel that it was a
'sexism' problem but the failure of the teacher to establish a climate of respect
and cooperation. Furthermore, the group as a whole agreed with the one teacher
who commented that what was depicted in the case study was so far from her own

experiences that it felt 'made up, because I just couldn't get in touch with this.' Several teachers confirmed this, expressing their perception that the case study did not have a 'real' quality because that kind of classroom conflict did not occur in their classrooms.

Despite this apparent singular voice in their responses, the teachers, as with the previous narrative, shared experiences that caused us to question the voice(s) in which they responded to these narratives. Despite the denial that gender equity operated at the elementary school level, one teacher shared that she asked her second graders to walk 'girl, boy, girl, boy' in line so that there was less misbehavior when the class was walking to a destination. She reported that the children called this being 'girl-trapped,' or 'boy-trapped.' This same teacher offered the comment that she has several boys who had 'special needs,' but that none of her girls had 'special needs.'

The conversation slipped from gender to sexuality when one of the two male elementary teachers in the group shared his experience with a male student who may have been gay. He was singled out by the other students as 'different,' and expressed his own awareness of this 'differentness.' The male teacher recounting the story told us how he held meetings with all of the parents of the students in class so that he could make clear that every child was to be respected regardless of perceptions. He held similar talks with his students. Even as he was offering this account, another teacher who taught at the same school commented how that child had always 'given her the creeps.'

The discrepancies between what the teachers' voice(s) said about gender in response to the narrative, and what they said about gender in their practice, again problematize notions of teacher voice(s) in response to teacher narratives. In this case, gender understood in normalized and standardized ways seemed invisible. That, coupled with pedagogical discourses of management, bound the teachers to limitation in critically talking about how gender and gender equity functioned in their practice. Gender seen as transgressive was visible. In a similar way, the understanding of gender linked to subject areas in the secondary school inhibited teachers from critically engaging in how the gender inequities at the elementary school contribute to those at the secondary level. The next example also takes up an issue of equity.

Critical appropriation of a social justice narrative

The text

Johanna Hadden's (2000) first-person narrative, 'A Charter to Educate or a Mandate to Train: Conflicts between Theory and Practice,' portrays a teacher voice calling on teachers to enact social justice and critical thinking in their practice. Hadden urges teachers to become change agents who teach students how to evaluate power relationships shaping policy and practice and who advocate for democratic and equitable participation at all levels of schooling. Teachers who do not, she claims, are disciples of the dominant regulatory and standardizing educational practices.

Hadden's narrative recounts how she took a stand against tracking her students in the name of social justice and found herself facing off with administrators. This teacher voice claims that good teachers promote social justice, resist the mandate to train instead of educate, and sometimes suffer from taking that stand. The inverse is implicit: teachers who accept the mandate to train are bad teachers who compromise their ethics and do not really care about their students.

The teachers' voice(s)

Faced with Hadden's ultimatum, the focus group teachers fashioned a critical appropriation of a 'virtual text' constructed of competing discourses from the very education establishment Hadden challenged. The focus group teachers used discourses of professionalism to question Hadden's professional judgment and shed doubt on her decision to recommend all of her fifth-grade students to the highest track for their new middle school. They interpreted that action as an effort to make the students feel good rather than as a demonstration of Hadden's concern for the students' 'strengths and weaknesses.' One veteran teacher remarked, 'I don't think that was really justice to her students even though it was a warm fuzzy.' With this comment, the teacher casts Hadden's decision as one of irresponsible misuse of authority and autonomy to make her students feel good about themselves – 'a warm fuzzy' – instead of using her authority and autonomy to make a considered judgment regarding each student's skills and abilities. Hadden's action was interpreted as using students to make a political statement, an irresponsible and unprofessional decision.

Hadden claimed that she shaped her decisions, which would include her professional judgment, on her commitment to liberatory pedagogy and critical theory. The source guiding her judgment was from outside of herself, from the theory and application she learned through her university classes. In contrast, the teachers in the response group located professional judgment within the individual teacher; one expressed the view, 'That's a very individual thing. And you can be a first-year teacher or you've had years of experience, but there's just something in you that you feel like this is going to work for this one ...' A second-grade teacher characterized professional judgment as an inquiry, 'Sometimes you're wrong .... But it's ... I'm just gonna try this and see.' These responses depict an understanding of teachers' knowledge as uniquely contingent and dependent on the events and characteristics informing their teaching practice. The teachers' comments reflect a distrust of outside influences such as university-based research or political or ideological convictions. In Hadden's case, these teacher/readers seemed to see it as distorting her judgment, and, by implication, her voice.

The teachers' conversation about this narrative has always been deeply disturbing to us because of the intransigent limitations revealed in their comments that foreclosed their ability to talk about social justice. Apparently they did not see the unintended consequences of tracking practices and could not understand Hadden's decision except as a 'warm fuzzy.' In our view, any individual voice was indistinguishable from the voice shaped in hegemonic technocratic pedagogy. This points to an urgent need for preservice teacher education and professional development programs to conscientiously and diligently create and sustain critical communities of teachers who identify social justice concerns and who feel comfortable talking about them. Social justice should not be defined and bound by what prevailing educational discourses tell us it is.

Implications for teacher voice(s)

From these examples of how teachers respond to teacher knowledge narratives three conclusions can be drawn that offer implications for teacher voice(s). The first conclusion is that this group of teachers objected strongly to the idea that teachers need to go outside of their practice to make good decisions, whether that be critical pedagogy, research on gender inequity, or systematic protocols for reflection. The teachers in the group valorized professional judgment forged in practice as something teachers 'have' and rely on to make judgments concerning students and teaching practice rather than finding 'solutions' in the voiced narratives found in teacher knowledge research.

The second conclusion is that teachers are political readers who are sensitive to how teachers are represented as professionals in research texts and how their voices may be misconstrued. Hole's narrative about the struggle to be a reflective practitioner was written in 1998, before the increased pressures of current accountability and 'highly qualified teachers' became the reality they are now. This narrative illustrates a teacher's anxious second-guessing about decisions made in the classroom, self-doubt, and lack of self-confidence – hardly the image of an educational professional or a 'highly qualified teacher.' Images of teaching such as this in research publications reinforce the notion that teachers should be more regulated and surveilled. Of course, most teachers would be very sensitive to that depiction when teachers are under so much public scrutiny. The focus group established that teachers can be a 'hard sell' if the narrative is reductive of practice, or disrespectful of teachers' professional image, or simplifies the variables, conditions, and concerns of classroom practice.

The third conclusion is that teachers are sophisticated readers about their work who are quick to disengage with a narrative that seems 'made up,' or 'not real.' Decontextualized case studies or narratives with a single focus that are simplistic or reductive of the complex context of teacher's work are easily dismissed, with the consequence that sometimes important issues or concerns such as gender equity or social justice are 'lost in translation.'

What are the implications of this analysis of teacher voice in teacher knowledge research? The first implication rests on the recognition that teachers and writers who choose to undergo the public evaluation that comes with publication of their stories do not choose arbitrary moments from teaching practice to write about. Teachers' writing about moments of practice will shape their interpretations of those moments with significance that resonates with the publishing community for whom they write and with voices that accordingly can be heard by the targeted audience. That means that these narratives reflect selected interests and representations of teacher voice that are not necessarily representative of every member of the larger teaching community. In fact, the narratives emerge from specific programs of teacher knowledge scholarship, each with its own epistemology and methodology regarding teacher practical knowledge. The consequence of this practice is that selected teacher voices come across as idealized and normative conflated into a singular teacher voice used in moral or romanticized narratives of teaching that support and illustrate the particular program's epistemology. Dissonant or jarring voices of teachers who resist these idealized notions of teaching, who do not put students first, who eagerly anticipate retirement are not selected for representation in teacher narratives.

The second implication builds on the first in that it compels teacher knowledge writers to more thoughtfully consider and reflect on the goals and purposes of their research. The normative teacher voice in the guise of the narrative format tells teachers what to do, and they are sophisticated enough readers to understand and resist that. If the intent is to understand teacher voice in its fullness of context, and richness of dimension, its constraints, its possibilities, then representations of teacher voice(s) must be indeterminate, messy, polyvocal, conflicting, ambiguous, and fragmented, allowing for an aesthetic stance on the part of the reader. Multiple perspectives on significant moments of classroom practices could be offered, representing the many interpretive communities of which teachers are members. To fashion teacher narratives as if teachers are a monolithic group is to replicate the attitude of the accountability movement toward teachers.

Finally, we can see that teacher voice(s) are profoundly shaped by the local district, region, and state in which teachers practice. Interpretive communities are formed not only by the broad influences of teacher education programs, and the social, historical, and cultural discourses of gender, race, class, and disability, but by the localized discourses of professionalism and 'best practices' sifted through the schools, central offices, and state departments of education. All of these shape teacher personal practical knowledge, which enables teachers to be flexible, innovative, informed, organized, and effective in their work. However, as seen in the responses of this particular teacher focus group, teachers' personal practical knowledge can also be limiting and constraining. Because teachers' practical knowledge is contingent and dependent on its surroundings, it can also become 'highly parochial and *impractical* knowledge' (Hargreaves, 1996, p. 15) that limits some teachers' willingness to consider issues of social justice or gender equity, or to challenge traditional educational practices.

This leads us to the questions asked at the beginning of this chapter about the challenges in researching and representing teacher voice(s). If the process of research on teacher knowledge is not innocent and if it does not culminate in conveying a final and definitive message to a passive consumer of this research, then the regulative ideal of creating authentic portrayals of the complexity of teachers' work – however noble – cannot in principle be accomplished. The process of representation is never complete in and of itself. Similarly, the process of interpretation – by anyone, but in this case the target audience of practicing teachers – is not innocent. Practitioners' interpretive frameworks are the products of their own culturally contingent socialization. Therefore any regulative ideal of 'respecting teachers' by accepting their interpretations of texts about teaching, without critical response, is likewise indefensible.

The alternative that remains is a conception of teacher knowledge research that focuses on the production of teacher research texts, not as an end product, but as a means to a more discursively distributed goal: that of engaging teacher readers in critical conversations with the voice(s) of the teachers in the narratives. Representations of the work of teaching can, and we argue should, be used to stimulate the interrogation of the goals and purposes of both teaching and writing about teaching. One way this can be accomplished is by exploring more open-ended genres of narrative representation such as readers' theater, poetry, or drama (Cahnman, 2005; Clark-Keefe, 2003; Saldana, 1995), or the experimental sonata case study form exemplified in the work of Sconiers and Rosiek (2000) that may open up new ways to talk about teaching.

If the goal of the teacher knowledge research movement of respecting teacher knowledge and teacher voice is to be retained, then the process of critical reflection must go both ways. Where dissonances occur between normative conceptions of teaching emerging out of academic discourses and the discourses of communities of teachers, the dissonance needs to be a provocation to further inquiry for both readers as well as writers. Writers of this research need to attend more closely to the enabling and constraining conditions that shape individual teacher voice(s) and explore ways to acknowledge the varieties of teaching contexts that shape dissonant and multiple teacher voice(s). Teacher education and professional development programs need to develop teachers in communities of critical thinkers and readers of research about their work. The important point is to enable a critical conversation between the writers of teacher narratives and the teachers who read them as a form of shared inquiry. This would differ from the one-sided norm of reflective practice often exported from university-based teacher educators to practicing teachers, which often implicitly or explicitly faults teachers for resisting this norm. It would, instead, draw teacher knowledge researchers into more substantive engagement with the institutional, cultural, and policy contexts in which teachers work and construct their voice(s). This, we offer, is where scholars interested in the practical side of teachers' work should want to be.

Notes

1 NCLB refers to congressional legislation passed in 2001 titled 'No Child Left Behind' that shaped school reform policies based on accountability and improved teacher quality. See www.ed.gov/policy/elsec/guid/states/index.html#nclb.

2 Four programs of teacher knowledge research include: scholarship of teaching (e.g., see Grossman, 1990; Shulman, 1987, 2000); narrative inquiry (e.g., see Clandinin & Connelley, 1995, 1996, 2000); teacher inquiry and action research (e.g., see Cochran-Smith & Lytle, 1993; Noffke, 1997); and cultural critical teacher research (e.g., see Giroux, 1992, 1997; Liston & Zeichner, 1996; Maher & Ward, 2002).

3 A reader-oriented approach was first conceptualized for the teaching of reading and literature by Louise Rosenblatt in 1938, and is still highly influential in that field. Based on her reading of John Dewey's theory of experience as transaction (1958), she proposed a transactional theory of literature (1938/1996), which emphasized the give and take between the reader and a text as one of 'Transaction . . . permits emphasis on the to-and-fro, spiraling, nonlinear, continuously reciprocal influence of reader and text in the making of meaning . . . (which) "happens" during the transaction between the reader and the signs on the page' (1938/1996, p. xvi).

4 The National Council for Accreditation of Teacher Education (NCATE) is a national program of accreditation standards for teacher education, http://www.ncate.org/. It is not an institution of the federal government.

References

American Association of University Women (AAUW) (1991). *Shortchanging girls, Short-changing America.* Retrieved September 13, 2007 from http://www.aauw.org/research/sgsa.cfm.

Barone, T. (2001a). Pragmatizing the imaginary: A response to a fictionalized case study of teaching. *Harvard Educational Review, 71*(4), 735–742.

Barone, T. (2001b). *Touching eternity: The enduring outcomes of teaching.* New York: Teachers College Press.

Barone, T. (2007). A return to the gold standard? Questioning the future of narrative construction as educational research. *Qualitative Inquiry, 13*(4), 454–470.

Barthes, R. (1975). *The pleasure of the text* (R. Miller, Trans.). New York: Hill & Wang.

Brooks, C. (1947). *The well-wrought urn: Studies in structure of poetry.* New York: Harcourt Brace.

Bruner, J. (1992). *Acts of meaning: Four lectures on mind and culture.* Boston: Harvard University Press.

Cahnmann, M. (2005). Poetry presentation. Qualitative Interest Group Annual Meeting, Athens, GA.

Clandinin, J. (2006). *Handbook of narrative inquiry: Mapping a methodology.* Thousand Oaks, CA: Sage Publications.

Clandinin, J., & Connelly, M. (1995). *Teachers' professional knowledge landscapes.* New York: Teachers College Press.

Clandinin, D. J., & Connelly, M. F. (1996). Teachers' professional knowledge landscapes: Teacher stories. *Educational Researcher, 25*(3), 24–31.

Clandinin, D. J., & Connelly, M. F. (2000). *Narrative inquiry.* San Francisco: Jossey Bass.

Clark-Keefe, K. (2003, November). *Mirror on my life.* Reader's theater presentation at the Fall Conference on Research on Women in Education. Knoxville, TN.

Cochran-Smith, M., & Lytle, S. (1993). *Inside outside: Teacher research and knowledge.* New York: Teachers College Press.

Cochran-Smith, M., & Lytle, S. (2006). Troubling images of teaching in No Child Left Behind. *Harvard Educational Review, 76*(4), 668–800.

Derrida, J. (1974). *Of grammatology* (G. C. Spivak, Trans.). Baltimore: John Hopkins University.

Elbaz, F. (1991). Research on teachers' knowledge: The evolution of a discourse. *Journal of Curriculum Studies, 23*(1), pp. 1–19.

Empson, W. (1930). *Seven types of ambiguity.* New York: New Directions Publishing Corp.

Fenstermacher, G. (1994). The knower and the known. In L. Darling-Hammond (Ed.), *Review of research in education* (pp. 3–56). Washington D.C.: American Education Research Association.

Fish, S. (1980). *Is there a text in this class? The authority of interpretive communities.* Cambridge, MA: Harvard University Press.

Gage, N. (1972). *Teacher effectiveness & teacher education: The search for a scientific basis.* Palo Alto, CA: Pacific Books.

Good, T., & Brophy, J. (1986). Teacher behavior and student achievement. In M. C. Wittrock (Ed.), *Handbook of research on teaching* (3rd edn, pp. 328–375). New York: Macmillan.

Giroux, H. (1992). Resisting difference: Cultural studies and the discourse of critical pedagogy. In L. Grossberg, C. Nelson, & P. Treichler (Eds.), *Cultural Studies* (pp. 199–212). New York: Routledge.

Giroux, H. (1997). *Pedagogy and the politics of hope: Theory, culture, and schooling.* Boulder, CO: Westview Press.

Grossman, P. (1990). *The making of a teacher: Teacher knowledge and teacher education.* New York: Teachers College Press.

Hadden, J. (2000). A charter to educate or a mandate to train: conflicts in theory and practice. *Harvard Educational Review, 70*(4), 524–536.

Hall, S. (1980). Encoding/decoding. In S. Hall, D. Hobson, A. Lowe, & P. Willis (Eds.), *Culture, media, language* (pp. 128–138). London: Hutchinson.

Hargreaves, A. (1996). Revisiting voice. *Educational Researcher, 25*(1), 12–19.

Hole, S. (1998). Teacher as rain dancer. *Harvard Educational Review, 68*(3), 413–421.

Iser, W. (1974). *The implied reader: Patterns of communication in prose fiction from Bunyan to Beckett.* Baltimore: Johns Hopkins University Press.

Iser, W. (1978). *The act of reading: A theory of aesthetic response.* Baltimore: Johns Hopkins University Press.

Liston, D., & Zeichner, K. (1996). *Culture and teaching.* Mahwah: Lawrence Erlbaum.

Maher, F., & Ward, J. (2002). Sexism in the classroom. In *Gender and Teaching* (pp. 1–18). Mahwah: Lawrence Erlbaum Associates.

Miller, J. (1990). *Creating spaces and finding voice: Teacher collaboration for empowerment.* New York: SUNY Press.

Noffke, S. (1997). Professional, personal, and political dimensions of action research. *Review of Research in Education, 22*, 305–343.

Ransom, J. (1941). *The new criticism.* New York: Harcourt Brace.

Richards, I. A. (1929). *Practical criticism: A study of literary judgment.* New York: Harcourt Brace.

Rosenblatt, L. M. (1938/1996). *Literature as exploration* (5th ed). New York: Modern Language Association.

Rosiek, J., & Atkinson, B. (2005). Bridging the divides: The need for a pragmatic semiotics of teacher knowledge research. *Educational Theory, 55*(4), 421–442.

Rowe, M. (1974). Wait time and rewards as instructional variables, their influence on language, logic, and fate control: Part 1-Wait time. *Journal of Research in Science Teaching, 11*, 81–94.

Sadker, D., & Sadker, M. (1994). *Failing at fairness: How America's schools cheat girls.* New York: Scribners.

Saldana, J. (1995). *Drama of color: Improvisation with multiethnic folklore.* Portsmouth, NJ: Heinemann Drama.

Sconiers, Z., & Rosiek, J. (2000). Historical perspectives an important element of teachers' knowledge: A sonata-form case study of equity issues in a chemistry classroom. *Harvard Educational Review, 70*, 370–404.

Shulman, J., & Mesa-Baines, A. (1993). *Diversity in the classroom*. Hillsdale, NJ: Research for Better Schools and Lawrence Erlbaum Associates.

Shulman, J., Lotan, R., & Whitcomb, J. (1998). *Groupwork in diverse classrooms: Casebook for educators*. New York: Teachers College Press.

Shulman, L. (1987). Knowledge and teaching: Foundations of the new reform. *Harvard Education Review, 57*, 1–22.

Shulman, L. (2001). From Minsk to Pinsk: Why a scholarship of teaching and learning? *The Journal of Scholarship of Teaching and Learning, 1*(1), 48–52.

Tompkins, J. (Ed.). (1980). *Reader-response criticism: From formalism to post-structuralism*. Baltimore: Johns Hopkins University Press.

Chapter 11

Life in Kings Cross

A play of voices

Bronwyn Davies

Introduction: Writing on an immanent plane of composition

Life in Kings Cross: A play of voices is a radio play in which I experience, and experiment with, a Deleuzian approach to writing. It is a play that sets out to evoke a particular place – Springfield Plaza and the surrounding streets and alleyways of Kings Cross, Sydney – and it brings that place to (an imagined) life through the people who live there and who pass through it. I used as my model Dylan Thomas's (1954) radio play *Under Milk Wood*, a play about the life of an imagined village in Wales. Like *Under Milk Wood*, the play covers a period of 24 hours, and contains the multiple voices and the dreams of an array of characters whose lives briefly intersect with those of others who inhabit Springfield Plaza and its surrounds.

Springfield Plaza is the place where I live, and I was curious about the possibility of writing that place – not as *my* place, but as a place with its own complex, rich, and often confronting life.[1] I wanted to use fiction to animate the multiple lives that make up that place in such a way that they were no longer strange, or incomprehensible in their difference. The imagined characters who appear in the play include, among others, homeless people, drug dealers, prostitutes, landlords, professors, shopkeepers, journalists, housewives, pickpockets, and backpackers. Each character is fictional, albeit inspired by the people I see around me. I do not presume to *represent* their lives as if my words could present a reality that pre-exists the act of writing; rather it is through the act of writing that lives are given space to emerge.

What I have tried to accomplish in this experiment with writing is a play of voices in which each character appears in his or her own separate life world, and in which each is a manifestation of the whole of that place. Each character is connected to history and to place in quite different ways, living in and passing through the plaza and its surrounds, sometimes aware of and interacting with others, sometimes not aware of anyone but themselves.

In writing this particular place I sought to write the people within it as co-extensive with the substance of it. Springfield Plaza became, in a Deleuzian sense, 'a juncture where the space of the world and the space of man [*sic*] unfold, between an interior and an exterior fold' (Buchanan and Lambert, 2005, p. 6). At the same time I was interested to open up the writing to include the multiplicity of the place, and the movement within it. Deleuze (1997) writes about a future composed of 'uncemented stones, where every element has a value in itself but also in relation to others: isolated and floating relations, islands and straits, immobile points and sinuous lines' (p. 86). As well, I was guided by two principles that I have drawn from the writing of Deleuze (2004): discarding the self-conscious 'I' and writing on an immanent plane of composition. These two principles together provide an approach to writing that is integral to the process of opening oneself to difference and to the movement of language, voice, and subjectivity toward the as-yet-unknown.

In conceptualising the authorial subject, Deleuze is not interested in the familiar self-conscious 'I', the one who is constituted as an isolated object that struggles to know itself and be known as one who has identity. He conceptualises the subject as a series of processes, as a place where thoughts can emerge: 'The individual is a series of processes that connect actual things, thoughts and sensations to the pure intensities and ideas implied by them . . . An individual is not a self-conscious 'I', it is a location where thoughts may take place' (Williams, 2003, p. 6). Both the authorial subject and the characters in the play are thus places, locations. The nature of those locations can be endlessly repeated, or, working with/in their extensities and intensities, they can open themselves to movement. The 'I' who writes a Deleuzian-inspired play is not the accomplished object of reflection with an identity to reveal in the writing, but a place where thoughts can emerge.

The writing itself thus opens the writer to becoming what is not yet known and to what can never be contained in words, or known completely. The play cannot be a realist tale that might capture one authoritative truth of the place, but an exploration with emergent voices and with movement toward the unknown. As writer, I can do no more than experience/experiment with seeing, hearing, touching, writing the deeply enfolded surfaces of an endlessly changing place, seeking to read/write what I might find written there as I myself pass through (Davies, 2000). My task as writer is thus to see/hear/think the folds in the social fabric as I move through it, as I go on becoming with/in it. I must open myself to the ongoing experience of finding within myself a fold of the social fabric, and at the same time open myself to re-foldings, each 'illuminating some little portion' of that place, 'each illuminat[ing] only one little aspect of the overall folding' (Deleuze, 1990, p. 157), all the while understanding that the folds are not static, not able to be captured once and for all with words. Each repetition may seem to be a static holding, but each repetition holds also the possibility of movement, since it can never be, according to Deleuze, the same as it was before.

I thus engaged in writing that would open me up to difference, to seeing differently, to being different, in my familiar place of living; on this immanent plane of composition, experience and experiment become part of the same process, a process of writing in which the world is not reduced through an attempt to re-present what I know already, but pushes me out into other ways of knowing, into the tangled possibilities of intersecting, colliding, and separate lives.

It is interesting to ask what part such experimental, transgressive writing might play in the social sciences. In what way does it facilitate the task of coming to know differently, and against the grain of dominant discourses? The authorial voice in more usual social science writing is dogged by the need to present itself as the one who knows, and in particular, the one who knows authoritatively (Davies, 1996). A risk in such authoritative writing is the colonisation of the lives one is attempting to unfold. In contrast Deleuze suggests writing in which there is

- a movement beyond the authorial self-conscious 'I' who is the centre of events;
- an abandonment of the illusion that the world can be fixed from a single perspective; and
- experimentation with writing such that the world is not reduced to the already known.

The very self-consciousness of 'writing a play' where the act of writing is to the forefront of one's mind makes it different from more usual social science writing where the idea is dominant and the act of writing subordinate, and where the compulsion to re-present what is taken to be real is almost irresistable. Because it was 'a play' I was able to give myself permission to allow my imagination free reign, at the same time as I worked from my body's deep surfaces as places to be read (Davies, 2000). These two strategies remove the gaze that lies outside oneself with its power to limit and contain, to freeze thought, and to dictate how the narration might be done.

The attempt to write on an immanent plane is accomplished against the formid-able weight of familiar language uses and patterns, the language whose task is to hold everything the same. Both Deleuze and Cixous see that familiar language as full of lies, of distortions of a particular truth or sets of truths that we might otherwise struggle to express:

> It is not only that words lie; they are so burdened with calculations and signi-fications, with intentions and personal memories, with old habits that cement them together, that one can scarcely bore into the surface before it closes up again. It sticks together. It imprisons and suffocates us.
>
> (Deleuze, 1997, p. 173)

The experimentation with language in the form of a play of voices offers a mode in which the burden of old habits, and the sticky surface of familiar language, might have their power displaced. As Cixous (1993) says, it is in experimentation with language that one can learn to 'unlie'. In learning to unlie one comes to know oneself as human, as a reflection, an instance of the human, and in moving beyond the known and the readily knowable, the individual glimpses the condition of humanity. In abandoning the self-conscious I, and the possibility of representation, the author is set adrift as and with/in an immanent plane of composition. In choosing to write a play, rather than, say, an ethnography of the Cross, I felt free to shed the burden of old habits, and the sticky surface of familiar language, to experience, and experiment with, language, in the struggle to make language unlie. My writing of the play was just such an experiment in breaking down my own sedimented perceptions, to make my own practice of language unlie. And what I found was that in opening oneself to the multiple lives in the Cross in this way, lives that intersect, diverge, and form part of a constant set of flows, what may have been threatening and alien, what may have been constituted as abject, to be cast out from myself, is instead able to be greeted with love.

In letting go of the familiar *explanatory devices* that manage the chaos of lives (one's own and others'), in trying to actively think as Deleuze has enjoined us to think, there is a surprising movement from repulsion to love that Cixous (1993) describes as the collision between light and blindness:

> The thing that is both known and unknown, the most unknown and the best unknown, this is what we are looking for when we write. We go towards the best known unknown thing, where knowing and not knowing touch, where we hope we will know what is unknown. Where we hope we will not be afraid of understanding the incomprehensible, facing the invisible, hearing the inaudible, thinking the unthinkable, which is of course: thinking. Thinking is trying to think the unthinkable: thinking the thinkable is not worth the effort. (p. 38)

A Deleuzian approach to writing gives voice to place, not as the backdrop to life but as life itself. The multiple, repetitive voices with/in that place, interwoven with the history of that place, constructing the present of that place, and its future, are always potentially locked into the limitations of the power/knowledge the place affords them. In writing a play that is open to those voices and to their repetitions, the artful act of writing opens a space of difference, a movement, a way of seeing that loves rather than abjects, that embraces rather than controls, that listens rather than tells.

In writing about that experience/experiment I hope to have opened a conceptual space for other researchers to work with in coming to know 'a place', 'a people' differently, through ridding themselves of the colonising authorial 'I' and opening themselves up to new modes of writing and of being.

Life in Kings Cross: A play of voices

A work of fiction

VOICE 1: It is late summer, early on a Saturday morning in Springfield Plaza. The night revelers are finally gone, leaving behind them the sad detritus of the night: a splatter of blood, broken bottles, vomit, bins and gutters overflowing with wrappers from MacDonalds, Sushi Hero, Garlo's Pies, The Best Kebabs, Indian Food . . . The revelers are unconscious in the lock-up, or at home in their suburban beds, oblivious to the day, and to whoever they might find curled up in their sweaty, rumpled, dream-filled beds. One lies safe, for the moment, snoring softly in the comforting arms of a lady of the night, who drifts softly on the enveloping waves of her latest hit.

Over by the freeway, old Professor Jones snorts and turns over, restless in his bed of rags beneath the footbridge. He dreams his complex six-legged formulae as the early morning traffic rushes past him, humming into his dreams.

(*Sound of seven lanes of traffic rushing past, mostly cars with an occasional truck, continuing as background to the professor's dreams.*)

PROFESSOR JONES: When I walk, you see, my back and front legs on one side move in phase with the middle leg, like this, on the other side. The other side . . . The suction cups on my feet hold fast to the wall, to the roof. Then, watch carefully, the other three legs move together, with a relative phase of half a cycle compared with the first set. The first set, you see, of the, game set and match. Match. Ratchet. Roach. Goddam! Cockroach. Yes, I have got the formula at last. Got it. Yes. The alternating sets of three legs make a triangular base of support on the ground. But when I slow down, my legs move in a metachronal-wave, the movement sweeping from front to back, like this. And when I am excited, beware the traffic, beware, I switch to a four-legged or a two-legged gait. A two-legged gait. They say I am only a two-legged animal, but I hold fast with my suction cupped feet. The cockroach moves fast and hides in the warm dark places in my nest. Infest. No. Listen to me. Listen to me. I have got it. My back and front legs on one side move in phase with the middle leg on the other side, like this . . .

VOICE 1: He drifts again into a dreamless early morning sleep.

VOICE 2: Back in Springfield Plaza, for the moment, as the day opens, it is quiet. Except for the birds who sing to each other in the song of the once green field with its bubbling spring and its view of the dazzled dappled water of the bay below.

The early morning golden light is filtered through the leaves of the Chinese Elms and Plane trees, and an ibis and several pigeons peck at the food on the black granite paving. A squawk of seagulls fights over a morsel abandoned at some lost point in the dark night.

A body lies on the pavement curled up in a patterned blue doona, oblivious to the passers-by.

VOICE 1: Wrapped up in his doona, Harald dreams of Vikings, sailing over the wild, cold sea. Steering through the narrow waters, with sheer cliffs on either side, his ship rolls over the huge, grey, pregnant waves. He stares out the ship window straight into the heavy deep waters, and when the ship turns on its side, as it slides down the wave, he stares at the ice-cold silver sky. He is wearing his Viking helmet with two cow horns and plays on his mouth organ a sweet nostalgic tune.

HARALD: I'm Harald the Great. I write poems that make the dead rise up from the deep, and I play music to rival the Sirens. I play for my Dadda who is lost at sea. I will play so sweet he cannot resist me. (*Music of the mouth organ and the creaking and groaning of the ship as it rolls on the waves.*) Why did you leave me Dadda? I'm stretching my hand down so deep into the roiling ice-cold water. Can't you take hold of it now? Take hold of it Dadda and I'll pull you up. Can you hear me Dadda? I can see your eyes, your two soft grey eyes. Can you hear my music Dadda? Just reach for my hand Dadda.

DADDA: Those are pearls that were my eyes. You cannot see me son, my bones are all disjoint and spread about on the floor of the wide, wide sea, and my eyes picked out by wee fish long long ago. Go home Harald, go home.

HARALD: Where is home Dadda? Don't leave me Dadda! I'll play you sweet music Dadda . . .

VOICE 2: An ancient landlord, bent over his brass filigreed walking stick, walks, slowly, along Darlinghurst Road, past Andersen's Danish Ice Cream and on towards Llankelly Place. He takes one step at a time, along the new black granite pavement with its black blobs of chewing gum and its brass inlaid histories of people he remembers only too well (drunken Christopher Brennan, crazy Bea Miles, the mad witch, Rosaleen Norton). Elegantly dressed in his ancient black suit, spotless starched white shirt and silk tie, he pauses to lean on his cane and catch his breath.

LANDLORD: (traces of a Polish accent) I am 98 years old, but there is life in the old dog yet. Not like my buildings.

VOICE 2: He jabs his cane in the air, pointing to the buildings in Llankelly place. He rests his cane down and leans both hands on it. He gazes for a long time along the lane, thinking . . .

LANDLORD: There are termites in my floorboards and the cockroaches swarm up my walls. The cockroaches seek the warm damp places. They lurk in the makeshift shelters put up each night by the dross that rises to the surface in the gaudy drug-filled nightlife of this rapidly decaying place. It is filled with the stench of the drunken youths (who should know better than to piss against my walls) and the derelicts (who no longer know the difference, poor souls, between a latrine and the walls of my buildings). The termites come in on the roots of the Plane trees. They follow the roots that travel along the surface of the sandstone in search of the sweet cool spring in the once-upon-a-time gardens of Springfield House.

VOICE 2: He walks slowly step by step toward the Plaza. He stops and jabs his stick at the brass inlaid plaque in the pavement, reading:

LANDLORD: 'Springfield House. Demolished in 1934'.

Such a beautiful house with its laughter and its music – those were the days of splendour and romance – the parties that went on all weekend, with artists, playwrights, actors, beautiful women . . . (he sighs) (A dance band strikes up a waltz.) I was 18 years old when I first danced with her. 1926. I remember as if it were yesterday . . .

VOICE 2: He holds his cane to his chest as if it were a beautiful woman, and sways to the music, dancing once again on the wide moonlit verandah of Springfield House, with Lily Littmann, magnificent dark-eyed beauty.

LANDLORD I: Ah Lily, Lily, my love.

VOICE 2: Another Professor steps out of her elegant white art deco apartment, down the white marble stairs and into the Plaza. She lifts her face to the morning sun, startled, as she is each morning, at the quality of the golden morning light. The soft breeze that finds its way up from the boat-bobbing bay caresses her bare skin still warm from sleep. Hair rumpled every which way, she is on her way to Bondi, to swim in the salt water and early morning light. Turning into Darlinghurst Road she sees the last of the revelers huddled in the street waiting for taxis – anxious taxis crowding the curb and vying to receive them – beautiful young people with bleary waxen faces and damaged livers, not quite ready to abandon the night. She walks past the door of the Massage King, now shut, the masseurs at home in their weary beds. The dying thumps of stale music escape with a whoosh of warm air from the opening door of the Empire Hotel. An old man hunched over his cane, walks along the pavement, one step at a time . . .

VOICE 1: Back along Darlinghurst Road, Gloria da Silva leans toward the mirror inside the doorway to inspect her lipstick. Carefully and precisely she tidies her face with the tip of her elegant long nailed little finger. Long shiny black boots, black bag over her shoulder, she is ready and waiting. Fresh as a dew-dropped daisy in the early morning light.

GLORIA DA SILVA: Ya want a lady darlin'?

VOICE 1: She says to a bleary, blond-haired youth heading for his lonely, bug-ridden backpacker bed.

VOICE 2: At the end of Darlinghurst Road, the El Alamein Fountain glitters in the early morning light, like a huge round dandelion, ready to blow a wish on. Next to the fountain is a sign that makes another sphere, locating this watery birth of wishes at the magnetic centre of desire: telling how far and which way to Athens, Berlin, London, Moscow, Tokyo, Seoul, New York, Rio, Auckland.

Running steadily and smoothly along Darlinghurst Road, up toward the Fountain, Georgie Delaney, dressed in a tight pink T-shirt and very short shorts, looking drop dead gorgeous, nods hello at Gloria. As she runs past the Plaza she sees a body wrapped up in its doona, dead to the world. She stops, and taking ten dollars from the pocket of her shorts, she gently tucks it into the shirt pocket of the slumbering man. She knows from her past work as policewoman on the beat how tough he'll be doing it. She smiles at the thought of him waking to find her small gift, and continues on her run.

VOICE 1: The street sweepers, dressed in navy trousers, heavy boots, and luminous lime green jackets are busy with their large brooms, sweeping up the rubbish, their hands protected in thick leather gloves against the needles and broken glass. The CCTV screen records a quick exchange between a sweeper and a shifty looking dealer, but the weary eyes of the young surveillance officer are glued to another screen. The street cleaning truck with its yellow whirring brushes begins cleansing in earnest. The drivers swerve around the sleeping body and drive on.

'Cleanse', rather than 'clean', is the word the city mayor uses to describe this work of cleaning the pavements. Cleanse: to remove dirt, filth, etc. To remove guilt from. Who is guilty here, and of what exactly?

After the whirring truck with its yellow brushes comes another noisy yellow water truck and men with the high-pressure hoses. Eventually the sleeping body and blue doona stir, and see that their hold on this piece of the Plaza is doomed. The sleeper staggers and slips on the watery pavement and two cleaners catch him before he falls, and help him to his feet. He gathers up his blue doona, and all that is left of the makeshift bed is the sheet of cardboard laid down against the cold of the black granite paving.

VOICE 2:   The trucks with the boxes of fruit and veg and bright-coloured flowers arrive for the street stall. The stall owners rapidly arrange its colourful display of fresh fruit and vegetables. The bright bunches of fresh summer flowers open their faces to the morning light and to the fine spray of water drifting on the air. The black granite paving glistens wet in the early morning sun, and the perfume from the flowers expands into the fresh, clean, glistening air.

A passer-by, elegant in her striped white silk trousers and cream jacket, newspaper tucked under her arm, pauses to buy a paw paw and strawberries for breakfast, and a bunch of white summer daisies. An investigative journalist, she relishes the quiet space in which she will read and reflect on the morning news, and later call her sister in Singapore to swap notes on current affairs. She jokes with the stall-owners, and barters over price, feeling utterly at home in the warm, moist, early morning light.

VOICE 1:   The staggering sleeper makes his way down to the Wayside Chapel for coffee and breakfast and fresh clothes – and maybe something to steady his nerves. He twitches his nose at the heavy stench of urine rising up from the pavement. Fresh out from a stretch in the clink, he's been all dried out and cleaned up. Last night was a grand celebration of freedom. He needs a hair of the dog. Each time he comes out, he's that bit weaker, that bit less sure of the ground. But he's ready to face anyone, and looking forward to the days of booze, and yarns with his mates, the wild nights of adventure, of impossible highs, and dramatic confrontations with any wanker who challenges him. He's got his rights. He slings his doona over his shoulder and as his feet slowly find their rhythm on the pavement he straightens up and squares his shoulders, and begins to rehearse the lectures to the young ones who need to know a thing or two about life. His mates are the local Aboriginal mob who hang out here in the Plaza.

HARALD: I read about land rights while I was away. Fuckin' awful days and nights of nightmares to make you fuckin' swear you were gonna die. Ya wanted to be dead anyway. Woke up one day and said all right. All right. But all right what? I thought I'd die of boredom. I done some reading in the prison library. About the way the early wild man was hunting right here, kangaroos and emus, outside that house – Springfield House. Seen the picture of it with me own eyes. The handsome black man with his spear, and the emus and kangaroos hopping about. That's where I slept last night, in those very bloody gardens – except the house is gone and so are the gardens. There's them boxes of plants on the wooden benches where Maisie and them bury their drugs when the pigs are coming. It's a riot when they forget where they are. All the plants get ripped out by the roots. Fuckin' dirt and bushes flyin' everywhere – shouting and yelling. Used to sleep on them wooden benches, all day in the sun, when they first done up the Plaza. Bloody beautiful. Can never soak in enough of that sun. Then they come along and plonked them dirty great plant boxes there to keep us off – put the chill in our bones sleeping on the pavement. Get piles in your arse from the cold tiles we sit on. We have a good laugh and the grog warms up muh bones.

VOICE 1: Harald's walk has developed a distinct limp since last time he was out. His hip is giving him buggery. But he concentrates on walking tall, walking smooth, imagines himself with a spear in hand and emus to hunt.

HARALD: The emu oil was good for the old arthritis. Wouldn't have had a gammy hip back then. Eh Dadda. You knew all them tricks. Learned them from the Aborigines you told me. Left me with them when you went to sea.

VOICE 1: He still looks grand. His grey hair is plaited neatly in a long plait down his back. He has new leather boots and a new black leather jacket. His handsome face is flushed and his eyes a bit rheumy. The edges of the buildings are fuzzy, but his feet know the way without having to look.

VOICE 2: All is quiet for the moment in the Plaza. Over in Orwell St, two men in their thirties are on their way to the Plaza to see what's happening. They spot two women walking toward them with backpacks. They split up and one of them approaches with a plan to distract them and do some useful pickpocketing. The women are on their way back from the Boy Charlton pool, and they pause to chat before going their separate ways.

MAN IN HIS THIRTIES: How far is it to the airport?

WOMAN: It's quite far. You could get the train.

MAN IN HIS THIRTIES: How long will it take me to get there? I'm going to Denmark. I'm running late.

WOMAN: Oh, you need to go to the International. It will take you about 20 minutes if you get a cab.

MAN IN HIS THIRTIES: Will I get there on time?

SECOND MAN IN HIS THIRTIES: Do you want me to smack him out? He's being a nuisance.

WOMAN: No he's OK.

SECOND MAN IN HIS THIRTIES: No I'll smack him out. He's being a nuisance. We're going to the Gold Coast stupid! I'll smack him out for ya.

WOMAN: No he's fine, really.

SECOND MAN IN HIS THIRTIES: No I'll smack him out. I'll smack him right out.

VOICE 2: The two women raise their eyebrows slightly at each other, say goodbye, and go their separate ways. The second man in his thirties gets out his brush from his bag, and brushes his long brown hair. There was nothing in the backpacks except wet swimmers. But he thinks he has a chance with that woman. Next time he meets her he'll tell her he smacked Jock right out, just like he said, and about his father who was a minister of the Church. Very strict with me he was. That'll impress her. But right now it is time to get up to the Plaza.

The Plaza is still for a moment. The busy stream of pedestrians has slowed. Strategically situated, so they can see the Plaza, but not be noticed themselves, half a dozen dealers are sitting or standing alone or in couples, watching, like hawks. So still they are invisible to the passers-by who stroll on their way to coffee, or the organic market, or to buy the weekend newspaper. Occasionally one of them moves, walking swiftly over to one of the others, steps a little too tense to be completely invisible. Then he goes back and sits and waits, disappearing again out of anyone's conscious gaze.

Half an hour passes. An hour. Passers-by who stop to chat to each other about the market, or the latest DA from Council, notice and remark on them, but they stay so still they pass out of awareness.

Silently a car pulls up right near the fruit stall. Stan-the-Man gets out, movements smooth as silk. He chats in a casual fashion to the people hanging out. One by one the hawks swoop in, so smoothly, so silently, nobody sees anything. The tension is gone, the hawks vanished, Stan chats on, joking with the guys who gather around him. Then he's gone. A group of three, two men and a woman, huddles on the steps of the Plaza, the woman doing a quick shoot up, and then they're gone. Two police officers stroll through the Plaza. Behind their backs large wads of money change hands, swiftly and silently; quiet smiles are also exchanged. The police officers walk on.

VOICE 1: Round the corner, Corinne the crow wakes. She's been sleeping in the warm alcove of the auto teller. She sits up, blankets still around her, her wild black hair all over the place. Her shimmy slipping down over her smooth brown round shoulder. She croaks at each passer-by:

CORINNE: Spare any change for a cuppa tea? Spare any change? Got any money for a cuppa tea? Got a coupla dollars for a cuppa tea?

VOICE 1: She needs a drink badly. The morning pedestrians barely notice her. Their worlds and hers run parallel and rarely meet. But now she needs money. She levers herself up to standing, using the wall of the abandoned bank to lean on, get herself steady. She needs a piss. Needs a change of clothes. Needs some grog. She grabs the bottle in its brown paper wrapper and tips it upside down. Empty. She is distracted by the vision of a young Aboriginal woman wheeling a stroller towards her. Sitting in the stroller is a gorgeous child with its black tumble of curly locks holding tight to a knitted elephant. She stares at the child, and moves out onto the footpath, out of her warm alcove, with steps remarkably like a big cat, despite her creaking bones. She holds out both her arms to stop the stroller. Danielle, on her way to the train, stops to watch, concerned. The baby hugs its knitted elephant and looks up at Corinne with interest. Corinne bends over toward the baby and croaks:

CORINNE: You're a little beauty. Aren't you? Eh? What a beauty!

VOICE 1: The child stares unafraid, and Corinne reaches down gently and takes hold of the baby's toes and waggles her foot.

CORINNE: I could kiss the earth you walk on.

VOICE 1: The mother smiles, and Corinne lets the foot go, and turns away to gather her gear and find some food and drink. But first a piss. Her bladder is busting.

Easy for the blokes who just piss in the potted plants. Just the right height. Or against the wall. She has to go all the way down to the toilets. The mother and child move on, and Danielle stands there amazed at the love that Corinne has expressed for the baby girl. Corinne is oblivious to her. She changes her top to start the day fresh, choosing a bright red one she got from the Wayside, and a blue and green striped beanie that she pulls out of an old plastic bag.

VOICE 2: At the Heavenly Café, in Llankelly Place, the morning crowd sits out on the pavement drinking their coffee and eating their breakfasts of pancakes and raisin toast, reading their papers. They chat to each other, and to the proprietor, who welcomes them each by name when they arrive. Marco is a moody man, given to bouts of gloom. For his customers, he is always friendly, witty, and welcoming. This morning he says in response to each query about his health:

MARCO: I am bursting with joy, it is oozing out of every pore.

VOICE 2: ... though he is deeply distressed by a dispute with his landlord over his demand for an increase in rent. For most of the customers, the warm welcome, the undemanding companionship, the smell of excellent coffee, the warmth of the dappled green sunlight filtering down through the Plane trees, entice them to let go for the moment of the everyday stresses of their insanely busy lives.

Inside the Heavenly Café, a toddler, no more than 18 months old, is squealing and squawking. She has finished the hot chocolate that Marco has made for her, in the tiny cup he keeps especially for her, and she is certain it is time to leave. On the way out she toddles independently ahead of her parents who wheel her stroller behind her. Suddenly she stops, transfixed, staring. Her gaze has alighted on a man, sitting out on the pavement next to the door of the café. He is exceedingly handsome with smooth brown skin and a neat grey pony-tail. He wears a black patch over one eye. She stands stock-still and stares. Her parents speak to her gently, encouraging her to move on. The exit from the café is blocked. They give her a slight nudge. She cannot be moved. She cannot hear them. She no longer hears or sees anything except the man with the eye patch. He looks back at her smiling, waiting. Everyone's attention is drawn to the transfixed child. Her parents nudge her, gently, again. Suddenly she starts, as if she is waking, becoming aware of the others around her. She starts to cry loudly, as if she is afraid of the man at whom she has been staring. The man with the patch and his companion laugh, and the child and her parents leave, calling out to the owners of the café.

PARENTS OF SMALL CHILD: See you Marco, see you Gemma.

VOICE 2: And peace descends again, in a quiet hum of voices, occasional laughter and the soft clink of coffee cup on saucer, and the background hum of traffic. The distant wail of a fire engine, grows louder and louder. The wailing red truck-in-a-hurry flashes past and rushes off, through the red light and down Macleay Street. All eyes lift, dreamily, and wonder for a second or two where the fire might be this time, and just as they let the thought go, a second truck wails, loud and insistent, overlaid on the first. In a moment, the wailing fades, the fire is forgotten, the sirens no more than an afterprint on memory (*sound of two sirens, one louder than the other, then fading into the distance*). The second Professor listens intently until the sound fades, seeing once again the smouldering embers of her beautiful house, burned to the ground. Twenty-five years ago, and still the sound of the fire truck triggers a buried memory of alarm. She turns back to her newspaper with a sigh. Perhaps it was only a false alarm, and there is no fire this time.

VOICE 1: An ancient blond woman in red high heels totters unsteadily by. Her hair is done up in a curious high swirling cone, with the texture of fairy floss. Her face is handsome, despite being deeply etched with wrinkles. It is painted with two perfect round patches of rouge on her high cheek-bones with matching lipstick. Her painted eyebrows are black and curve up in a surprising flourish on the outside edges. She evokes another place, another time. The Pigalle, perhaps, fifty years ago. Did she ever encounter Sartre and his friends?

VOICE 2: Mollie sips her coffee and chats to her two ageing gay friends. She is 74, single, and always elegantly dressed with a special flair for gorgeous hats. The boys ask her about her will, and what she has decided to do about it.

MOLLIE: I'm going to leave my house to the accountant. The apartment will go to my niece.

BOYS: It must be worth at least a million! How can you leave it to the accountant? Can't you think of someone more deserving?

MOLLIE: I wouldn't know how to choose. It's too hard to think of which charity. How do I know if they're any good? Probably rip off all your money instead of using it for the people who need it. And anyway, he's very good to me. He looks after me. He makes sure I don't have to worry about money.

BOYS: That's crazy Mollie. You don't have to leave him the house . . .

MOLLIE: (*Sighs*) I have to go home now to clean the apartment. It takes me all day.

BOYS: All day? It shouldn't take more than a couple of hours, that small apartment.

MOLLIE: I like to do it properly. I move all the furniture and vacuum under it. It takes a long time to do it properly. I like it to be clean.

VOICE 1: She stands to leave and the boys protest that she should relax, but she is determined. She wants the apartment to be perfect. Then she'll put on her very best clothes and jewels and hat, and be ready for her date with her handsome ageing accountant. He'll take her to an extravagant restaurant, with a view of the Harbour, and he'll buy her a bottle of '85 Piper Heidsieck, which costs a fortune she can tell, from the unctuous face of the waiter, and real caviar, and kiss her fingertips, and tell her that her beauty is as compelling as it ever was. Her, who was only ever a milliner. She sighs, and walks slowly and carefully on her way home to clean the apartment.

VOICE 2: There is still a faint chill on the air, and the sun is warm. An early autumn leaf drifts down from the Plane tree, landing softly among the coffee drinkers. A young man shuffles along Llankelly place toward the café. Silently he thrusts a card at the second Professor that reads 'I am deaf and cannot speak. Please help me'. She takes five dollars out of her bag and gives it to him.

Old Jen, once a barmaid and now a widow, sits down at the table with the gay boys, taking a while to catch her breath. She puts her stick out of the way and signals to the waiter inside that she wants her usual. She carefully counts out the money and puts it on the table beside her. Her short silver hair is perfectly coiffed. Her bright red lipstick is immaculate and perfectly matches her bright red shirt. She has on her smart tweed jacket against the chill in the air. Her diamond rings glitter in the dappled light. The gay boys chat to her for a while, invite her to their party, then finish their coffee and leave.

SECOND PROFESSOR: Hi Jen. How are you?

JEN: I'm fine thanks love. How are your boys?

SECOND PROFESSOR: Pete is still not talking to me.

JEN: I told you that would happen. You're too soft. I saw you giving money to that beggar, pretends he's deaf. He's no more deaf than I am. He can hear what you say y' know. I've spoken to him when he's not looking and he heard alright. Those boys are always asking me to their parties. You wouldn't want to know the goings on there!

VOICE 2: The second Professor takes her leave of Jen and wanders back home pondering the paper she is working on. As she cuts through the dilapidated, soon-to-be-demolished Village Centre, she comes upon a tiny old woman who looks up at her with an intent expression.

TINY OLD WOMAN: Can you help me?

VOICE 2: She points toward the stairs.

SECOND PROFESSOR: Yes, of course.

VOICE 2: Gently she tucks her hand under the arm of the tiny old woman and walks with her down the stairs. The tiny old woman holds onto the railing with her other hand and makes it down the stairs with ease. They walk towards a stretch of wet paving.

SECOND PROFESSOR: They've been hosing the floor. We'll need to go carefully.

TINY OLD WOMAN: There's no railing here on these stairs.

VOICE 2: She says as she points toward the next set of stairs. The second Professor tucks her hand under her arm again, and the tiny old woman nestles into it. Her small body is soft and warm, like the feathery under-wing of a bird. At the bottom of the stairs she says:

TINY OLD WOMAN: That's nice.

SECOND PROFESSOR: Yes . . . Are you OK now? Can you manage these next stairs?

VOICE 2: The tiny old woman gestures toward the small supermarket, soon to be demolished and says:

TINY OLD WOMAN: I'm going shopping.

VOICE 2: The second Professor relinquishes the soft warm fragile body, and continues home to her computer and writing, her hand still holding the surprising soft feathery warmth and the gentleness of the tiny old woman.

VOICE 1: Back in Llankelly place three young men walk purposefully past the Heavenly Café toward Happy Hockers. They have white handkerchiefs tied around their faces. Quick as a flash they smash the window of Happy Hockers and scoop the jewellery into bags and leg it off back down Llankelly Place. The people sitting in the café, and at the vegetable juice shop, and the pedestrians walking up the alley, stare in amazement, jaws dropped down in a frozen moment of surprise. An enterprising young boy, standing idly by, dives in and grabs the jewellery that dropped on the pavement, and runs off up Darlinghust Road.

One of the coffee drinkers, Dee-Dee, an office manager, whips out her mobile and rings the police, offering a detailed description of clothing and hair colouring, while the owner of Happy Hockers and everyone else stare dumbfounded after the brazen young men who are scooting off round the corner into Springfield Mall. After long seconds of silence, broken only by Dee-Dee's call, the pedestrians begin to walk on their way, resuming the pattern of the day that had for the moment been interrupted. Everyone in the café begins to talk at once about their surprise, their failure, apart from Dee-Dee, to do anything, and the utter brazenness of the three young men. They cannot agree on what they were wearing or even what they were carrying. Some said metal bars, others baseball bats. Others had noticed nothing at all, imagining somehow, without paying it any attention, that it was perfectly normal for three young men to wear handkerchiefs round their faces at noon in the Cross.

VOICE 2: The Ecstasy Adult Shop is next door to the Heavenly Café. Janni emerges from Ecstasy and makes his way to the Café. He is looking very elegant in his spotless white trousers and open-necked white shirt. He sits next to the entrance, under the Plane trees, and orders a coffee. He drinks it slowly to make it last. He orders another. Danielle is walking fast towards the coffee shop. Will she turn in? She does! Janni asks her:

JANNI: Would you like to sit at my table?

VOICE 2: She looks startled, looks around imagining that there must be no spare tables and that he is mindful of this fact. But she spots an empty table, thanks him graciously, and takes her seat. She is really hungry as it's past lunch-time. She picks up the menu and studies it intently. Janni comes over with his almost empty coffee cup and asks if he can sit at her table. Again she assumes there must be a limited number of tables and without taking her nose out of the menu, gestures toward the empty chair, saying:

DANIELLE: Yes, of course, go ahead.

VOICE 2: Gemma takes Danielle's lunch order, and she pulls out of her shopping bags the colour cards and tiles and pieces of fabric she has spent the long morning hunting for, and begins to lay them out on the table. She is deeply absorbed in the colours and colour combinations and in the decisions she has to make. Janni is watching her closely.

JANNI: You live around here?

DANIELLE: Yes I do.

JANNI: Are you new to Sydney?

DANIELLE: Yes, I just arrived two weeks ago.

JANNI: Have you bought an apartment?

DANIELLE: Yes, I have.

VOICE 2: Her lunch arrives and she sighs and moves the samples over to the side of the table. She is ravenous and sinks her teeth thankfully into her delicious sandwiches.

JANNI: I have a new apartment too.

It's a bachelor apartment and it has a view of the Bay.

It is over at Rushcutters Bay.

I've had my name down for a long time, and finally it's come up.

I don't have to pay anything for it.

I'm writing a book.

It's about the voices, the yammer in the mind.

It's about how to ignore them.

I have just been to Ecstasy.

I used to be a real man for the women.

Whenever I saw a beautiful woman walking by, I would know she found me attractive. I could make love to her. I would know it straight away.

But lately everything has been flat.

I have had no desire. I thought if I went to Ecstasy my body would wake up again.

When I saw you walking towards me, down the lane, I couldn't believe it.

And then you turned into the café.

You are new here. Have you got a boyfriend? You don't?

Well, you know, I am not a bad-looking guy. I'm 59 but I have still got a good body. I am strong and I am very good to look at.

My teeth are not good, you might be worrying about that, but I'm going to get them fixed. Then you'll see that I look very good.

I can help you with your apartment. Are you painting it? I'm good with a paintbrush. You need furniture moved? I am strong.

My name is Janni.

I came originally from Czechoslovakia when I was 20 years old. I have a good apartment. You would like it, and I am writing a book.

DANIELLE: You know Janni, it's true I don't have a boyfriend, but, you know, I'm not actually looking for anyone. I'm sorry.

JANNI: I was really afraid you were going to say that.

VOICE 2: Danielle gathers up her samples and goes into the café to pay. She realizes the café was holding its collective breath while it waited for her answer. They have all relaxed back into their own separate worlds. Janni sits despondent with the last half inch of his coffee now stone cold. He stares into the cup and doesn't notice Danielle leave the café. When she reaches her apartment she checks behind her to see that he is not following. She sighs thankfully that there is no sight of him, and lets herself inside, sighing at the peacefulness of the hallway with its wood-paneled walls and lead pane windows.

VOICE 1: The afternoon stretches peacefully, with a string quartet playing for a couple of hours, the pedestrians strolling through, the homeless sitting on the benches listening to the music and occasionally talking to each other, and taking a swig out of a bottle in a brown paper bag. The second Professor works at her computer, window wide open, and occasionally glances down at the Plaza. Two police officers stroll through and approach a man holding a bottle in a brown paper bag.

POLICE OFFICER: You know it is illegal to drink in this zone.

DRINKER: No man I'm not drinkin'. Jus' holding the bottle for someone else. For me mate.

POLICE OFFICER: Who are you holding it for?

DRINKER: I dunno 'is name man. 'E just went down there for a piss. 'E'll be back any minute. Told me to hold the bottle.

POLICE OFFICER: I thought you said he was a mate.

DRINKER: Yeah man 'es me mate. Just gone for a piss. I'm not drinking man, no way!

VOICE 1: The police officers move on and right behind their backs the bottle-holder takes a swig and smiles and wipes his mouth on his sleeve (*sighing with satisfaction*).

At the automatic teller, Professor Jones is struggling to comprehend how the card works. His baggy tracky pants are hanging low around his hips revealing the cleft of his buttocks. He struggles with the buttons and then extracts his card and walks off. The young woman standing behind him calls after him.

YOUNG WOMAN: Excuse me, excuse me, you've left your money in the machine.

PROFESSOR JONES: I have?

YOUNG WOMAN: Yes, here, this twenty is yours.

PROFESSOR JONES: But I asked for fifty. It can't be mine.

YOUNG WOMAN: Yes, it is yours.

VOICE 1: He looks doubtful, but takes the money and puts it in his pocket, and the young woman smiles and makes her withdrawal.

As the afternoon draws toward its end, Janey Lovejoy strides jerkily up Llankelly Place, legs stiff and puppet like, moving at great speed yelling loudly:

JANEY: Leave me alone alright, ya fuckin' cunt! leave me alone alright ya fuckin' cunt! Leave me alone! Go an' live somewhere else! Go and live somewhere else alright! Leave me alone! Ya fuckin' cunt.

VOICE 1: She stares straight ahead walking at great speed, her voice swelling magnificently in her rage, filling up the whole alley, bouncing off the walls and drowning all other sound and thought. Her boyfriend doesn't dare to follow her, darting up Orwell Street and back down to the Wayside Chapel.

VOICE 2: Peace descends again in Llankelly Place and the tailor, standing in his doorway having a smoke, and the investigative journalist on her way home with her groceries continue to chat about the pleasure they each take in their work, in the combination of pressure and satisfaction at a job well done.

VOICE 1: Walking swiftly up Darlinghurst Road, a young man in an elegant suit has an erect penis in his hand. Too much crystal meth and this persistent source of urgent need simply cannot wait until he gets home.

VOICE 2: In the Plaza, Maisie has made contact with a buyer. She strides out toward Earl Lane, the buyer, looking a little uncertain, ten metres behind. Maisie has her stash in the electrical box of a private hotel. She whips it out swiftly, totally ignoring the pedestrian who walks by.

The uncertain young backpacker, fresh from his bug-ridden bed, makes his purchase without seeing quite where it had been stashed.

VOICE 1: As the sun sinks behind the tall buildings and the dusk begins to settle, some currawongs begin their evening song, calling to each other, chi-di-ch-laa, and melodious falsetto wails, uh-waaah, float on the puffs of cool evening air.

Thousands of fruit bats begin their nightly exodus from the Botanical Gardens, flying silently over the Cross, on the way to their nightly feeding grounds. The white cockatoos screech and swoop in their complex aerobatics, sailing on their broad white wings over the pedestrians then up on a puff of warm air to sit on the rooftops and watch.

VOICE 2: The ageing bikies begin to gather in Darlinghurst Road, revving up their motors to announce their Saturday night presence. The fairy lights in the plane trees flicker on, and the Plaza tranquilly prepares itself for the nightly onslaught of young and beautiful people coming to the nightclubs, and desperate people looking for something, for thrills, for entertainment, for drugs, for companionship, for sex. All intent on doing Saturday night in style. The groups of young and beautiful walk swiftly, chatting and laughing to their mobiles, small groups of people not so sure of their destinations walk less purposefully, looking for something to entertain them. Some residents walk by with shopping bags, looking forward to cooking a nice dinner and quietly watching The Bill, or listening to good music, or reading a book.

The ones who sit all day in the Plaza, who vanished for a while, have returned and taken up their positions on the ledge outside Hungry Jacks. They sit silently, and, only occasionally, there is an outburst when one of them falls into uncontrollable rage at another.

VOICE 1: The second Professor walks through the Plaza to the Massage King. (*Sound of the opera Orphée et Eurydice drifts out into the night. Dois-je finir mes jours sans un regard de ce que j'aime.*) She sighs as she hears her favourite song. The sweet contralto singing the part of Orpheus. Fits into this part of the world where beautiful women who were once men stroll through the streets.

On the massage table the hours at the computer are kneaded out of her shoulders and neck with loving care, with hard probing fingers and elbows. The masseurs chat softly to each other in Chinese as they work on the extraordinary array of bodies brought to them, some stoic, sighing at the release of stress, others groaning and crying out in pain. Outside there is a commotion. Three young men, swaying back and forth on their feet, yell from the pavement:

DRUNKEN YOUTH 1: How much does it cost?

DRUNKEN YOUTH 2: Ya do the full body? Ya know what I mean? Do blow jobs?

VOICE 1: Their faces are leering and their voices are slurred. One holds a large bottle of beer in his right hand, wrapped in a brown paper bag. He keeps trying to fit it, absent mindedly, into the pocket of his skin tight jeans, looking vaguely puzzled when it does not fit. The head masseur, a slight and beautiful young woman, comes to the door and shakes her head slightly and frowns. She says softly:

MASSEUR: You want massage?

VOICE 1: She points to the board on which the prices are listed.

DRUNKEN YOUTH 2: Whaddya do? The lot. Ya know?

VOICE 1: He staggers, and leers, his thick red lips are loose and wet. One of his companions feels sure in some blurry space in his brain that it is time to unzip his tight trousers and get some relief. He hunkers forward to pull the zip down in such a way that his precious jewels do not get snagged. He fumbles his flaccid dick out of his trousers, and waves it at the masseur, realizing as he does so an unbearable need to urinate. He urinates on the floor of the Massage King. The masseurs freeze and stare at him in horror. They do not have the words in English to tell him to leave. Unabashed his friend asks:

DRUNKEN YOUTH 2: How much does it cost? The massage?

VOICE 1: The second Professor gets up from the massage table to speak to them and they stagger off round the corner into the Plaza. The masseurs wash the stinking urine from their entryway. The second Professor goes with the head masseur to the police station to make a report on these three young men looking for trouble, but the masseur does not have the words in English, and the professor cannot remember what they were wearing. She only remembers the staggering gait, the thick slobbering red lips, the too tight jeans and the bottle of beer in the brown paper bag. The police point out that this is not an adequate description – it could fit any one of the hundreds of drunken men out there on the streets. When they get back, the drunken youths have vanished into the dark night.

VOICE 2: Harald has a Viking hat turned up side down on the pavement, with a few coins in it. He plays his mouth organ in a desultory fashion, distracted by the conversations going on around him amongst his mates. When he listens to the music it seems sweet, and capable of melting the hardest heart, bringing tears to the eyes of those whose faces are sealed over against him (*sound of mouth organ*).

VOICE 1: The pavement is thick with fun-seekers on their way to nightclubs and to sex joints. Most of them are young and look much the same as each other, the girls with their long fingernails, bare midriffs, perfect teeth and mobiles glued to their ears; the boys with their jeans and T-shirts and identical expressions on their faces. All laughter and excitement, switched on and oblivious to each other. Scattered amongst them are the usual familiar faces, each eccentric and exotic in its own way: the biker gang, the guy with the Mohawk, the old bloke who shuffles about in his baggy pants and pisses wherever it takes his fancy, the tall elegant tranny, who stops the hearts of both men and women when they see her, and Jancy, who is addicted to the internet and hasn't washed in a year, hanging about outside the internet joint having a quick drag on his fag, leaving the butt on the doorstep so he can light it up again when he comes back out. He stinks so bad you can smell him, even after he goes inside. And then there's 60-year-old Maisie, sitting on a milk-crate, with her breasts like watermelons, her low-cut dress revealing those beauties in all their extraordinary magnificence. Maisie drives a flash Mercedes and spends most of her time with blokes from the top end of town. She hangs out here because she loves the electric buzz of it, the sleaze, the unpredictability. And Poppet, who shouldn't be here. Dressed up as a naughty school girl, with her blonde hair tied in bunches on either side of her head. She's on the verge of passing out, struggling to stay upright, her head dropping and body sagging every few seconds. Then Queenie, who turns everyone's head as they walk by. Queen of the night, tall and slender, leopard skin mini-skirt, long gorgeous legs in soft leather thigh-high boots, a low-cut glittering gold top that reveals the kind of breasts that some would die for. Her face is crowned with a magnificent tumble of tightly coiled bronze ringlets.

QUEENIE: I'm the Queen of the night. When I'm as high as a kite, and a man takes me in his arms, and buries his face in my glorious breasts, he's king of my world. His rippling muscles, his large erect organ, his joy in my breasts, my softly rounded white body, the secret throbbing place between my legs, longing for him. A union fit for the gods – not weighed down by guilt or anxiety – by the what ifs, and is this real love? The questions of good middle-class people, their sex killed dead by their relentless quest for meaning. Here, in this union, my body is completely uninhibited. We can do whatever it is lust drives us to do, and ride on the high of an orgasm that dissolves the particles of your body and sets them adrift among the stars. It is heavenly love. And afterwards I will stand down there on the street and entice another god who will go with me into that uninhibited space of pure body, pure lust, pure joy. They are more than happy to pay well for it – for the pleasure of that moment of pure lust. That state of pleasure can last through ten such gods at least, sometimes twenty and on a good night I can do that many in a couple of hours. Afterwards, they enjoy the furtive looks at each other, in the urinals, over a beer, chatting up their girlfriends, who didn't notice they were gone. They know where each other has been, they know the moment of abandonment, the grunting, thrusting, groaning explosion of unrestrained pleasure. At least that's what they imagine. Some shy boys can't get over their inhibitions. Most have had a few drinks too many, or shot up too much dope to be able to get it up. No matter, they pay up anyway, and can still go out in the street and exchange the glances that suggest that amongst men they too know that moment of pure conquest.

Want a lady darling?

Both my kids are at Uni. I've paid off the mortgage. I'm paying their fees up front. They want for nothing. The trick is not to depend on the dope. The grind of sex without it is grim – fat sweaty bodies stinking of beer and cigarettes, flabby tummies, flaccid dicks having to be encouraged into life, missing teeth, bad breath, guilt, anxiety. When I'm coming down it's tempting to get another hit. They look and behave like goblins and monsters. But I don't. I resist.

Want a lady darling?

No, well that's his loss. Pete's nearly finished his medical degree. Gina's writing a PhD on the sex trade, for god's sake, about the girls in the clubs who are putting themselves through Sydney Uni. There's an irony for you.

The other trick is not to share your money with pimps and madams – or the police. You have to be in control, not the other way round.

Want a lady darling?

It's slow tonight. A few more hours to go, then home to a nice hot bath in my claw foot tub, with candles lit, Edith Piaf singing *Je ne regret rien*, and a view of the ocean with the sun rising up through the early morning clouds.

Want a lady love?

Here we go.

VOICE 1: The Plaza is a theatre full of life's dramas, the surrounding walls creating an amphitheatre in which each player loudly performs for whoever is listening:

MULTIPLE OVERLAPPING VOICES: Give me m'money! (*shove*)

Leave me alone will ya!

Give me m'money! (*shove*)

Leave me alone will ya!

Give me m'money! (*shove*)

Leave me alone!

(*Sound of a metal bar clanks and reverberates on the granite paving*)

Haw haw!

A technicolour yawn that went from the top of William Street all the way to the bottom. Five hundred metres man . . .

Haw haw!

A technicolour yawn!

Haw haw!

All the way down! Fuckin' amazing man.

(*Crash and clank of metal bar, wail of a siren, squabble and squawk of seagulls*)

You should have seen me man I was going like the clappers!

I did, I did. Where were you? (*screams*) Did you really? Where are you? We're in Springfield Plaza heading for the Empire. We'll meet you outside.

I was crying so hard, the tears were just streaming down my face and I just wanted to tell everyone to fuck off!

When I was a kid I had this pair of blue dancing shoes.

Yeah?

I'm going to MacDonalds. Want anything? I'll bring ya some chips.

I'm bloody starving.

Ya wanna joint?

Ya wanna fix?

Ya wanna hit?

Ya wanna lady love?

Ya got any change for a cuppa tea?

I know this guy right, all his veins are shot. He shoots up in his dick man. It's the truth, the only veins he's got left. Has to get an erection, then . . .

Fuckin' get out of m' face will ya!

(*sound of glass breaking*)

Give me m' money now ya mongrel or I'll kill ya
(*sound of footsteps running*)
Come back here ya mongrel
(*Metal bar clanking on the paving, siren wailing, sound of vomiting*)
What's going on here?
No I don't talk to police.
What's going on?
No I'm serious, I don't talk to police.
It's a Sydney Melbourne thing (*laughter*).
He's legged it with my American Express
Come down to the station and make a report.
(*Laughter*)
It's just a Sydney Melbourne thing.
I was crying and crying so hard . . .
Ya wanna hit?
Spare any change for a cuppa tea?

VOICE 1: A young woman in Earl Lane is dragging the garbage out of the bins, scattering it on the ground. She is searching, searching, endlessly through all the bins, for presents she can give people, for interesting things she can take home to her room already thick with rubbish.

A young man is out looking for some Ice, and he's in a hurry. The ice worms are in his flesh, digging down to his bones.

The ageing bikies turn on their engines and rev them up loudly, vrrmm, vrrmm. One rolls out slowly onto the street, and a second, wearing a skeleton mask, rolls out and blocks the traffic, gesturing to the others to roll out while he holds the traffic at bay. They rev up in a pack, and the last one who held the traffic, falls in at the end.

(*Loud sound of twenty engines revving up and taking off, a brief silence, a distant siren wailing, silence. Then a short sharp screech of breaks followed by a thud.*)

Llewellyn Jones lies crumpled on the roadway.

The traffic has stopped. The pedestrians have stopped. Life has stopped in this frozen frame of disbelief.

One of the pedestrians whips out her mobile and dials 000.

DEE DEE: An ambulance, quick, Darlinghurst Road, just outside the needle exchange – yes yes – the needle exchange. He just stepped out in front of the car. He's on the road. For god's sake hurry up.

VOICE 1: She shuts up her phone and stares at the white-faced driver climbing out of his car, in slow motion. He doesn't want to see what is there, he doesn't want to be there, he does not want to see up close the body lying sprawled across the road.

Crowds gather, the area is cordoned off, the sirens wailing. But it's too late. Too late. Too late to find his beloved Norma. Too late to spend the twenty dollars he found in the auto teller.

VOICE 2: All is quiet in the Plaza. Occasionally furtive men come and piss long flowing streams of stinking yellow liquid against the wall. Always in the same spot.

At 3 am the young and beautiful burst out of their nightclubs to catch the last train or get the last cabs. Groups of young men hang about, and some find a plastic bottle and turn the Plaza for a few brief minutes into a soccer field, and themselves into stylish, sexy, world-class soccer players.

At 4 am there is a young man too drunk to move, who sinks down on the steps and cannot get up, even though his friends prod and poke him and encourage him to get up. They wait patiently, then pull him to his feet. He gingerly tries out his legs and finds they will work in a sort of a fashion, and they stagger off.

The man in the elegant suit is pacing back and forth, trying not to look as if he is expecting anyone, pacing, pacing. A couple of men come and wake Harald who has bedded down for the night, to see if he's got anything they can use. And then they too move on.

The garbage truck roars up the Lane and men bounce out and open up mysterious doors and pull out the hidden wheelie bins.

Someone has found some flowers and put them in the gutter where Professor Jones fell.

VOICE 1: Harald dreams yet again of his lost Dadda and whimpers in his sleep. The second Professor dreams of her Uncle Llewellyn throwing back his head and laughing his huge belly laugh, in the days before he was sent from home in disgrace. Danielle dreams of a small girl whose feet she kisses. Georgie Delaney dreams of Judgement Day, and discovers to her amazement that God is Chinese. Janni writes in his journal of his new-found libido, and Jen dreams of her husband, who loved her so much, and died at sea when she was only thirty. Mollie dreams of a magnificent hat with sweeping feathers and a dress that shows off her magnificent cleavage. Corinne dreams of walking, walking endlessly, her weary feet taking one step after another, the silver mirage of her destination slipping out of sight each time she thinks she is home. The backpacker scratches himself and dreams of Queenie's breasts and sobs with pleasure as he buries his face in them.

And so the dreams weave their way in and out of the flow of traffic in the Cross, in and out of intersecting lives that do and do not touch each other.

The song of a currawong, chi-di-ch-laa summons the faintest wash of pink into the deep night sky.

All is quiet in the Plaza.

The El Alamein fountain flows over, and the water runs down to the sea.

Note

1 This desire to write the place I lived was inspired by a collaborative research project funded by the Australian Research Council called *Enabling place pedagogies in rural and urban Australia*. My co-researchers are Susanne Gannon, Margaret Somerville, and Kerith Power.

References for the introduction

Buchanan, I. and Lambert, G. (2005). Introduction. In I. Buchanan and G. Lambert (Eds.), *Deleuze and space*. Edinburgh: Edinburgh University Press.

Cixous, H. (1993). *Three steps on the ladder of writing* (Trans. S. Cornell and S. Sellers) New York: Columbia University Press.

Davies, B. (1996). *Power/knowledge/desire: Changing school organisation and management practices* (pp. 1–259). Canberra: Department of Employment, Education and Youth Affairs.

Davies, B. (2000). *(In)scribing body/landscape relations*. Walnut Creek: AltaMira Press.

Deleuze, G. (1990). *Negotiations*. (Trans. M. Joughin) New York: Columbia University Press.

Deleuze, G. (1997). *Essays critical and clinical* (Trans. D.W. Smith and M.A. Greco) Minneapolis: University of Minnesota Press.

Deleuze, G. (2004). *Difference and repetition* (Trans. P. Patton, first published 1968, France). New York: Columbia University Press.

Thomas, D. (1954). *Under Milkwood*. New York: New Directions Publishing Corporation.

Williams, J. (2003). *Gilles Deleuze's difference and repetition. A critical introduction and guide*. Edinburgh: Edinburgh University Press.

Afterword

Decentering voice in qualitative inquiry

Elizabeth Adams St.Pierre

From the very beginning of my career as a qualitative researcher and methodologist I have had trouble with *data* (St.Pierre, 1997a) as described in what I have recently been calling 'conventional' qualitative inquiry, a methodology turning toward interpretivism but still very dependent on positivism – actually unthinkable without positivism. My troubles with data, especially with the privileging of interview data – the voices of participants transformed into written text – were immediately evident in two research projects grounded in poststructural theories of subjectivity and language. The first project was a combination of an ethnography and an interview study (St.Pierre, 1995) that used Foucault's ethical analysis, care of the self, to study the construction of subjectivity in a group of older white southern women who live in my hometown. The second was an interview project (unpublished) with expert readers who read texts that are too hard to read.

Readers of the essays in this collection must, by now, be aware that a research methodology that privileges *voice* as the truest, most authentic data and/or evidence has to be problematic for those with a poststructural bent because voice is part of the humanist discursive and material formation poststructuralism works against. Voice is especially troublesome for those who are wary of the supposed conscious, stable, unified, rational, coherent, knowing, autonomous, and ahistoric humanist individual who is 'endowed with a will, a freedom, an intentionality which is then subsequently "expressed" in language, in action, in the public domain' (Butler, 1995, p. 136). To be fair, I will out myself here at the beginning of this chapter and confess that I find the unexamined celebration of voice in qualitative research increasingly tiresome. I believe we have burdened the voices of our participants with too much evidentiary weight. I suggest we put voice in its place as one data source among many from which we produce evidence to warrant our claims and focus for a time on other data we use to think about our projects that we've been ignoring for decades.

I came to this conclusion early in my own work after studying Deleuze and Guattari's (1980/1987, 1991/1994) radical ontology and poststructural theories of subjectivity (e.g., Butler, 1992; Derrida, 1967/1974; Foucault, 1984/1985). In my research projects I found that I no longer knew who either the researcher(s) or the participants in my studies *were* if, in fact, we could even *be*, as described in the 'philosophical system that begins with Plato and continues through Descartes, Husserl, and Sartre and supports an ontological distinction between soul (consciousness, mind) and body' (Butler, 1990, p. 12) and, I might add, between the human and the non-human. Simply pluralizing subjectivity or talking about split subjects or 'subjects-in-process' did not begin to account for a subject I found myself ~~being~~ (and had always ~~been~~) and trying to write. I have written elsewhere that during the research project on subjectivity in my hometown 'such a subject was almost too hard to think, and it's still too hard to think except when I am that subject. Such a subject breaks down every conceptual order I know' (St.Pierre, 2004, p. 332), especially the conceptual order upon which voice relies for its meaning.

Troubles with subjectivity are bound to lead to troubles with language, and after studying poststructural theories of language (e.g., Deleuze, 1993/1994, 1967/1974; Foucault, 1971/1972), I no longer believed, first, that meaning was a 'portable property' (Spivak, 1974, p. lvii) or, second, that language could transport meaning, unmediated, from one unified subject to another, say, in an interview. Butler's (1987) 'linguistic misfires' (p. 183) are all too common in ordinary speech, so how could someone's voice provide evidence that could warrant scientific claims? We know that people say all sorts of things, so why is what they say treated as more authentic than, for example, something they write or draw? I am reminded here of an old *New Yorker* cartoon taped to my office door in which a woman stands in the middle of her garden and says, 'The garden is my resume.' Indeed. She doesn't have to say anything. So why do we privilege voice as the carrier of the truest meaning?

My troubles with the subject and language were compounded by my troubles with poststructural theories of space/time (e.g., Augé, 1992/1995; Deleuze & Guattari, 1980/1987; Hardt & Negri, 2000; Serres, with Latour, 1990/1995). The voice in its presentness, if there is such a thing, vanishes immediately, and our poor attempts to capture it on tape or in fieldnotes always fail. So where/when is the interview – the exchange of voices? Does it occur in the space/time of the 'official' tape-recorded conversation as my institutional review board assumes? Or does it continue in other 'unofficial' conversations with that participant in other spaces – in dreams – and in other times – in a 'memory of the future' (Deleuze, 1986/1988, p.107). The fairly straightforward interview described in qualitative textbooks became impossible to think or do. Voices could no longer reliably secure the truth.

Presence and voice

My troubles with data (in qualitative inquiry, data collected in observations and interviews), with the subject, with language, and with space/time emerged from my troubles with *presence*, Derrida's bane. Presence, 'being there,' is what makes qualitative inquiry unique because we believe that our face-to-face interactions with people make our work especially valid. We are not armchair researchers, running statistical programs on data several times removed from living, breathing people. We qualitative researchers are very present in our research, in the thick of things, talking with and observing our participants. Qualitative inquiry is not distant; it's live and in person; it happens right now. And, of course, extended time in the field – being there and being there longer – makes our work even more valid.

For poststructuralists, however, presence and other related concepts of qualitative inquiry – for example, voice, interview, narrative, experience – cannot secure validity, the truth. A rather long quote from Derrida (1972/1981) describes the economy of the metaphysics of presence, *phonocentrism*, that forces us to completely rethink qualitative inquiry:

> *Phoné,* in effect, is the signifying substance *given to consciousness* as that which is most intimately tied to the thought of the signified concept. From this point of view, the voice is consciousness itself. When I speak, not only am I conscious of being present for what I think, but I am conscious also of keeping as close as possible to my thought, or to the 'concept,' a signifier that does not fall into the world, a signifier that I hear as soon as I emit it, that seems to depend upon my pure and free spontaneity, requiring the use of no instrument, no accessory, no force taken from the world. Not only do the signifier and the signified seem to unite, but also, in this confusion, the signifier seems to erase itself or to become transparent, in order to allow the concept to present itself as what it is, referring to nothing other than its presence. The exteriority of the signifier seems reduced. Naturally this experience is a lure, but a lure whose necessity has organized an entire structure, or an entire epoch; and on the grounds of this epoch a semiology has been constituted whose concepts and fundamental presuppositions are quite precisely discernible from Plato to Husserl, passing through Aristotle, Rousseau, Hegel, etc. (p. 22)

In phonocentrism, presence is 'treated as a centering, grounding force, or principle' (Culler, 1982, p. 93). As Culler (1982) remarked,

> the authority of presence, its power of valorization, structures all our thinking . . . To claim, as in the Cartesian *cogito*, that the 'I' resists radical doubt because it is present to itself in the act of thinking or doubting is one sort of appeal to presence. Another is the notion that the meaning of an utterance is what is present to the consciousness of the speaker, what he or she 'has in mind,' at the moment of utterance. (p. 94)

It is as if signifiers aren't separate from thought, as if they somehow emerge in voice miraculously, spontaneously *as* thought. In this phenomenological system, voice is pre-discursive and 'asserts the "truth" of a kind of physiological understanding of the immediacy and interconnectedness of the world before the mind learns how to 'talk' itself into an understanding based on an "I-Thou" division' (Watts, 2001, pp. 181–182). Moreover, because it seems that the listener can actually hear in the voice of the speaker her breath, the life force of her being, we begin to believe that speech is the purest, most direct, natural, and authentic form of communication. The 'voices of our participants,' subjective witnesses whose 'experiences are offered not only as truths, but as the most authentic kinds of truths' (Williams, 1976, p. 128), are the centerpiece of our work. In this way, presence, and especially voice, structures the economy of conventional qualitative inquiry as it structures other humanist projects.

With the critique of phonocentrism in mind, I found in my research that all the interdependent and interlocking concepts of qualitative inquiry, its entire structure, its 'grid of intelligibility' (Foucault, 1976/1978, p. 93) – grounded as it is in particular descriptions of the subject, of language, of knowledge, of reality, and so forth – concepts that rely on a metaphysics of presence, must be deconstructed (see, e.g., Garrick, 1999). I also learned that other poststructural qualitative researchers had had troubles similar to mine, and that the peculiarities of their projects had demanded that they deconstruct other humanist concepts used in qualitative inquiry. Lather deconstructed *validity* (1993), the presumed *clarity* of language (1996a), in addition to *empathy*, *voice*, and *authenticity* (see this volume). Jackson (2003) deconstructed *voice*. Scheurich deconstructed *validity* (1993) and the *interview* (1995). Pillow (2003) deconstructed *reflexivity*. I deconstructed *data* (St.Pierre, 1997a) and the *field* (1997b).

Because of this kind of work, qualitative inquiry is no longer itself – it is not one thing. If a researcher self-identifies as 'qualitative,' we cannot be sure what that means because qualitative inquiry, the methodology, is reinvented within various epistemologies as well as in systems of thought, like poststructuralism, that critique the hermeneutical rage for meaning and doubt the epistemological project itself. As a result, poststructural qualitative inquiry may bear little semblance to conventional qualitative inquiry.

Much has changed since the publication in 1985 of Lincoln and Guba's classic book, *Naturalistic Inquiry*, and since the publication in 1986 of Erickson's classic essay, 'Qualitative Methods in Research on Teaching.' These texts are only two markers of the beginning of the qualitative movement that took up the 'interpretive turn' (Hiley, Bohman, & Shusterman, 1991) initiated in cultural anthropology, for example, by Geertz's (1973) *The Interpretation of Culture*. These texts retain features of the logical positivism they worked against that had dominated the philosophy of science since World War II, because the correction or critique of a prior system of thought cannot escape that system. As Derrida (1966/1978) wrote about the critique of metaphysics,

> There is no sense in doing without the concepts of metaphysics in order to attack metaphysics. We have no language – no syntax and no lexicon – which is alien to this history. We cannot utter a single proposition which has not already slipped into the form, the logic, and the implicit postulations of precisely what it seeks to contest. (p. 250)

Creating a new language may or may not help in such critique, for example, substituting 'trustworthiness' for 'validity,' because both words refer to legitimation or truth. As Spivak (1974) wrote, 'to make a new word is to run the risk of forgetting the problem or believing it solved' (p. xv), and even if we doubt it is possible or desirable, truth matters, especially in research. It follows, then, that there is no need to give up on *voice* but rather to bring into question its authorizing power and, as I wrote earlier, to put it in its place.

To repeat, my point here is that qualitative inquiry is no longer stable or coherent, and the work of poststructural researchers may not be recognizable as *qualitative* as that signifier is usually described in introductory qualitative textbooks. Think about the following scenario. If, in a research project, one were able to deconstruct even one, much less several, of the humanist concepts that organize the coherence of conventional qualitative inquiry, that is, if one were able to accomplish the 'over-turning and displacing of a conceptual order, as well as the nonconceptual order with which the conceptual order is articulated' (Derrida, 1972/1981, p. 329), how would one then describe that project? Would it be *qualitative*? Would it be *research*?

And, perhaps more importantly, given federal policy that insists that educational researchers do 'scientifically based research,' would it be *science*? Grover J. Whitehurst, the Director of the U.S. Institute of Education Sciences and the creator of its What Works Clearinghouse, said in a session (Session 29.001) at the 2003 annual meeting of the American Educational Research Association that we need less theory and more of what works and, further, that postmodern methods, in particular, will not help us learn what works. He was very clear that research that smacks of postmodernism is not science. But if Whitehurst and others who are very sure they know what science is have been reading widely during the last 40 years (and many of us doubt they have), they might justifiably fear that science is being deconstructed, that it is increasingly unrecognizable, which means, of course, that the power they maintain within the old structure is likely to be diminished. That could be good news indeed for the rest of us.

Narrative

So what has poststructuralism done to conventional, interpretive/positivist qualitative inquiry? For one thing, it has critiqued narrative, as have, interestingly, some of those (Shavelson, Phillips, Towne, & Feuer, 2003) who have recently tried to re-install randomized experimental trials as the gold standard of scientifically based research in education. These particular authors, who may or may not be educational researchers, asked the following questions about narrative (with my comments in brackets) in order to point out its supposed shortcomings:

> To what extent can rival narrative accounts of the same action be ruled out? [Why should rival accounts be ruled out – to silence disagreement?] To what extent would another narrator replicate the account? [Can human activity ever be replicated?] To what extent does the narrative generalize to other times and places? [Why is generalizability privileged?] There is nothing in the use of narrative form, by itself, that guarantees the veracity of the content of the account or which vitiates the need for the usual epistemic warrants used in science. [But isn't science itself simply another narrative?]
>
> (Shavelson et al., 2003, p. 27)

Agreeing with Carnap (1966), a logical positivist, they refer to narrative work as 'pre-scientific' (p. 28) and unable to warrant scientific claims.

Ironically, poststructuralism also critiques, but differently, the narrative impulse, the 'narrative fixing of reality and subjective identity' (Clough, 1998, p. 11), what Ricoeur (1983/1984) described as the pulling together of temporally distributed, disparate events and supposedly intentional actors into the coherent comfort of narrative. In his *Poetics*, Aristotle put forth the idea, summarized by Miller (1990), that 'plot is the most important feature of a narrative. A good story has a beginning, middle, and end, making a shapely whole with no extraneous elements' (p. 66). All this smacks of the familiar Hegelian triumph of Same over Difference as well as Lyotard's (1979/1984) terror of consensus, and poststructuralists are suspicious of what must be excluded to create the equilibrium, totality, unity, and pleasing closure that mark narrative. In fact, Lyotard (1979/1984) defines postmodernism as 'an incredulity toward metanarratives' (p. xxiv), and he identifies the 'liberation of humanity and the speculative unity of all knowledge' as great legitimating 'myths' (Jameson, 1984, p. ix) that spawn smaller narratives we use to make sense of our lives.

But some people say that everything is narrative – that it is the 'central instance of the human mind (Jameson, 1984, p. xi) – and qualitative inquiry certainly embraced the 'narrative turn' (see, e.g., Chase, 2005, Connelly & Clandinin, 1990; Maines, 1993; Nespor & Barylske, 1991).

> The flight of intellectuals to 'story' – and away, one might say, from treatise – [was] prompted by the belief that 'story' (quickly ossified into the more portentous 'narrative' by scholars) remained an academic-free zone, where life's events and lessons might be directly encountered without professorial vices, like murdering to dissect.
>
> (Romano, 2002, p. B12)

Here, the narrative, the most 'natural' form, the unmediated brute fact, the tale of the experience itself, is above analysis, critique, or interpretation even though it is always already interpretation piled on interpretation, or, as Geertz (1973) wrote, 'turtles all the way down' (p. 29).

Narrative seems to accompany 'nostalgia for the presence of the one true Word' (Haraway, 1988, p. 590), a desire to recover a lost origin – 'the point where the truth of things corresponded to a truthful discourse, the site of a fleeting articulation that discourse has obscured and finally lost' (Foucault, 1971/1984, p. 79) – a return to the real, which might, however, be a simulacrum (Baudrillard, 1981/1988). On the other hand, narrative is a 'way of *consuming* the past, a way of forgetting' (Jameson, 1984, p. xii) – ordering and completing the past so it can be more easily put aside. In any case, the narrative impulse cannot be privileged in poststructural research.

Occasionally, I have read lovely, theory-laden stories (e.g., Chaudhry, 1997) that serve as exemplars of what narrative might accomplish in qualitative inquiry. Most often, however, it seems that qualitative researchers 'find' stories in their data and call that work analysis. I have read too many research reports prefaced by a solid review of the theoretical literature, which presumably will be used in data analysis, only to find that theory abandoned and the 'analysis' section an unreflexive description of participants followed by a collection of stories. I believe, with Lather (1996b), that 'methodology often diverts attention from more fundamental issues of epistemology' (p. 2) and that researchers disregard theory convinced that a simple story can substitute for a more rigorous analysis. They may believe that analysis would sully the pure, the natural, the sacrosanct voices of participants, the data story that 'speaks for itself.' I suspect that the organization of the typical qualitative research report (borrowed from the natural sciences) may encourage the tendency to suspend theory because theory and data are separated into different sections of the paper. Theory, once reviewed, is simply forgotten by the time the author presents data, voices. It could be that the researcher may be unable to use the theory they've studied as an analytic; if so, she may need different theory or instruction in analysis. And, of course, there is the inevitable lack of fit between theory and data. But that disconnect should be an alert that fruitful theoretical work is possible and should be attempted rather than a reason to abandon analysis. I find I am less and less interested in the simple data 'stories' I read in qualitative research reports.

Experience

Narrative goes hand-in-hand with another concept that grounds qualitative inquiry, *experience*, as in the common phrase, 'the everyday lived experiences of participants.' Participants often embed their experiences in stories they tell us in interviews. Experience thus becomes data and then foundational evidence that warrants our claims.

But Derrida (1970/1974) explained that experience is a metaphysical construct that 'has always designated the relationship with a presence' (p. 60). In the metaphysics of presence, either experience or identity is assumed to be prior to the other, depending on one's project, and so can serve as a foundation. But Nietzsche (1887/1992) wrote that 'there is no such sub-stratum; there is no "being" behind doing, effecting, becoming; "the doer" is merely a fiction added to the deed' (p. 481). In her work on performativity, Butler (1995), following Nietzsche, wrote that even though a 'performative appears to "express" a prior intention, a doer *behind* the deed, the prior agency is only legible as the effect of that utterance' (p. 134). In this way, identity and experience produce each other and cannot be thought separately; therefore, neither can be a foundational authority, and as Scott (1992) explained,

> it is not individuals who have experience, but subjects who are constituted through experience. Experience in this definition then becomes not the origin of our explanation, not the authoritative (because seen or felt) evidence that grounds what is known, but rather that which we seek to explain, that about which knowledge is produced. (pp. 25–26)

Thus, experience is not simply material, what 'happens'; it is also discursive. Of course, this is not to say that nothing happens, but that what happens is recognized and made meaningful only through available discourses that 'systematically form the objects of which they speak' (Foucault, 1971/1972, p. 49), including identities. Rather than being the ground of our knowing, experience is a valorized, regulating fiction and a 'shaky basis for epistemology' (Fuss, 1989, p. 17).

But appeals to experience abound in qualitative inquiry where it serves as the origin, the final warrant for a claim; and the 'authority of the "lived"'' (Spivak, 1999, p. 39) is celebrated rather than problematized as a window onto, for example, the workings of the discursive and material practices of ideology (Althusser, 1970/1971). 'Although a phenomenological inquiry into the conditions of speaking keeps us in close correspondence with lived experience, concerns with the linguistic [in poststructuralism] lead one to comprehend signification as primarily symbolic, having little to do with the ontic' (Watts, 2001, p. 182). In his history of sexuality, Foucault (1976/1978) wrote that truth in our society, and in scientific discourse, is 'faced with a theoretical and methodological paradox: the long discussions concerning the possibility of constituting a science of the subject, the validity of introspection, lived experience as evidence, [and] the presence of consciousness to itself' (p. 64). Poststructuralists doubt that truth, as described in humanism, can begin to contemplate these paradoxes. It follows, then, that a radical critique of the primacy of voice as the teller of experience and truth in qualitative inquiry is overdue.

Qualitative inquiry

Over ten years ago, I wrote that I wanted 'to produce different knowledge and produce knowledge differently' (St.Pierre, 1997a, p. 175). At that time, researchers had already begun to deconstruct concepts central to qualitative inquiry – *voice*, *narrative*, and *experience* – and others I mentioned earlier that they believed were overcoded with presence. Since then, we've made various attempts to produce knowledge differently. For example, we've written 'messy texts' (Marcus, 1994, p. 567) to trouble the transparency of realist tales, though in retrospect quite a few just seem messy rather than innovative. To address bias and objectivity – positivist concepts still evident in so-called interpretive qualitative inquiry – we've asked our students to write 'subjectivity statements' in which they 'reflect' on their 'subjectivities' as if 'subjectivity' is, first, something that can be pluralized and, second, as if the subject is a stable entity upon which one can reflect. Even if we claim to be poststructural, we continue the positivist practice of coding data and calling that work analysis. Further, except for writing a brief description of coding data or describing the miraculous 'emergence of themes,' seldom does a researcher tackle the difficult task of describing data analysis – perhaps because it would be virtually unrecognizable as what we now think of as analysis, for how does one describe *thinking about an object of knowledge* like teacher preparation, dropouts, or teen pregnancy.

Even though we write theoretically about fractured, shifting subjects, participants in our reports retain the characteristics of humanist subjects – we organize them under proper names, 'pseudonyms,' and we write rich, thick descriptions of their appearances, personalities, and experiences embedded in stories. We continue to serve them up as whole as possible for our readers, believing that richer and fuller descriptions will get us closer and closer to the truth of the participant. And, of course, we celebrate their voices, trying to stay as close to their original spoken words as possible, not worrying about editing out the 'you know's and 'um's in our written transcripts.

We may attempt to complicate matters by saying that we are practicing deconstruction by simultaneously 'doing it and troubling it,' but it seems to me that *we might just stop doing it* – qualitative research, that is – in the same way, particularly if we want to produce different knowledge by 'rupture and restructuration' (Derrida, 1993/1994, p. 13). But I think it is very, very difficult to produce knowledge differently because I believe we are still deeply mired in the conceptual order of the metaphysics of presence. And it is very, very difficult to muster all those deconstructive learnings at once, ours and everyone else's, and then do something we might still want to call 'inquiry' or even 'science.' Who would recognize it? Where would we begin?

Derrida (1967/1974) wrote that we must begin '*Wherever we are*; in a text where we already believe ourselves to be.' And, indeed, my meager deconstruction of conventional qualitative inquiry has occurred *in the texts I have written*, where I noticed after the fact and *in the writing* (Richardson & St.Pierre, 2005) that I had refused fundamental categories of qualitative inquiry – the subject, data, representation, and so forth. Here, I am reminded of Foucault's (1982) admonition that we should 'refuse what we are . . . we have to promote new forms of subjectivity through the refusal of this kind of individuality' (p. 216). Subjectivity has always been the focus of my work, the linchpin that, once put under erasure, topples every other supposed stable referent. And, because I believe writing is thinking – analysis, if you will – writing has been the site of my struggle.

Of course, it is almost impossible to say or write a sentence without using 'I' to refer to 'me,' no matter how I think about 'myself.' We are always bound by the language and the 'I' of humanism. But Butler (1992) explained this very well in the following:

> My position is mine to the extent that 'I' – and I do not shirk from the pronoun – replay and resignify the theoretical positions that have constituted me, working the possibilities of their convergence, and trying to take account of the possibilities they systematically exclude. (p. 9)

Over the course of many years, I have worked hard to resignify those theories that described a subjectivity I was born into but never believed. An accomplishment of this refusal is that I *no longer think of myself as I did before poststructuralism*, and the following passage by Rorty (1986) was pivotal in this work:

> The urge to tell stories of progress, maturation and synthesis might be over-
> come if we once took seriously the notion that we only know the world and
> ourselves *under a description*. For doing so would mean taking seriously
> the possibility that we just *happened* on that description – that it was not
> the description which nature evolved us to apply, or that which best unified
> the manifold of previous descriptions, but just the one which we have now
> *chanced* to latch onto. If we once could feel the full force of the claim that
> our present discursive practices were given neither by God, not by intuition
> of essence nor by the cunning of reason, but *only* by chance, then we would
> have a culture which lacked not only a theory of knowledge, not only a sense
> of progress, but *any* source of what Nietzsche called 'metaphysical comfort.'
> (p. 48)

Until I read those words, I thought I was essentially real. It had never occurred to me
that I was a very real *effect of a description*, that I was living my life and producing
myself, others (and the world) according to someone's description, and that there
had been through the centuries of the past and would be through the centuries of
the future other descriptions of the person, the individual, the subject, whatever
signifier we choose. I found this idea terrifically freeing, though, of course, I soon
understood that escaping the 'I' is impossible. Nonetheless, Rorty's words have
enabled me to look at most anything, any structure – the subject, qualitative inquiry,
science – as a *description* that can, has been, and will be rewritten with more or
less ease.

And I use the word 'rewritten' deliberately, because, as I explained earlier, it
is in the writing – about qualitative research, subjectivity, language, data, and so
forth – that I learn refusal. So I write, and then I analyze my writing to see what I've
done and not done. For example, when writing a paper (unpublished) about the
reading hard texts project mentioned earlier, I found that I had refused the primacy
of voice – of interview data – by including data from participant interviews in the
literature review, the review of theory. I did not write a separate literature review
section in which I quoted only published (written) scholars followed at some point
by an interpretation or data section in which I assigned pseudonyms to participants,
described them individually, quoted their voices at length, and so on. Here's an
example of that writing with words from participants presented in both quotes
and italics and embedded in what is commonly called the literature review, the
discussion of theory and epistemology that guides the study:

> It is understandable that words that cannot be understood in isolation (or even
> in the context of a single text) may put off readers who expect language to
> be immediately transparent and clear. What happens is that texts dense with
> '*special language*' are sometimes dismissed as deliberately obfuscatory and
> full of jargon. But, as Terry Eagleton (1990) explains, 'jargon just means a
> language not natural to me' (p. 35). Perhaps the failure to read occurs because
> we seldom teach students that even experts do not 'understand' certain words,
> even after much struggle. No doubt, it is '*frustrating for people who want an*

answer' to be told that a concise definition of *subjectivity* or *race* or *reading* is not available. '*You have to learn the lingo so you can get the expertise to read,*' and learning the lingo could take years of reading – not a happy prospect for readers who rebel when they encounter a text that doesn't 'beg to be understood.'

(Sommer, 1994, p. 542)

Remember that the topic I studied was how expert readers read texts that are too hard to read. That is what I was thinking about as I wrote and produced knowledge using (1) comments of the scholars whose work I had read in published texts – the conventional theory section of a report – and (2) comments of the scholars I had interviewed – the conventional data section of a report. I thought simultaneously with everyone's ideas as I attempted to make a different sense of the object of my inquiry. So separating their comments into different sections of the report no longer made sense; in fact, I couldn't do it. Participants' comments were no more present, no more foundational, no more authentic, no truer than the comments of Eagleton or Sommer. Writing up my study in this way was not deliberate but rather an unintended effect of many years of attempting to refuse *presence*. Deconstruction just happens.

But, as Spivak (1974) explained, we continue to write about voices, particularly in qualitative inquiry, as if they are originary and present even though they can never be:

> The text of philosophy (of the so-called 'sciences of man,' of literature . . .) is always written (we read it in books, on tape, through the psychic machine): yet that text is always designated by philosophy (and so forth) to be speech ('Plato says . . . ,' or at most, 'it is as if Plato said . . . '). 'Writing' is 'immediate(ly) repressed'. What is written is read as speech or the surrogate of speech. 'Writing' is the name of what is never named. (p. lxx)

I suggest that continuing to privilege the 'voices' of our participants as if they are present and as if that presence is somehow sacred will continue to limit qualitative inquiry. And that brings me to the conclusion of this chapter.

And back to data (and evidence)

I think it bears repeating that in my research I have not studied participants; rather, I have investigated a topic – an object of knowledge – subjectivity in older women or how expert readers read texts that are too hard to read. And I have used comments from everyone I could find, from published researchers and theorists, from participants, from colleagues, from characters in film and fiction, from anyone and everyone to help me think hard about that topic. Thus, I believe all those comments are data – Foucault's words are data just as much as the 'voices of participants' – and should be treated as such. I also believe we should seriously rethink the organization of the conventional qualitative research report because it artificially isolates those data in different sections and thus contributes to weak analyses – too many voices, too little analysis.

In addition to people's comments, I have used data that are not easily identified, some of which I named over a decade ago: dream data, sensual data, emotional data, response data (St.Pierre, 1997a), and memory data (St.Pierre, 1995). One must, following Rorty, give up the conventional description of data to think these (always already) data. Some escape the human/non-human binary. Some escape humanism's measured, chronological time. In my research, just as in my life, time is always out of joint, 'disarticulated, dislocated, dislodged' (Derrida, 1993/1994, p. 18). I agree with Deleuze (1990/1995) 'that it is possible to experience events which have not yet taken place' (p. 48). But data always deferred, never present, cannot be thought in the economy of phonocentrism.

It seems to me that if we are steeped in poststructural theories – if they are in our very bones – we do indeed find ourselves doing it differently. But I think we could be more deliberate in this work of rupture, especially around 'voice.' I think we are ethically obliged to think hard about how we are thinking; and, in the case of data – what (data) we are thinking with. Foucault can help us here. He wrote,

> Thought is not what inhabits a certain conduct and gives it meaning; rather, it is what allows one to step back from this way of acting and reacting, to present it to oneself as an object of thought and to question it as to its meaning, its conditions, and its goals. Thought is freedom in relation to what one does, the motion by which one detaches oneself from it, establishes it as an object, and reflects on it as a problem.
>
> (Foucault, 1984/1997, p. 117)

To reflect on it, as Rorty might say, as one description among others we might think and do.

Jane Flax (1990), agreeing with Rorty, reminded us that the 'philosophy post-modernists seek to displace is a fiction, chosen (in some sense) as a maximally effective rhetorical device' (p. 195). I suggest that we treat conventional qualitative inquiry – mired as it is in the metaphysics of presence – as simply another description, a useful but inadequate fiction – one that may have reached the limits of its effectiveness.

The rigor of qualitative inquiry has been questioned for some time, often by positivists and neo-positivists, but I question its rigor for different reasons: (1) its obsession with the voices of participants as the primary, most authentic data (evidence), which results in (2) the eclipse and disappearance of other data (evidence) that is surely unacknowledged and unaccounted for in a study and, thus (3) weak analysis and the recycling of old ideas. Thinking with Derrida, I look forward to an overturning of the hegemony of presence, of voice, in qualitative inquiry – to what Lather (2007) might call a 'post-methodology' (p. 70), a methodology-to-come in which we begin to do it radically differently wherever we are in our projects. Whether we will call this work 'qualitative' remains to be seen.

References

Althusser, L. (1971). Ideology and ideological state apparatuses (Notes towards an investigation). In L. Althusser, *Lenin and philosophy and other essays* (B. Brewster, Trans.) (pp. 127–186). New York: Monthly Review Press. (Reprinted from *La Pensée,* 1970).

Augé, M. (1995). *Non-places: Introduction to an anthropology of supermodernity* (J. Howe, Trans.). London: Verso. (Original work published 1992).

Baudrillard, J. (1988). Simulacra and simulations. In M. Poster (Ed.), *Jean Baudrillard: Selected writings* (P. Foss, P. Patton, & P. Beitchman, Trans.) (pp. 166–184). Stanford, CA: Stanford University Press (Original work published 1981).

Butler, J. (1987). *Subjects of desire: Hegelian reflections in twentieth-century France.* New York: Columbia University Press.

Butler, J. (1990). *Gender trouble: Feminism and the subversion of identity.* New York: Routledge.

Butler, J. (1992). Contingent foundations: Feminism and the question of 'postmodernism.' In J. Butler & J. W. Scott (Eds.), *Feminists theorize the political* (pp. 3–21). New York: Routledge.

Butler, J. (1995). For a careful reading. In S. Benhabib, J. Butler, D. Cornell, & N. Fraser (Eds.), *Feminist contentions: A philosophical exchange* (pp. 127–143). New York: Routledge (Essay dated 1994).

Carnap, R. (1966). *An introduction to the philosophy of science.* (M. Gardner, Ed.). New York: Dover Publications (Original work published 1966 by Basic Books under the title *Philosophical foundations of physics: An introduction to the philosophy of science*).

Chase, S. E. (2005). Narrative inquiry: Multiple lenses, approaches, voices. In N. K. Denzin & Y. S. Lincoln (Eds.), *Sage handbook of qualitative research* (3rd ed.) (pp. 651–679). Thousand Oaks, CA: Sage Publications.

Chaudhry, L. N. (1997). Researching 'my people,' researching myself: Fragments of a reflexive tale. *International Journal of Qualitative Studies in Education, 10*(4), 441–453.

Clough, P. T. (1998). *The end(s) of ethnography: From realism to social criticism* (2nd ed.). New York: Peter Lang.

Connelly, F. M., & Clandinin, D. J. (1990). Stories of experience and narrative inquiry. *Educational Researcher, 19*(5), 2–14.

Culler, J. (1982). *On deconstruction: Theory and criticism after structuralism.* Ithaca: Cornell University Press.

Deleuze, G. (1988). *Foucault* (S. Hand, Trans.). Minneapolis: University of Minnesota Press (Original work published 1986).

Deleuze, G. (1994). He stuttered. In C. V. Boundas & D. Olkowski (Eds.). *Gilles Deleuze and the theater of philosophy* (pp. 23–29). New York: Routledge (Original work published 1993).

Deleuze, G. (1995). *Negotiations: 1972–1990.* (M. Joughin, Trans.). New York: Columbia University Press (Original work published 1990).

Deleuze, G., & Guattari, F. (1987). *A thousand plateaus: Capitalism and schizophrenia.* (B. Massumi, Trans.). Minneapolis: University of Minnesota Press (Original work published 1980).

Deleuze, G., & Guattari, F. (1994). *What is philosophy?* (H. Tomlinson & G. Burchell, Trans.). New York: Columbia University Press (Original work published 1991).

Derrida, J. (1974). *Of grammatology.* (G. C. Spivak, Trans.). Baltimore: Johns Hopkins University Press. (Original work published 1967).

Derrida, J. (1978). Structure, sign and play in the discourse of the human sciences. In J. Derrida (Ed.), *Writing and difference* (A. Bass, Trans.) (pp. 278–293). Chicago: University of Chicago Press (Lecture delivered 1966).

Derrida, J. (1981). *Positions* (A. Bass, Trans.). Chicago: University of Chicago Press (Original work published 1972).

Derrida, J. (1994). *Specters of Marx: The state of the debt, the work of mourning, and the new international* (P. Kamuf, Trans.). New York: Routledge (Original work published 1993).

Eagleton, T. (1990). *The significance of theory.* Oxford: Blackwell.

Erickson, F. (1986). Qualitative methods in research on teaching (3rd ed.). In M. C. Wittrock (Ed.), *Handbook of research on teaching* (pp. 119–161). New York: Macmillan.

Flax, J. (1990). *Thinking fragments: Psychoanalysis, feminism, and postmodernism in the contemporary West.* Berkeley: University of California Press.

Foucault, M. (1972). *The archaeology of knowledge and the discourse on language* (A. M. S. Smith, Trans.). New York: Pantheon Books (Original work published 1971).

Foucault, M. (1978). *The history of sexuality: Volume 1: An introduction* (R. Hurley, Trans.). New York: Vintage Books (Original work published 1976).

Foucault, M. (1982). The subject and power. In H. L. Dreyfus & P. Rabinow (Eds), *Michel Foucault: Beyond structuralism and hermeneutics* (pp. 208–226). Chicago: University of Chicago Press.

Foucault, M. (1984). Nietzsche, genealogy, history. In P. Rabinow (Ed.), *The Foucault reader* (pp. 76–100). New York: Pantheon Books (Reprinted from *Hommage à Jean Hyppolite,* pp. 145–172, 1971, Paris: Presses Universitaires de France).

Foucault, M. (1985). *The history of sexuality. Volume 2. The use of pleasure* (R. Hurley, Trans.). New York: Vintage Books (Original work published 1984).

Foucault, M. (1997). Polemics, politics, and problematizations: An interview with Michel Foucault (P. Rabinow, Interviewer; L. Davis, Trans.). In P. Rabinow (Ed.) *Ethics: Subjectivity and truth* (pp. 111–119). New York: The New Press (Interview conducted 1984).

Fuss, D. (1989). *Essentially speaking: Feminism, nature & difference.* New York: Routledge.

Garrick, J. (1999). Doubting the philosophical assumptions of interpretive research. *International Journal of Qualitative Studies in Education, 12*(2), 147–156.

Geertz, C. (1973). *The interpretation of cultures: Selected essays.* New York: Basic Books.

Haraway, D. J. (1988). Situated knowledges: The science question in feminism and the privilege of partial perspective. *Feminist Studies, 14*(3), 575–599.

Hardt, M., & Negri, A. (2000). *Empire.* Cambridge, MA: Harvard University Press.

Hiley, D. R., Bohman, J. F., & Shusterman, R. (1991). *The interpretive turn: philosophy, science, culture.* Ithaca, NY: Cornell University Press.

Jackson, A. Y. (2003). Rhizovocality. *International Journal of Qualitative Studies in Education, 16*(5), 693–710.

Jameson, F. (1984). Foreword. In J.-F. Lyotard, *The postmodern condition: A report on knowledge* (pp. viii–xxi). (G. Bennington & B. Massumi, Trans.). Minneapolis: University of Minnesota Press (Original work published 1979).

Lather, P. (1993). Fertile obsession: Validity after poststructuralism. *Sociological Quarterly, 34*(4), 673–693.

Lather, P. (1996a). Troubling clarity: The politics of accessible language. *Harvard Educational Review, 66*(3), 525–545.

Lather, P. (1996b, April). *Methodology as subversive repetition: Practices toward a feminist doubled science*. Paper presented at the annual meeting of the American Educational Research Association, New York City, New York.

Lather, P. (2007). *Getting lost: Feminist efforts toward a double(d) science*. Albany, NY: SUNY Press.

Lincoln, Y. S., & Guba, E. G. (1985). *Naturalistic inquiry*. Newbury Park: Sage Publications.

Lyotard, J-F. (1984). *The postmodern condition: A report on knowledge* (G. Bennington & B, Massumi, Trans.). Minneapolis: University of Minnesota Press (Original work published 1979).

Maines, D. R. (1993). Narrative's moment and sociology's phenomena: Toward a narrative sociology. *The Sociological Quarterly, 34*(1), 17–38.

Marcus, G. E. (1994). What comes (just) after 'post'?: The case of ethnography. In N. K. Denzin & Y. S. Lincoln (Eds.), *Handbook of qualitative research* (pp. 563–574). Thousand Oaks, CA: Sage Publications.

Miller, J. H. (1990). Narrative. In F. Lentricchia & T. McLaughlin (Eds.), *Critical terms for literary study*. Chicago: University of Chicago Press.

Nespor, J., & Barylske, J. (1991). Narrative discourse and teacher knowledge. *American Educational Research Journal, 28(4),* 805–823.

Nietzsche, F. (1992). On the genealogy of morals. In *Basic writings of Nietzsche* (W. Kaufmann, Ed., & Trans.). New York: Modern Library (Original work published 1887).

Pillow, W. S. (2003). Confession, catharsis, or cure? Rethinking the uses of reflexivity as methodological power in qualitative research. *International Journal of Qualitative Studies in Education, 16*(2), 175–196.

Richardson, L., & St.Pierre, E. A. (2005). Writing: A method of inquiry. In N. K. Denzin & Y. S. Lincoln (Eds.). *Handbook of qualitative research* (3rd ed.) (pp. 959–978). Thousand Oaks, CA: Sage.

Ricoeur, P. (1983/1984). *Time and narrative*. Vol. 1. (K. McLaughlin & D. Pellauer, Trans.). Chicago: University of Chicago Press.

Romano, C. (2002). Is the rise of 'narratology' the same old story? *Chronicle of Higher Education, XLVIII*(42), p. B12.

Rorty, R. (1986). Foucault and epistemology. In D. C. Hoy (Ed.), *Foucault: A critical reader* (pp. 41–49). Cambridge, MA: Basil Blackwell.

Scheurich, J. J. (1993). The masks of validity: A deconstructive investigation. *International Journal of Qualitative Studies in Education, 9*(11), 49–60.

Scheurich, J. J. (1995). A postmodernist critique of research interviewing. *International Journal of Qualitative Studies in Education, 8*(3), 239–252.

Scott, J. W. (1992). Experience. In J. Butler & J. W. Scott (Eds.), *Feminists theorize the political* (pp. 22–40). New York: Routledge.

Serres M. (with B. Latour). (1995). *Conversations on science, culture, and time* (R. Lapidus, Trans.). Ann Arbor: University of Michigan Press (Original work published 1990).

Shavelson, R. J., Phillips, D. C., Towne, L., & Feuer, M. J. (2003). On the science of education design studies. *Educational Researcher, 32*(1), 25–28.

Sommer, D. (1994). Resistant texts and incompetent readers. *Poetics Today, 15*(4), 523–551.

Spivak, G. C. (1974). Translator's preface. In J. Derrida (Ed.), *Of Grammatology* (G. C. Spivak, Trans.) (pp. ix–xc). Baltimore: Johns Hopkins University Press.

Spivak, G. C. (1999). *A critique of postcolonial reason: Toward a history of the vanishing present*. Cambridge, MA: Harvard University Press.

St.Pierre, E. A. (1995). *Arts of existence: The construction of subjectivity in older, white southern women.* Unpublished doctoral dissertation, The Ohio State University, Columbus.

St.Pierre, E. A. (1997a). Methodology in the fold and the irruption of transgressive data. *International Journal of Qualitative Studies in Education, 10*(2), 175–189.

St.Pierre, E. A. (1997b). Nomadic inquiry in the smooth spaces of the field: A preface. *International Journal of Qualitative Studies in Education, 10*(3), 363–383.

St.Pierre, E. A. (2004). Care of the self: The subject and freedom. In B. Baker & K. E. Heyning (Eds.), *Dangerous coagulations?: The uses of Foucault in the study of education* (pp. 325–358). New York: Peter Lang.

Watts, E. K. (2001). 'Voice' and 'voicelessness' in rhetorical studies. *Quarterly Journal of Speech, 87*(2), 179–196.

Whitehurst, G. J. (2003, April). *The Institute of Education Sciences: New wine in old bottles.* Paper presented at the annual meeting of the American Educational Research Association, Chicago, IL.

Williams, R. (1976). *Keywords: A vocabulary of culture and society.* New York: Oxford University Press.

Author index

Subject index